THE ORIGINS OF
OṂ MAṆIPADME HŪṂ

THE ORIGINS OF *OṂ MAṆIPADME HŪṂ*

A Study of the Kāraṇḍavyūha Sūtra

Alexander Studholme

State University of New York Press

Published by
State University of New York Press, Albany

Printed in the United States of America

For information, address State University of New York Press,
90 State Street, Suite 700, Albany, NY 12207

Production by Kelli M. Williams
Marketing by Jennifer Giovani

Library of Congress Cataloging-in-Publication Data

Studholme, Alexander, 1967–
The origins of Oṃ maṇipadme hūṃ : a study of Kāraṇḍavyūha sūtra/ Alexander Studholme.
p. cm.
ISBN 0-7914-5389-8 (alk. paper) – ISBN 0-7914-5390-1 (pbk. : alk. paper)
1. Tripiṭaka. Sūtrapiṭaka. Kāraṇḍavyūha Sūtra. Oṃ Maṇipadme Hūṃ.

BQ2240.K347 S78 2002
294.3'437—dc21 2002020933

10 9 8 7 6 5 4 3 2 1

To my grandmother J. J. M. S. (1898–2002)

CONTENTS

ACKNOWLEDGMENT

I would like to give particular thanks to Professor Paul Williams and Dr. Rupert Gethin of the Centre for Buddhist Studies at Bristol University for their tuition and to the British Academy for its funding.

INTRODUCTION

The Importance of *Oṃ Maṇipadme Hūṃ*

The six-syllable Buddhist formula *Oṃ Maṇipadme Hūṃ* needs little introduction. Its form and meaning have long been discussed, though seldom, it must be said, with great accuracy, by European travelers to Tibet and its surrounding regions. In 1254, in what would appear to be the earliest such reference to the formula, the Franciscan friar William of Rubruck remarked of the Mongolians of Karakoram: "Wherever they go they have in their hands a string of one or two hundred beads, like our rosaries, and they always repeat these words, *on mani baccam*, which is 'God, thou knowest,' as one of them interpreted it to me, and they expect as many rewards from God as they remember God in saying this."[1]

At the end of the twentieth century, following the Tibetan diaspora of the last forty years, the influence of *Oṃ Maṇipadme Hūṃ* is no longer confined to the outer reaches of Central Asia. Just as the single syllable Oṃ has become almost universally understood as a symbol of things both Indian and religious, so too has *Oṃ Maṇipadme Hūṃ* begun to establish a place for itself in the popular consciousness of the West. That is to say, it is familiar not merely to Western Buddhists. Increasingly, as the formula appears in a wider and wider variety of different contexts, people with no obvious allegiance to Buddhism will admit to some sense of recognition at the sound or sight of the syllables *Oṃ Maṇipadme Hūṃ*.

In Tibetan Buddhist culture, of course, the formula is ubiquitous: it is the most important mantra associated with the bodhisattva Avalokiteśvara, the Buddhist equivalent of the patron deity of Tibet. *Oṃ Maṇipadme Hūṃ* is, to begin with, a prominent visual feature of the landscape, carved and painted onto the rocks that line a road or a path, written in huge letters high up on a hillside, or present in monumental form in the so-called *maṇi*-walls (in Tibetan, *maṇi gdong*) the glorified dry-stone walls that are constructed entirely out of rocks each inscribed with a sacred formula, which, as the name of these edifices would suggest, is most often *Oṃ Maṇipadme Hūṃ*. *Oṃ Maṇipadme Hūṃ* is also (with few exceptions) the formula that, in printed form, fills the "prayer wheels" (*maṇi chos 'khor*) of the Tibetan religious world. These are the cylinders or drums—sometimes large and sometimes small—which line the outside walls of monasteries and temples, waiting to be spun around by visitors, as well as the personal, hand-held contraptions, kept revolving by a gentle flicking of the wrist. Prayer wheels are also found, in different shapes and sizes, harnessed to the power of mountain streams, to the currents of hot air rising from butter lamps, and even, in modern times, to the flow of electric currents.[3]

The simple recitation of *Oṃ Maṇipadme Hūṃ*, usually accompanied, as William of Rubruck observed, by the counting of prayer beads, is also the most popular religious practice of the Tibetan Buddhist system. The formula, it would be true to say, constitutes an essential part of the texture of Tibetan life. Its sound can be heard at any time of the day and in any kind of situation.[2] It is almost as if, as the following rather lyrical passage by the German Lama Govinda suggests, the Tibetan world is constantly humming with the subtle vibration of Avalokiteśvara's six-syllable mantra. Govinda writes:

> "The deep devotion with which this hopeful message was accepted and taken to heart by the people of Tibet is demonstrated by the innumerable rock-inscriptions and votive-stones on which the sacred formula of Avalokiteśvara is millionfold engraved. It is on the lips of all pilgrims, it is the last prayer of the dying and the hope of the living. It is the eternal melody of Tibet, which the faithful hears in the murmuring of brooks, in the thundering of waterfalls and in the howling of storms, just as it greets him from rocks and *maṇi*-stones, which accompany him everywhere, on wild caravan tracks and on lofty passes."[4]

As well as being an essential component of the exoteric side of Tibetan religious life, *Oṃ Maṇipadme Hūṃ* is also an important constituent of the more private or esoteric part of Tibetan religious practice. It would be practically impossible, for instance, to count every occasion on which the formula is used, incidentally, in the course of all the many different rites and rituals of Tibetan Buddhism.[5] In general, however, the use of *Oṃ Maṇipadme Hūṃ* is regarded not as an adjunct to other, more vital forms of religious procedure, but as a powerful means of spiritual development in its own right. It is a basic, foundational practice taught to children and beginners.[6] Yet it is also a practice that not even the most advanced practitioner would ever wish to leave behind.[7] Its recitation is one of the central pillars of the Tibetan religious system.[8]

In order to give a particular focus to this recitation, a large number of *sādhana* texts—step-by-step invocations of supernormal beings—connected to the formula were composed, each culminating in a concentrated session of the repetition of *Oṃ Maṇipadme Hūṃ* in conjunction with the visualization of a particular form of Avalokiteśvara. The Tibetan *bsTan 'gyur* contains a number of *ṣaḍakṣara* (or *ṣaḍakṣarī*)—"six-syllable"—*sādhanas.*[9] These works continued to be composed in Tibet long after the definitive creation of a fixed Tibetan Buddhist canon in the first part of the fourteenth century.[10] But, possibly the most extraordinary and most mysterious application of *Oṃ Maṇipadme Hūṃ* is its use in the so-called Black Hat (*zhva nag*) ceremony of the *Karma bKa' brgyud* school of Tibetan Buddhism, during which the Karmapa, the lama who sits at the head of that particular sect, is believed to manifest as a form of Avalokiteśvara while slowly reciting the six-syllable formula and while wearing a special black crown, given to the fifth Karmapa by the Chinese emperor at the beginning of the fifteenth century.[11]

Finally, *Oṃ Maṇipadme Hūṃ* plays another important role in Tibetan life as a mode of collective religious practice. On particular occasions and over the course of several days, people will gather together to recite the formula as many times as they are able. Again, though this is a form of practice which may be performed with regard to a variety of different mantras, the one most often used in this respect is, undoubtedly, *Oṃ Maṇipadme Hūṃ*. I myself saw this activity going on while staying at the Tibetan refugee settlement at Clement Town in North India during the winter of 1992–93, when, at the time of the Tibetan New Year, everyone in the colony was encouraged to recite *Oṃ Maṇipadme Hūṃ*. A large tent was set up in the forecourt of one of the three monasteries of the settlement precisely for this purpose and each person engaged in the practice was asked to keep a record of the number of recitations he or she had achieved, so that, at the end of the week, a grand total might be calculated and this number conveyed to Dharamsala, the seat of the Tibetan government-in-exile, where the blessings accumulated in the process might be dedicated to the well-being of the Dalai Lama. During this time, I would be woken, early each morning, by the sound of my landlord and his two young children busily muttering the formula. Later that year, in the course of a trip into Tibet itself, I discovered a group of people, mainly elderly, gathered in the courtyard of a temple in Lhasa occupied in precisely the same way, reciting *Oṃ Maṇipadme Hūṃ* in order that the accumulated number of recitations might be sent to the Dalai Lama.[12]

Given the great importance of *Oṃ Maṇipadme Hūṃ* in Tibetan Buddhism, an academic study devoted entirely to the history of the formula did not seem unwarranted. To this end, my original intention had been to trace the complete historical trajectory of the formula, from its original inception in India to its establishment as one of the linchpins of the Tibetan Buddhist system. Some preliminary research was, therefore, conducted into the avenues by which the formula reached Tibet from India and into the means by which it was subsequently promoted by the Tibetans themselves. However, it soon became apparent that the *Kāraṇḍavyūha Sūtra*, the earliest textual source for any mention of *Oṃ Maṇipadme Hūṃ* and a text that has, hitherto, been largely overlooked by Western scholarship, does not just mention the formula in passing, but may, in fact, be seen as a work whose central concern is the dissemination of the formula. It seemed justifiable, then, to devote all my energies to an analysis of this sūtra, in order to see what this might reveal about the place of *Oṃ Maṇipadme Hūṃ* within the development of Mahāyāna Buddhism. What findings I managed to make on the later history of the formula are, occasionally, used in the support of this more modest project. Meanwhile, a complete history of *Oṃ Maṇipadme Hūṃ* must remain a thing of the future, involving as it would, the mastery of a wide range of Tibetan literary sources.

The first chapter of this book, then, introduces the reader to the *Kāraṇḍavyūha Sūtra*, discussing both the internal and external evidence for its likely date and place of origin and providing a brief survey of its treatment, to date, in Buddhist academic studies. A detailed, annotated précis of the sūtra, made from the Sanskrit edition of the text produced by P. L. Vaidya and published as part of the *Mahāyāna Sūtra Saṃgraha* by the Mithila Institute of Dharbanga in 1961,[13] with reference, also, to the Tibetan version of the text found in the Peking edition of the *bKa' 'gyur*,[14] forms an appendix to the thesis. The making of this précis was, naturally, essential to my own analysis of the sūtra. It is, I believe, worthy of inclusion here not only because, without it, my own presentation and argument might seem a little obscure to a reader unfamiliar with the text, but also, because I hope it will be of some interest and use to scholars working in this field. No definitive Sanskrit edition of the *Kāraṇḍavyūha* has yet been produced—the language of the work is difficult and the text exists in a number of subtly different versions—putting a proper English translation of the sūtra beyond the scope of the present, historical study.[15]

Chapters 2, 3, and 4 set out to show that, from an historical point of view, the six-syllable formula *Oṃ Maṇipadme Hūṃ* represents a Buddhist adaptation of the five-syllable Śaivite formula *Namaḥ Śivāya*. Chapter 2 establishes, initially, that there is a strong connection between the *Kāraṇḍavyūha Sūtra* and the non-Buddhist purāṇic tradition. The discussion dwells principally on an analysis of different versions of the *vāmana-avatāra*—the story of Viṣṇu's incarnation as a dwarf—found both in the sūtra and in various different purāṇas. The *Kāraṇḍavyūha,* the chapter concludes, seems to have been written in a religious milieu in which Śiva was the dominant god, complemented harmoniously by the other great purāṇic deity Viṣṇu. More specifically, it is argued, the evidence suggests that there may be a particular relationship between the sūtra and the Śaivite *Skanda Purāṇa*.

Chapter 3 shows that, in the *Kāraṇḍavyūha*, Avalokiteśvara appears as an *īśvara* (lord) and *puruṣa* (cosmic man or person) in the mold of the two great purāṇic deities. In keeping with the findings of the previous chapter, though, certain details of this conception of the bodhisattva betray a distinctively Śaivite, rather than Vaiṣṇavite, influence. We discuss the way in which this presentation of the bodhisattva is tailored to the demands of accepted Buddhist doctrine and integrated with the roles and attributes of Avalokiteśvara already established in earlier Mahāyāna sūtras. The chapter ends by tracing the evolution of the bodhisattva, from his first appearance under the original name of Avalokitasvara as an attendant of the Buddhas Amitābha and Śākyamuni, to his emergence as the supreme Buddhist *īśvara*.

Chapter 4 examines the similarities—and differences—between the treatment of *Oṃ Maṇipadme Hūṃ* in the *Kāraṇḍavyūha Sūtra* and the treatment of *Namaḥ Śivāya* in Śaivite texts (principally the *Skanda Purāṇa* and *Śiva Purāṇa*). Both the five- and the six-syllable formulae are presented as the *hṛdaya*, or "heart," of their respective *īśvaras*. Both are said to be *sui generis* methods of attaining liberation. Both are promoted as forms of practice that are available to everyone, regardless of social or religious status. At the same time, both are shown to be somewhat secret and difficult to obtain. Furthermore, just as *Namaḥ Śivāya* is explicitly presented as a developed form of the Vedic *praṇava Oṃ*, so too is *Oṃ Maṇipadme Hūṃ* described in terms that indicate that it, too, is to be regarded as a kind of *praṇava*. The presentation of *Namaḥ Śivāya*, however, is illustrated in the purāṇas by a story about the marriage between a king and queen, presupposing, I suggest, an understanding of the Śaivite formula in terms of the doctrine of *śakti*, the energetic, female dimension of the male deity. Such a story is noticeably absent in the sūtra.

Chapter 5 argues that the treatment of *Oṃ Maṇipadme Hūṃ* in the *Kāraṇḍavyūha* represents the reconfiguration, by the Mahāyāna monastic establishment, of a practice first propagated by lay Buddhist tantric practitioners. The sūtra is clearly written from the monastic point of view. Instead of a story about an (eventually) happy marriage, the sūtra's long section on *Oṃ Maṇipadme Hūṃ* is prefaced by a story about the shipwreck of the seafaring king Siṃhala and his subsequent escape from the clutches of a band of *rākṣasīs*, man-eating demonesses, who are disguised as beautiful women—a tale more obviously in tune with the monastic temperament. More conclusively, the end of the sūtra also includes a teaching on monastic discipline, laying heavy emphasis on the importance of preventing non-celibate practitioners from making their homes in the monastery. Yet, the preceptor who grants initiation into the use of *Oṃ Maṇipadme Hūṃ* is said to be married. The characteristics of this man are those of an antinomian, free-living tantric yogin. This reading is supported by an association made, in the sūtra, between *Oṃ Maṇipadme Hūṃ* and the idea of the *vidyādhara*, the "holder of knowledge," a figure almost synonymous with the *mahāsiddha*, the archetypal tantric practitioner.

The presentation of *Oṃ Maṇipadme Hūṃ* in the *Kāraṇḍavyūha*, it seems, describes the adaptation of a practice that originated in tantric circles to the doctrinal and ethical framework of Mahāyāna monasticism.

Doctrinally, then, the sūtra is the result of a process of creative religious synthesis. Significantly, for example, *Oṃ Maṇipadme Hūṃ* is presented in a number of different ways as analogous to the Perfection of Wisdom and, finally, as greater than the Perfection of Wisdom. This would appear to express the idea that *Oṃ Maṇipadme Hūṃ*, as a form of the *praṇava*, supercedes the Perfection of Wisdom as the supreme principle of the Mahāyāna. Then, certain aspects of the tantric-style origins of the formula are preserved. Initiation into the use of *Oṃ Maṇipadme Hūṃ*, for instance, is said to be dependent on the use of a tantric-style maṇḍala. However, the central figure of this maṇḍala is not Avalokiteśvara, but the Buddha Amitābha. This is symbolic of the fact that the concise formula of Avalokiteśvara is now located within a Mahāyāna doctrinal system in which rebirth in Sukhāvatī, the pure land of Amitābha, is the overarching religious goal and, also, of the fact that the use of the formula is now to be understood as one of the many Mahāyāna practices that are believed to lead to this goal. Recitation of *Oṃ Maṇipadme Hūṃ* is no longer presented as a means of engagement with the *śakti* of the *īśvara*, but is reconfigured as a form of the traditional Mahāyāna practice of the *nāmānusmṛti*, or "bringing to mind the name," of Avalokiteśvara, commonly associated with the goal of Sukhāvatī.

The sūtra manages to avoid, almost entirely, any allusion to the conception of the concise formula as *śakti*. This, I suggest, is deliberate. With its sexual connotations, the characteristically tantric doctrine of *śakti* is perhaps not best suited to the training of monastic practitioners. Instead, the *Kāraṇḍavyūha* roots the use of *Oṃ Maṇipadme Hūṃ* in a scheme borrowed from the *bhakti*, or "devotional," side of the purāṇic tradition. Recitation of the formula is said to lead to rebirth in worlds contained within the hair pores of Avalokiteśvara's body. This is a reworking, I suggest, of a doctrine classically expressed in chapter eleven of the *Bhagavadgītā*. There, Arjuna "sees" (*paśyati*) a cosmic form of the *īśvara* Kṛṣṇa that contains the whole universe and is then taught the doctrine of *bhakti* as a means of making this experience his own. By the time the *Kāraṇḍavyūha Sūtra* was constructed, of course, the theology of the *Bhagavadgītā* was common to both the Vaiṣṇavite and the Śaivite tradition alike. The so-called *Īśvaragītā* of the *Kūrma Purāṇa*, for instance, presents a Śaivite version of the teaching.

In the sūtra, the cosmic form of the Buddhist *īśvara* is expressed anew in Mahāyāna terms. The amazing attributes of Avalokiteśvara's body mimic those of Samantabhadra, the great bodhisattva of the *Avataṃsaka Sūtra*, a debt that the *Kāraṇḍavyūha* explicitly acknowledges by alluding several times to Samantabhadra and even, at one point, describing a kind of duel—a *samādhi* contest (*samādhivigraha*)—between the two bodhisattvas, which Avalokiteśvara, naturally, wins. Just as the *Bhagavadgītā* promotes *bhakti*, through the use of the Vedic *praṇava Oṃ*, as a means of entering the vision of the Vaiṣṇavite *īśvara*, so the *Kāraṇḍavyūha* promotes the *nāmānusmṛti* of the Buddhist *praṇava Oṃ Maṇipadme Hūṃ* as a means of entering the vision of the Buddhist *īśvara*. The vision of the cosmic Avalokiteśvara is itself assimilated with the central Mahāyāna doctrine of Sukhāvatī, when this manifestation of the bodhisattva is said, in the sūtra, to lead beings to Amitābha's pure land: the purāṇic doctrine of "seeing" (*darśana*) the *īśvara* is syncretized with the Mahāyāna doctrine of rebirth in the Buddha's pure land.

Finally, chapter 6 turns to the vexed issue of the meaning of the six-syllable formula. The true meaning of *Oṃ Maṇipadme Hūṃ*, it is argued, reflects this syncretism. The middle four syllables of the mantra, "*maṇipadme*," are not, as has been variously suggested, to be translated as the (grammatically unfeasible) "jewel (*maṇi*) in the lotus (*padme*)" or even as the vocative "(O thou) with the jewel and lotus," but as the locative compound "in the jewel-lotus," or "in the lotus made of jewels." Variations of the same brief phrase are used, throughout the Mahāyāna, to describe the manner in which a person is said to appear in Sukhāvatī or in the pure lands in general. The image given in the sūtras is that of a practitioner seated cross-legged in the calyx of a lotus flower made of jewels, which then unfolds its petals to reveal the splendour of one or other of the pure lands. The formula, therefore, the *hṛdaya*, or "heart," of Avalokiteśvara, the Buddhist *īśvara*, is also an expression of the aspiration to be reborn in Sukhāvatī.

In conclusion, then, the question remains open as to whether *Oṃ Maṇipadme Hūṃ* was, in fact, the original six-syllable formula of Avalokiteśvara or whether this particular form, which meshes so well with the overall design of the Mahāyāna sūtras, replaced an earlier mantra, used in the period before the incorporation of this doctrine into the Mahāyāna system, which has now been forgotten. The possible identity of such a mantra is considered.

CHAPTER 1

Background to the *Kāraṇḍavyūha Sūtra*

There are two separate and quite distinct versions of the *Kāraṇḍavyūha Sūtra*, one in prose and another in verse. With respect to editions kept, respectively, at the Bibliothèque Nationale and the Société Asiatique in Paris,[1] the one is a text of sixty-seven leaves, or one hundred and thirty-four pages, comprising two sections (*nirvyūha*) of sixteen and twelve chapters (*prakaraṇa*),[2] while the other is a very much longer work of one hundred and eighty-five leaves or three hundred and ninety pages, containing about four thousand five hundred verses (*śloka*), composed mainly in the thirty-two-syllable *anuṣṭubh* meter,[3] in a total of eighteen chapters.

Neither version should be confused with a work by the name of the *Ratnakāraṇḍa* that appears in the Tibetan canon, translated by a certain Rinchen 'Tshos bsgyur. This is an entirely different text, consisting mainly of a discussion of moral and doctrinal matters in connection with the bodhisattva Mañjuśrī. This work, the *Ratnakāraṇḍa*, or a very similar one, whose title is translated as *Ratnakāraṇḍavyūha*, is also to be found in the Chinese canon, translated once in 270 C.E. by Dharmarakṣa and again, sometime between 435 and 468 C.E., by Guṇabhadra.[4]

The *Kāraṇḍavyūha Sūtra,* which is the concern of this thesis, is almost wholly devoted to the glorification of the Bodhisattva Avalokiteśvara, as is made clear by the full title sometimes given to the work: *Avalokiteśvaraguṇa-kāraṇḍavyūha*.[5] This might provisionally be translated as "The Magnificent Array, (Contained in a) Casket of the Qualities of Avalokiteśvara." A discussion of this translation of the title of the sūtra follows.

In a recent English translation of the two *Sukhāvatīvyūha Sūtras,* Luis Gomez renders the term *vyūha* as the "magnificent display" of the wondrous qualities of the land of Sukhāvatī.[6] This meaning might easily be attached to the use of the term in the titles of other Mahāyāna works.[7] *Vyūha,* though, is also used in the Vaiṣṇavite tradition to signify both the "successive emanations" of Viṣṇu, as well as part of the "essential nature" of the god.[8] In actual fact, the *Kāraṇḍavyūha Sūtra* does, as we shall see, share many of the characteristics of the Śaivite and Vaiṣṇavite purāṇas and does describe a succession of different appearances by Avalokiteśvara (as an *asura*, as a brahmin, as a bee and as a flying horse) comparable to the different manifestations of Viṣṇu. It seems possible, therefore, that the *vyūha* of the sūtra is also being used with the Vaiṣṇavite sense in mind. "Magnificent array," then, is perhaps better than "magnificent display."

The term *kāraṇḍa*, in this particular context, has usually been translated as "basket."[9] It might, though, be better to choose a word that conveys a sense of greater solidity and gravitas. Monier Monier-Williams also offers "covered box of bamboo wicker work."[10] P. C. Majumder suggests "casket."[11] The latter translation certainly befits the way in which the related term *karaṇḍaka* is employed in the Prajñāpāramitā literature. In his *Materials for a Dictionary of the Prajñāpāramitā Literature*, Edward Conze also translates this term as "basket" (he makes no mention of *kāraṇḍa*).[12] However, the passages in which the word occurs indicate that it describes a container used for keeping relics, an object that it seems more natural to call a "casket." In the *Aṣṭasāhasrikā*, for instance, the effect of placing a wishing-jewel (*cintāmaṇi*) in a *karaṇḍaka* is compared to the way in which the Prajñāpāramitā pervades the relics of the Tathāgata. The *karaṇḍaka*, in this context, is said to be "an object of supreme longing," which "emits radiance" and which "should be paid homage to."[13]

The Tibetan rendering of *Kāraṇḍavyūha* is *Za ma tog bkod pa'i mdo*, where *za ma tog* also seems to refer to a kind of casket. The term appears, for instance, in the *Tshig gsum gnad du brdeg pa*, or "The Three Statements That Strike the Essential Points," a *gter ma*, or "discovered" text of the *rNying ma*, or "Old," school of Tibetan Buddhism, dating from the late thirteenth or early-fourteenth century. The text is said to be the last testament of the early *rDzogs Chen* master dGa' rab rDorje, comprising an oral commentary on the *rDo rje'i tshig gsum*, or "three *vajra* verses."[14] The three verses themselves, we read, were written in melted lapis luzuli on gold, fell from the sky into the palm of dGa' rab rDorje's disciple Mañjuśrīmitra and were then put into a tiny thumbnail-sized vessel, which itself was then "placed within a casket," or *za ma tog*, "of precious crystal" (*rin po che shel gyi za ma tog sen gang ba cig snod du babs pa*).[15] There is no such thing, surely, as a "basket" made of crystal.

The *Kāraṇḍavyūha Sūtra*, then is a "casket" containing the "magnificent array" of the manifestations and works of Avalokiteśvara. The implication of this title is that the sūtra is comparable, in its function, to a relic casket, which may then be made an object of homage. This is consistent with the fact that the sūtra, in the manner of the earlier Prajñāpāramitā sūtras and other Mahāyāna works, refers to itself as something to be set up and worshipped. At the end of a passage in which Avalokiteśvara is said to teach the *Kāraṇḍavyūha* to the *asuras*, the sūtra is compared to a wish-fulfilling jewel (*cintāmaṇi*). The *asuras* are then said to turn with happiness towards it, to listen to it, to develop faith towards it, to understand it, to write it, to have it written, to memorize it and to recite it, to worship it (*pūjayiṣyanti*), to reflect on it (*cintayiṣyanti*), to explain it in full to others (*parebhyaśca vistareṇa saṃprakāśayiṣyanti*), to meditate on it (*bhāvayiṣyanti*) and to bow to it (*namaskurvanti*) with great joy, respect and devotion.[16]

The longer verse *Kāraṇḍavyūha* is later than the prose version, probably by as much as a thousand years. In the opinion of Giuseppe Tucci, this verse text is representative of the worst kind of Mahāyāna sūtra. It adds little of note to the prose, he writes, and exemplifies the somewhat banal tendency within Mahāyāna Buddhism to rejoice in the simple virtue of the prolixity of a work, not exactly for its own sake, but for the sake of the increased amount of merit earned by those who wrote, read, or recited it.[17] The greater part of this padding out process is achieved by the addition of certain passages from the *Śikṣāsamuccaya* and of almost half of the *Bodhicaryāvatāra*. These are both works that have been attributed to the Indian master Śāntideva, who is said to have lived in the eighth century.[18] This, as we shall see, would be enough to show that the verse *Kāraṇḍavyūha* is the later text, as the earliest known manuscripts of the prose sūtra have been dated to a time no later than the early part of the seventh century C.E.

The most significant evidence supporting the much later date of the verse sūtra, however, is the number of striking similarites between it and a Nepalese work, the *Svayaṃbhūpurāṇa*, which scholars agree was composed around the middle of the second millennium. The most obvious of these similarities, as Tucci points out, is the fact that both works are framed by similar extended prologues and epilogues. These consist of dialogues between, first, a Buddhist sage named Jayaśrī and a king named Jinaśrī, and, second, between the great Buddhist emperor Aśoka and his Buddhist preceptor Upagupta. Both this prologue and this epilogue are entirely absent from the prose sūtra.[19]

The *Svayaṃbhūpurāṇa* survives today in several different recensions. This, as Tucci remarks, compounds the difficulty of deciding whether the debt of influence is owed by it to the verse *Kāraṇḍavyūha* or vice versa, or even if the two works have borrowed from a third, unknown source.[20] Both works are popular in Nepal. Despite the usual association of the purāṇas with the non-Buddhist religious traditions, the *Svayaṃbhūpurāṇa* is, in fact, a Buddhist work. There is some reason to believe that it was originally referred to as an *uddeśa*, or "teaching," a word more commonly associated with Buddhist texts.[21] The content of the work, though, is actually more akin to that of a *māhātmya*,[22] a sort of guide for pilgrims, describing the holiness of certain important shrines and temples, in this instance, chiefly, the Svayaṃbhū, or "self-existent," temple in the Kathmandu Valley.

At one point, however, the verse *Kāraṇḍavyūha* elaborates on a section in the prose sūtra, in which various gods are said to be produced from different parts of the body of Avalokiteśvara.[23] Avalokiteśvara himself, the verse sūtra adds, is an emanation of the *Ādibuddha*, or "primordial buddha," a term that is explicitly said to be synonymous with *Svayaṃbhū* and *Ādinātha*, "primordial lord."[24] It seems reasonable to suggest, then, that the verse *Kāraṇḍavyūha* was composed as an adjunct to the *Svayaṃbhūpurāṇa*, as part of a process synthesizing the cult of Avalokiteśvara with the cult of the *Svayaṃbhū*. The sūtra, therefore, seems likely to be the later of the two works.

The oldest surviving manuscript of the *Svayaṃbhūpurāṇa* is considered to have been created in 1557 or 1558.[25] The present scholarly consensus, however, is that the very first version of the text was composed in the fourteenth century.[26] David Gellner writes that it probably dates from the period of king Jayasthitimalla, the ruler of the Kathmandu Valley between 1382–1395.[27] John K. Locke concludes, too, that the text belongs to the late Malla period.[28] Allowing a certain interval, then, between the creation of the *Svayaṃbhūpurāṇa* and that of the verse *Kāraṇḍavyūha*, we may perhaps conclude that the latter was composed not long after the beginning of the fifteenth century. Siegfried Lienhard suggests that it was written in the sixteenth century.[29]

The fact that the verse sūtra is later than the prose is also supported by the linguistic character of the two texts. The Sanskrit of the verse text, despite the inclusion of some peculiarly Buddhist vocabulary, is written in almost pure classical Sanskrit, a considerable stylistic refinement of the prose text. The prose sūtra is written in a form of hybrid Sanskrit. F. Edgerton, for instance, includes the prose text in his third class of Buddhist Hybrid Sanskrit.[30] Constantin Régamey comments: "According to the more detailed classification of John Brough, the [prose] *Kāraṇḍavyūha* would present the characteristics of the late Avadāna style and of the medieval Buddhist Sanskrit, frequent in tantric works, though not confined to them."[31]

The earliest existent copies of the prose *Kāraṇḍavyūha Sūtra* belong to the collection of Buddhist texts unearthed, during the 1940s, in a *stūpa*, situated three miles outside the town of Gilgit in northern Kashmir. Fragments of two different manuscripts of the sūtra have been identified amongst this find.[32] These are both written in much the same type of script, which, according to the expert palæographic analysis conducted on one of these texts, became obsolete around 630 C.E.[33] It is less easy to gauge when the sūtra was actually composed: this must remain, for the time being, a matter of some conjecture. In 1955, Nalinaksha Dutt, without giving any grounds to substantiate his opinion, stated simply that the sūtra is "of about the fourth century."[34] Such an estimate, however, would seem to be broadly supported by Adelheid Mette, who has recently produced an edition of the Gilgit fragments of the text.[35] Where these fragments correspond, Mette observes, their wording is not always identical, indicating that the history of the text tradition had begun much earlier. She writes: "Many of the seeming peculiarities of language are due to corruption which, perhaps already in the fifth or sixth century A.D., affected a formerly more correct Sanskrit text."[36]

This view would also be compatible with another aspect of the *Kāraṇḍavyūha*, namely, that it is representative of that stratum of Buddhist literature in which the categories of sūtra and tantra are somewhat blurred. The work is, as its name declares, very obviously a sūtra, laying great stress, for instance, on the central Mahāyāna doctrine of rebirth in Sukhāvatī. However, the promotion of the formula *Oṃ Maṇipadme Hūṃ*, together with other features of the text such as the use of a maṇḍala, the role of a guru figure and the motif of the conversion of Śiva to *Buddhadharma* are all more characteristic of the tantra genre.

Following a discussion of this issue by the fifteenth century Tibetan lama mKhas grub rje, David Snellgrove cites three works in which the forms of sūtra and tantra seem to overlap: the *Suvarṇaprabhāsa Sūtra*, which includes a presentation, common in the tantras, of a fivefold arrangement of buddhas and long sections on the use of mantras, the *Mañjuśrīmūlakalpa Tantra*, sections of which refer to themselves as sūtra, and the *Sarvatathāgatatattvasaṃgraha Tantra*, which, similarly, is said to be a sūtra in the colophon of its Sanskrit manuscript.[37] This list is, of course, by no means exhaustive. However, while these texts were, subsequently, classified as tantras by the Tibetans, the *Kāraṇḍavyūha* has, as far as I can tell, always remained a sūtra. In this respect, it might be grouped alongside texts such as the late Prajñāpāramitā works, the *Prajñāpāramitā Hṛdaya*, or "Heart Sūtra," and the *Svalpākṣarā Prajñāpāramitā Sūtra*. Despite their propogation of such well-known formulae as, respectively, *Gate Gate Pāragate Pārasaṃgate Bodhi Svāhā* and *Oṃ Mune Mune Mahāmunaye Svāhā*,[38] these last two texts have generally—though not always—been regarded as sūtras. mKhas grub rje, for instance, writes that it seems reasonable that the *Svalpākṣarā* should belong to the "mantra" category and that some assert that the *Hṛdaya* should also belong to the same category.[39]

The dating of these texts, too, is a matter of informed guesswork. Snellgrove, for instance, implies that the *Mañjuśrīmūlakalpa* was written in the fifth century,[40] N. Dutt (suggesting that the text postdates the *Kāraṇḍavyūha*) the sixth century,[41] and Yukei Matsunaga, in a more recent study, the seventh century.[42] The tantric-hued Prajñāpāramitā texts are probably earlier than this. Conze suggests a fourth century date for the *Hṛdaya* and *Svalpākṣarā*.[43] Sounding a more definite note, R. E. Emmerick reports that, while the earliest surviving Sanskrit manuscript of the *Suvarṇaprabhāsa* can be no earlier than the middle of the fifth century, a more primitive version of the text seems to have been used by its first Chinese translator Dharmakṣema, a figure who arrived in China in 414 C.E.[44] In the company of such texts, a late fourth century or, perhaps, early-fifth century date for the *Kāraṇḍavyūha Sūtra*, does not, then, seem unreasonable.

This dating would, furthermore, be consistent with the traditional account of the earliest appearance of the *Kāraṇḍavyūha Sūtra* in Tibet. The text is said to have been one of the first two Buddhist works ever to have reached the Land of Snows during the reign of Lha tho tho ri, arriving either (depending on which account you read) in a casket which fell from the sky onto the roof of the king's palace, or in the hands of missionaries from the country of Li, modern day Khotan.[45] King Lha tho tho ri, said to have been born five generations before the first of the three great Tibetan religious monarchs, Srong btsan sgam po, who died in 650 C.E., is deemed to have lived some time between the end of the fourth and the end of the fifth century.[46]

This putative connection with missionaries from Khotan would also fit in with the most likely place of origin of the *Kāraṇḍavyūha*. The text makes one mention of the Indian province of Magadha, where Avalokiteśvara is said to bring an end to a twenty year famine.[47] It also refers several times to the city of Vārāṇasī, itself situated on the borders of that province, where Avalokiteśvara is said to manifest in the form of a bee,[48] where the preceptor, who grants initiation into the practice of *Oṃ Maṇipadme Hūṃ*, is said to live,[49] and where those who abuse the customs of the *Saṃgha* are said to be reborn as the lowliest creatures living on filth.[50] I do not think, however, that we can conclude from these references that the sūtra was composed in the region of either Magadha or of Vārāṇasī. Much of the *Kāraṇḍavyūha* reflects a close interaction between Buddhism and Śaivism. The use of Vārāṇasī, the great Śaivite city, as the backdrop to the drama of the sūtra, may surely be seen simply as a symbolic means of acknowledging the confluence of the two traditions. Similarly, the use of Magadha as a location for the action of the sūtra may merely be a way of linking the activity of Avalokiteśvara to the holy land of northeast India.

It seems more likely that the sūtra originated in Kashmir. The evidence for this, I must admit, is rather slim and highly circumstantial. First, the earliest manuscripts of the sūtra were found, at Gilgit, in Kashmir. Second, Kashmir is strongly associated with the development of Śaivite tantra and the influences of both Śaivism and of tantric-style practice are, it will be argued, strongly apparent in the sūtra. Third, as we shall see, the sūtra gives Avalokiteśvara some of the characteristics of Samantabhadra,[51] the great bodhisattva of the *Avataṃsaka Sūtra*, a work whose origins are associated with the Central Asian regions bordering Kashmir.[52] Finally, it is not very far from Kashmir to Khotan, from whence the *Kāraṇḍavyūha Sūtra* may first have reached Tibet.[53]

Scholars working in the first part of this century would have been resistant to the idea of a late fourth or early-fifth century date for the sūtra. They would, similarly, have been surprised to learn that the Gilgit manuscripts of the text were attributed to a period no later than the beginning of the seventh century. Their preconceptions would even have been disturbed by an examination of various editions of the Tibetan canon, where the prose *Kāraṇḍavyūha* is clearly shown to have been one of the many texts brought to the Land of Snows during the first great period of Buddhist transmission, that is, at the end of the eighth century. In the colophons of the Derge and Lhasa editions of the *bKa' 'gyur*, the translators of the work are named as Jinamitra, Dānaśīla, and Ye shes sde, all of whom are well-known figures from that time.[54] A third colophon lists different translators,[55] Śākyaprabha and Ratnarakṣita, who may also have been working at that time: one Śākyaprabha is said, in Tāranātha's early seventeenth-century *History of Buddhism in India*, to be a contemporary of Dānaśīla's.[56] The prose *Kāraṇḍavyūha* is also listed in a Tibetan catalog of translated Buddhist texts, the *sTong Thang lDan dKar*, or "White Cheek of the Empty Plain," which was probably compiled in 812 C.E.[57]

For up until the 1940s, western Buddhistic scholars had consigned the *Kāraṇḍavyūha Sūtra* to an imaginary corpus of late, "corrupted" Mahāyāna literature, belonging to the ninth or tenth century.[58] Linguistically, according to Régamey, there were good reasons for thinking that the work was written towards the end of the first millenium C.E.[59] Also, the only known manuscripts were of Nepalese origin, the earliest of which came from the twelfth century. On top of that, the Chinese translation of the sūtra, by T'ien Si Tsai, did not take place until as late as 983 C.E.[60] (The verse sūtra is not found in Chinese translation, a fact which is quite in accord with the probability that it was not written until the fifteenth or sixteenth century. It is, likewise, not found in Tibetan translation, having, almost certainly, yet to have come into existence by the time the Tibetan *bKa' 'gyur* was first compiled by Bu ston in 1322.)

Another factor taken to support a late ninth or tenth century date for the sūtra was the absence of any copy of the work and, it seemed, of any mention of *Oṃ Maṇipadme Hūṃ*, from among the hoard of manuscripts collected from the Silk Road oasis town of Tun Huang, whose libraries were sealed up in the tenth century.[61] In 1979, however, Yoshiro Imæda announced that the formula (slightly altered as *Oṃ ma ni pad me hūṃ myi tra sva hā*, *Oṃ ma ma ni pad me hum mye*, and *Oṃ ma ma ni pad me hum myi*) did, in fact, appear in three different Tun Huang manuscripts. These are all versions of the same text, a treatise known as the *Dug gsum 'dul ba*, or "The Purification of the Three Poisons," which describes how a dead person may be prevented from taking an unfavourable rebirth by the practice, performed by relatives on his or her behalf, of purifying (*'dul ba*) the three poisons (*dug gsum*) of greed, hatred, and delusion. *Oṃ Maṇipadme Hūṃ* (or its approximation) is associated in this text with the activity of Avalokiteśvara and is said to purify the third poison of delusion.[62] It remains a mystery, however, as to why the six-syllable formula is only found in these semicorrupted and elaborated forms and why no copy of the *Kāraṇḍavyūha* has been found in the hoard of sūtras and tantras discovered at Tun Huang. The caves, after all, contain a painting (executed in 836 C.E.) of the thousand-armed Avalokiteśvara,[63] an iconographic form that is, as we shall see, central to the dogmatic purpose of the *Kāraṇḍavyūha Sūtra*.

Nonetheless, this mistaken assumption that the *Kāraṇḍavyūha* was such a very late and, by implication, such a very heterodox Mahāyāna sūtra was probably the principal cause of a distinct lack of scholarly interest in the text. The number of academic articles on the sūtra remains small: there are four by Régamey, three on linguistic peculiarities and one on the Vaiṣṇavite and Śaivite influences discernible in the sūtra; one by Tucci, editing short passages from the verse sūtra and pointing out its connection to the *Svayaṃbhūpurāṇa*; one by Majumder on the verse sūtra that does little more than give a short précis of its contents; one by Jeremiah P. Losty on a twelfth-century Indian manuscript of the sūtra,[64] and, lastly, a piece by Siegfried Lienhard focusing on an obscure lexicological detail. More recently, Adelheid Mette has published her edition of the Gilgit fragments (including a brief introduction to the text) and another short article on the history of the text. And that, apart from the cursory treatment given to the sūtra in the early literary surveys of Eugène Burnouf and Maurice Winternitz, is that.[65]

No critical edition has been made of either the prose or the verse version of the Sanskrit text. Tucci seemed to have abandoned his ambition to edit the verse sūtra as soon as he had discovered it added little of value to the shorter prose version.[66] The lack of a critical edition of the prose text is also explained, to some extent, by the difficulty and obscurity of much of the language and the many inconsistencies found between the different manuscripts.[67] The sheer volume of these documents attests to the great popularity of the *Kāraṇḍavyūha Sūtra* in Nepal. Scholars have long been familiar with Nepalese manuscripts in the libraries of Calcutta, Cambridge, London, Munich, Oxford, Paris, and Tokyo. But, as Mette adds, a team of German scholars has recently photographed more than one hundred and twenty additional Nepalese manuscripts, "some of them very early."[68] Jean Przyluski began, but never managed to complete, an edition of the Sanskrit prose version, using three manuscripts available to him in Paris at the time.[69] Similarly, Régamey was prevented by illness from producing editions of the prose and verse versions of the sūtra.[70] A complete edition of the Tibetan text was, however, completed by Lalou, who consulted a number of different recension of the *bKa' 'gyur*, as well as the Chinese tradition. This remains unpublished.[71]

The most well-known edition of the *Kāraṇḍavyūha*, that of Satyavrata Sāmaśrami, first published for the *Hindu Commentator* in Calcutta in 1873 and based on a late-twelfth-century Nepalese manuscript, cannot be regarded as "critical."[72] Reproduced by the Mithila Institute at Darbhanga in 1961, it is described by its editor P. L. Vaidya as "very corrupt." Régamey pronounces it "noncritical" and "very peculiar": its readings differ in almost every line from the majority of manuscripts. Moreover, Régamey writes, it is impossible to know to what degree these readings are based on a particular (and obviously very corrupt) manuscript or whether they represent Vaidya's own emendations.[73] This is also Mette's view: "It seems that Vaidya too has altered the text, but without consulting any further manuscripts."[74]

This, however, for convenience's sake, is the edition which I have used in order to produce a précis of the *Kāraṇḍavyūha Sūtra*. I have also referred to the Tibetan translation of the text found in the Peking *bKa' 'gyur*. There exists no published translation of the sūtra in any modern European language. I have, though, been able to consult a handwritten French translation of the sūtra, made by Eugène Burnouf in 1837.[75] I cannot pretend, however, to have made any more than the occasional, fairly rudimentary comparison between the Sanskrit and Tibetan versions of the text. Nor have I referred in any great detail to the recent edition of the Gilgit fragments prepared by Mette. The first Gilgit text, Mette remarks, shows some slight differences between the later Nepalese versions, but corresponds "on the whole," as regards content and length.[76] Fortunately, for present purposes, these fragments do include parts of the section of the sūtra devoted to the subject of the six-syllable formula, where the mantra's form is unambiguously confirmed as: "*Oṃ Maṇipadme Hūṃ*."[77]

The *Kāraṇḍavyūha Sūtra*, then, on the balance of the available evidence, is a work that was composed in Kashmir at around the end of the fourth and beginning of the fifth century C.E. In the following chapter, we begin our examination of the different religious influences brought to bear on the construction of the text.

CHAPTER 2

Purāṇic Influence on the *Kāraṇḍavyūha Sūtra*

In his study, published in 1971, of the various Vaiṣṇavite and Śaivite motifs found in the *Kāraṇḍavyūha*, Constantin Régamey suggested that there was a definite link between the sūtra and the purāṇas, the name given to those non-Buddhist texts that, together with the *Mahābhārata* and *Rāmāyaṇa*, underpin the so-called mytho-epic period of Indian religion. Meaning literally "belonging to old or ancient times," the purāṇas contain a great variety of different types of religious teaching, mixing discourses on philosophy, theology and doctrine with history, myth, and fable.

Régamey's conclusion was largely based on his discovery that a verse couplet from the sūtra was almost the exact replica of a couplet found in the Śaivite *Skanda Purāṇa*.[1] The verse itself is a concise statement of the doctrine of the *liṅga*, the central, phallic symbol of the Śaivite cult and might be translated into English as: "It is said that space is (his) *liṅga* and the earth his pedestal. He is the ground of all and is called *liṅga* because all beings dissolve into him." The *Kāraṇḍavyūha* is denigrating this doctrine: the verse is said, in the sūtra, to be uttered by "the foolish common people" (*īdṛśapṛthagjaneṣu sattveṣu*).[2] A comparison of the two versions shows that the only differences between the Buddhist and non-Buddhist presentations are one word and one syllable. In the sūtra, we find:

> *ākāśaṃ liṅgam ity āhuḥ pṛthivī tasya pīṭhikā*
> *ālayaḥ sarvabhūtānāṃ līyanāl liṅgam ucyate*[3]

and in the purāṇa:

> *ākāśaṃ liṅgam ity āhuḥ pṛthivī tasya pīṭhikā*
> *ālayaḥ sarvadevānāṃ lāyanāl liṅgam ucyate*

The *Kāraṇḍavyūha* replaces the word *devānāṃ*, "gods," with *bhūtānāṃ*, "beings," expressing a more inclusive view of the domain of the *liṅga's* creative power. It also changes *lāyanāl* to *līyanāl*, a unique Buddhist hybrid word derived, like the other, from the Sanskrit root *lī-*, "to dissolve." This, according to Régamey, because of its closer phonetic resemblance to the word *liṅga*, provides a more satisfying folk etymology than the more orthodox Sanskrit word.[4] This close similarity, then, between a verse from the sūtra and a verse from the *Skanda Purāṇa*, Régamey decides, is proof that sources for the *Kāraṇḍavyūha Sūtra* are to be sought among the purāṇas.[5] We might, to begin with, wish to be a little more cautious. In reproducing what was, in all likelihood, a fairly common definition of the word *liṅga*, the sūtra simply reveals that it springs from a Śaivite-influenced religious milieu.

In a recent survey of the purāṇas, Ludo Rocher remarks only that these texts "have a number of points in common with Buddhist literature."[6] In the Pali canon, he notes, the *jātaka* tales detailing the previous lives of Śākyamuni Buddha "often treat material very similar to those of the purāṇas."[7] The *Mañjuśrīmūlakalpa*, a Mahāyāna sūtra which, like the *Kāraṇḍavyūha*, also contains tantric-style material, contains prophetic history similar in character to the history found in some of the purāṇas.[8] The *Lalitavistara*, the Mahāyāna sūtra detailing the life of Śākyamuni Buddha, refers to itself, as Maurice Winternitz also observed, as a purāṇa.[9] There is only one major work in Buddhist literature, Rocher adds, that actually bears the name purāṇa in its title. This is the *Svayaṃbhūpurāṇa*, the *māhātmya* of the sacred places of Nepal, which, as we have seen, shares certain features with the verse *Kāraṇḍavyūha*.[10] But, both these works, as we have seen, are so late that any remarks made about them cannot be said to shed any light on the putative influence of the purāṇas on the original prose sūtra.

Rocher omits Winternitz's comment that, "by reason of the boundless exaggerations but also on account of the extravagance in the praise of *bhakti*," parts of the *Mahāvastu*, a non-Mahāyāna work describing the life and past lives of the Buddha, as well as Mahāyāna sūtras such as the *Saddharmapuṇḍarīka* and the *Kāraṇḍavyūha* itself, "remind us of the sectarian purāṇas."[11] He might, too, have added that the use of stories and myths in works such as the *Lalitavistara*, the *Mahāvastu* and the *Divyāvadāna* (part of the vinaya corpus of the Mūlasarvāstivādins) is also reminiscent of the purāṇic tradition. The same might be said for the *Kāraṇḍavyūha* itself.

The story found in the sūtra, for instance, about the shipwreck of king Siṃhala and his team of five hundred merchants bears some resemblance to one of the central episodes of the *Rāmāyaṇa*. In the sūtra, Siṃhala is helped to safety by Bālāha, the magical flying horse, from the *rākṣasī* inhabitants of an island, also known as Siṃhala. In the *Rāmāyaṇa*, Sītā is rescued by Rāma from the monstrous Rāvaṇa and the *rākṣasīs* of Laṅkā, an island traditionally referred to as Siṃhala Dvīpa, "the island of Siṃhala." These similarities are, however, only really significant enough to show that the sūtra is connected to a very broad, pan-Indian tradition of storytelling. The main elements of the two tales—the idea of an offshore island inhabited by demons and the danger of being shipwrecked there—are almost archetypal. The story of Siṃhala as found in the *Kāraṇḍavyūha* may, in fact, be accounted for purely in terms of the Buddhist tradition. The tale also appears, as Lienhard points out, as one of the Pali *jātakas*, as part of the *Mahāvastu* and as part of the *Divyāvadāna*.[12] The same basic theme is also reproduced in the *Saddharmapuṇḍarīka Sūtra*, where those who have set off onto the ocean in search of treasure and who have been blown onto the shore of *rākṣasīs* are among those who are said to be protected by calling on the name of Avalokiteśvara.[13]

Another chapter in the *Kāraṇḍavyūha*, however, looks very much more like the actual reworking of a purāṇic story. Avalokiteśvara, at one point, is said to appear in the realm of the gods in the form of the brahmin beggar Sukuṇḍala. One of the gods, being asked for alms by Sukuṇḍala, tells him that he has nothing to give. Sukuṇḍala replies that the god must give him something. When the god enters his palace, he discovers that his vessels have been miraculously filled with jewels, delicious food, and fine clothes. He then invites Sukuṇḍala inside to share in these things. This is then the cue for a discourse from Sukuṇḍala on the wondrous nature of the *vihāra* at Jetavana (it is strewn with jewels, inhabited by a *tathāgata*, full of wish-fulfilling trees, beautiful flowers, lotus pools and so on). Sukuṇḍala also explains that he is neither a god nor a man, but a bodhisattva, who feels compassion for the wretched and miserable and points out the path to awakening.[14]

Although my research has failed to discover any specific source for this story, there seem to be good reasons to understand it to be the somewhat clumsy adaptation of a purāṇic folktale.[15] First, the fact that the protagonist, Sukuṇḍala, is a brahmin suggests that this was not, originally, a Buddhist story. Second, the link between the action and the concluding sermon, which contains the doctrinal message of the piece, seems rather contrived, the sign of a crude ad hoc treatment of an old tale. Third, the chapter ends with another verse couplet, sung by the god to Sukuṇḍala, that is somewhat reminiscent of the use of the couplet commented on by Régamey. "In a meritorious field free of all faults," the god declares, "today a seed has been sown and today an abundance of fruit has been harvested."[16] Again, I remain ignorant of the use of this couplet anywhere else. But it seems quite plausible that, like Régamey's verse, it was originally a well-known saying associated with one or other of the two great purāṇic deities. If so, it is being used here, not as part of a Buddhist attack on purāṇic doctrine, but as a means of showing that Avalokiteśvara has, in some sense, usurped the position of these deities, an idea we will take up in earnest in the next chapter. The inclusion of Sukuṇḍala's statement to the effect that he is neither a god nor a man, but a bodhisattva, might, similarly, be a reminder that the brahmin beggar is now to be regarded as a manifestation of Avalokiteśvara and not, as seems quite likely to have been the case in an earlier version of the story, an emanation of one of the two main purāṇic gods.

That the *Kāraṇḍavyūha* is reworking elements of the purāṇic tradition is, however, conclusively demonstrated in the encounter that takes place between Avalokiteśvara and Bali, the king of the *asura*s. This chapter represents a Buddhist adaptation of what is often referred to as the *vāmana-avatāra* of the Vaiṣṇavite tradition, the story of Viṣṇu's appearance as a *vāmana*, or "dwarf." This mythical episode, which appears in many different versions, describes how Bali, who has overthrown the god Indra (or Śakra) as ruler of the world, is tricked into giving up his position by Viṣṇu. Appearing as a dwarf, the god asks Bali to be given as much land as he can cover in three strides. When Bali agrees to this proposal, Viṣṇu suddenly adopts a vast form, big enough to cover both the heavens and the earth in two strides. Bali, therefore, is stripped of his dominion. He is also, in some versions of the story, bound and taken off into captivity, because he is considered to be guilty of the further crime of being untrue to his word: having given everything he has in order to satisfy Viṣṇu's first two strides, he is simply incapable of living up to his promise of offering the god a third stride's worth of land.

Much of Régamey's 1971 piece on the *Kāraṇḍavyūha* was devoted to an analysis of the use of the *vāmana-avatāra* in the sūtra. It was, however, beyond his scope to search the purāṇas for similar treatments of the story and he ended the article by wondering whether "connoisseurs" of those texts might be able, eventually, to discover a "source" for the Buddhist version of the tale.[17] Happily, since then, a detailed study of the *vāmana-avatāra* has been published by Deborah A. Soifer, making this task a good deal easier.[18] As we shall see, an examination of different presentations of the myth does contribute to the sense that a connection might indeed exist between the *Kāraṇḍavyūha Sūtra* and the *Skanda Purāṇa*, the "source" of Régamey's verse couplet.

Soifer lists thirty different occurrences of the myth, twenty-four of which are taken from thirteen different purāṇas. The remaining six come from the great epics: three from the *Mahābhārata*, one from the *Rāmāyaṇa* and two from the *Harivaṃśa*, the long poem that is regarded as a supplement to the *Mahābhārata*, describing the life of the Vaiṣṇavite *avatāra* Kṛṣṇa.[19] Approximately half of all these are really only allusions to the story, describing its events in a few sentences. Of the other, fuller versions, two—one from the Vaiṣṇavite *Bhāgavata Purāṇa* (VIII. 15–23) and the other from the Śaivite *Skanda Purāṇa* (I. i. 18–19)—correspond in one very important respect to the presentation of the story found in the *Kāraṇḍavyūha Sūtra*.

The story, revolving as it does around the central event of the making of an offering by Bali to Viṣṇu, is almost bound to be linked, in any context, to the generalized religious virtue of "giving." However, what is distinctive about these three versions (in the two purāṇas and the one sūtra) is the overwhelming extent to which this theme is emphasized. Unlike other purāṇas, the *Bhāgavata* and the *Skanda* use the myth very much as a kind of moral fable designed to encourage the making of donations to religious institutions. This theme, common enough in Buddhist discourses to the laity, appears also to be the main purpose behind the inclusion of the story in the sūtra. In the course of this presentation of the myth, all three of these different versions punctuate the narrative with reflections on the limited worth of material possessions and the uselessness of such things at the time of death.

In the Vaiṣṇavite *Bhāgavata Purāṇa*, first of all, the dwarf responds to Bali's greeting with the words:

> Never was any such coward king in your family who at the time of religious donations turned his face against persons who, deserving the gift, had requested for it . . .[20]

Bali responds to the dwarf's request for three paces of land by saying that he should ask for as much land as he needs. Viṣṇu replies:

> All the desired-most objects (or lands) that are available in the three worlds cannot be enough to satisfy a person who has not subdued his senses or the mind, oh king! He who is dissatisfied with three feet of land, cannot have his desire fulfilled with an island-continent consisting of nine *varṣas* (sub-continents), as he will crave to possess all the seven island-continents. . . . A contented person leads a happy life, while a discontented person who has no control over himself, is never satisfied even if the three worlds be possessed by him. It is said that non-contentment with reference to wealth and objects of enjoyment, is the cause of transmigration of man in this world, and that contentment with what one happens to get by (one's predestined) luck, is the way to emancipation (from *saṃsāra*).[21]

Bali's preceptor Śukra recognizes that the dwarf is really Viṣṇu in disguise. Fearing the potential consequences of the god's demands, he argues that it is better to temper the urge to make charitable or religious offerings with an element of worldly prudence:

> They (i.e. the wise) do not commend that gift as good if it endangers the means of livelihood of the donor. For in this world, charitable gifts, performance of sacrifices, austere penances and religious acts can be performed by persons with means of subsistence. A person who divides his wealth in five shares (and invests it) for the purpose of religious acts, glory, getting economic return, personal pleasure and provision of one's relatives, becomes happy here and hereafter.[22]

Bali agrees with these sentiments. "What has been stated by your worship is true," he says.[23] But, nonetheless, he goes on to argue that he must fulfill his promise. Even if the dwarf does prove to be Viṣṇu, he adds, and he is forced to give away everything he has, this will still be a good thing:

> O *brāhmaṇa* sage! Those who lay down their lives without retreating from the battlefield are easily available, but not so the donors who, when approached by worthy recipients, reverentially give away their wealth. Poverty and affliction in consequence of satisfying the desires of (ordinary) supplicants appear graceful to a magnanimous and merciful soul. Need it be said that it is much more so in cases like yours who know the Brāhman or Vedas?[24]

Then, at the end of the story, after he has been bound for failing to keep his promise, Bali says:

> What is the use of the body which abandons one ultimately (at the time of death)? Of what worth are the robbers, designated as one's own people (e.g. sons, kith and kin), who take away our property? Of what purpose is the wife who is the cause of transmigration in the *saṃsāra*? What is the use of houses to a mortal? It is sheer waste of life here.... It is sheer good luck that I too am brought to the presence of yourself—you who are the destroyer of both subtle and gross bodies ... and that I am forcibly made to give up my wealth (and glorious position). And it is wealth (and position) that deprives man of his judgment and makes him incapable of understanding the uncertainties of life, due to its being within the clutches of death.[25]

Finally, similar sentiments are voiced by Bali's grandfather Prahlāda. He says:

> I consider that great divine grace has been shown unto him (Bali) in that he has been relieved of his fortune which infatuates the mind and bewilders the soul. By wealth, even a self-controlled learned person gets deluded (and forgets the essential nature of the soul, even though known previously).[26]

In much the same way, the *vāmana-avatāra* is also used to extol the virtue of making religious donations in the Śaivite *Skanda Purāṇa*. There, an imaginative solution is found to the problem of how a story about an offering made to Viṣṇu might be used to promote the giving of donations to Śiva. In a previous life, we read, Bali had been a roguish and sinful gambler who, undergoing a sudden change of heart, had become a great donor of gifts to

Śiva. It is this relationship with Śiva, the purāṇa says, that is both the cause of the gambler's auspicious rebirth as Bali and, also, what eventually saves him, as Bali, from being punished. The story is preceded by some general remarks on charitable giving and the cult of Śiva. For instance:

> A man seeks something and gains his object. Know that immediately (after getting the result) a sort of niggardliness besets him. Afterwards he dies and his merit becomes exhausted. . . . Hence there is nothing more conducive to liberation than charitable gifts. From charitable gifts, knowledge is acquired and from knowledge, liberation is achieved undoubtedly. Devotion unto the Trident-bearing Lord (Śiva) is greater than liberation, O *brāhmaṇas*. Sadāśiva, the lord of all, gives away everything when his mind is pleased. Śaṅkara becomes satisfied with even a very little thing that is offered, say, even water of a very little quantity. In this connection they cite this ancient legend.[27]

There then follows the story of the gambler. On his way to a prostitute, he is robbed of all his ill-gotten gains and left with only a loin cloth and the flowers, betel leaves and sandal paste he had planned to take to the woman. Clasping his shoulders with his hands to cover his nakedness, he makes the sign of the swastika. Then, running on, he stumbles and falls to the ground, going into a swoon. When he regains consciousness, he finds that his mind is naturally directed towards wholesome thoughts. He is disgusted with worldly objects and repents of his past. "The scent, the flowers etc. that had fallen on the ground," we read, "were dedicated to Śiva by that gambler unconsciously and unintentionally."[28] Later, when he dies, it is this action that prevents him from being reborn in hell. Instead, he is given, for a short time, the position of Indra. The purāṇa then asks:

> What then in the case of those people who are actuated by faith to offer large quantities of scents, flowers etc. always with great devotion to Śiva, the Supreme Spirit? (i.e. they deserve much greater reward). They will attain *Śivasāyujya* (identity with Śiva). They will be accompanied by Śiva's army and acquire great joy. Indeed Śakra is the servant of such people. . . . Mahādeva is (i.e. deserves) to be worshipped and adored by all living beings knowing the truth. Thus the gambler attained the status of Indra for a period of three *ghaṭikās*.[29]

In this new and exalted position, the gambler behaves very generously. As a result, when Indra retakes his throne, the former sinner is reborn as Bali. Bali, in turn, continues to express the same generous impulse. We read: "Thus, O *brāhmaṇas*, Bali became eagerly devoted and engaged in munificent charitable gifts due to the previous practice which the gambler had, because he was engaged in the worship of Śiva."[30] Bali's father, Virocana we read, was also very generous, to the extent that he even cut off his own head and offered it to Śakra. This prompts the following remarks:

> There is nothing greater than a charitable gift anywhere. That charitable gift offered to persons in distress is highly meritorious. Anything whatsoever within one's capacity, (if offered) is capable of infinite results. There is nothing greater than a charitable gift in all the three worlds.[31]

The purāṇa then tells the story of the *vāmana-avatāra*. At the end of the story, Bali escapes punishment. After some intercessionary pleading by his wife, Vindhyāvalī, he is told to go to the heavenly realm of Sutala. The same ending is also described in the *Bhāgavata Purāṇa*, where Vindhyāvalī is joined by Prahlāda and the god Brahmā in pleading for clemency. Bali's redemption in the *Skanda Purāṇa* is said to be due to the "favour of Śaṅkara"[32] (a synonym of Śiva). The merit earned by the gambler's original, unintentional offering to Śiva has, it seems, been enough to save both the gambler and Bali from going to hell. The chapter ends with a repeat of an earlier refrain and further praises to Śiva:

> In his former birth as a gambler, fragrant flowers and other things that had fallen on dirty ground were offered by him to the great *ātman*. What had fallen down was dedicated to Śiva, the great spirit, by him. What then in the case of those who worship Maheśvara with the greatest devotion? Those who devoutly offer sweet scents, flowers, fruits or even water go to Śiva's presence . . . Mahādeva should be worshipped in the form of *liṅga* by those who desire salvation. There is no greater bestower of worldly pleasures and liberation than Śiva.[33]

The same overriding emphasis on the virtue of charitable giving is also found in the version of the *vāmana-avatāra* in the *Kāraṇḍavyūha*, where the story is presented as if told by Bali to Avalokiteśvara. Both at the beginning and at the end, the bodhisattva discourses on the value of making religious donations and on the uselessness of material possessions at the time of death. First, after he has been greeted by Bali, the bodhisattva describes the various benefits of filling Buddhist alms bowls. They who regularly fill the bowls of those belonging to the Buddhist order, he says, will never be overwhelmed by sloth, will write and have written the *Kāraṇḍavyūha Sūtra*, remember its name and listen to *Dharma*-teachings from it.[34] They who fill the alms bowl of a single bodhisattva will remember, talk about, write, and listen together to the *Dharma*-teachings of a *dharmabhāṇaka*, or "*Dharma*-preacher."[35] They who, asking for a *Dharma*-teaching from a *tathāgata*, fill his bowl with a daily meal, will become *cakravartin* kings, will never experience the suffering of hunger and thirst, of hell, and of being separated from loved ones, and will go to Sukhāvatī, where they will appear before Amitābha, listen to the *Dharma* and receive predictions of their enlightenment.[36] Avalokiteśvara then gives a list of comparisons and examples showing the extraordinary amount of merit earned by filling the alms bowl of a *tathāgata*.[37] At the end of the story, Avalokiteśvara turns his attention to the perils of clinging to worldly wealth in the face of death. Material possessions, he says, are dreamlike and will offer no protection at that time. As people are dragged down into hell, the bodhisattva explains, they will be told by the henchmen of Yama, the lord of death, that one of the causes of their suffering is the fact that they failed to make offerings to the alms bowl of a *tathāgata*.[38]

Bali is also saved from final punishment in the *Kāraṇḍavyūha*. Having promised to do whatever Viṣṇu ordains, Bali then supplicates Avalokiteśvara, begging him to be his protector.[39] This leads the bodhisattva to make a *vyākaraṇa*, or "prediction," typical of the Mahāyāna sūtras: Bali will become a *tathāgata* called "Śrī"; all the *asura*s will be converted to the true way; there will be neither greed, nor hatred nor delusion in Bali's buddha-field and the six-syllable formula will be obtained, the first reference to *Oṃ Maṇipadme Hūṃ* in the entire sūtra.[40]

The *Kāraṇḍavyūha* is perhaps less ingenious than the *Skanda Purāṇa* in the way it adapts the Vaiṣṇavite story to a non-Vaiṣṇavite polemic. In the sūtra, the solution to this problem lies not in an account of Bali's previous lives, but in reconsidering what Bali's crime really is. This is now deemed to consist not, as in the traditional version, of being unable to keep his promise, but rather, in having made his offering to the wrong being. According to the *Kāraṇḍavyūha*, Bali should not have given to Viṣṇu at all, but to the Buddha instead. As Régamey points out, the Buddhist version of the story is framed, at the beginning and end, by a lament of Bali to precisely this effect. The same Sanskrit phrase is used twice: *kukṣetre mayā dāṇaṃ dattam*, meaning: "I have put my gift in the wrong place."[41] Bali declares he has acted in the manner of a *tīrthika* (*tairthikadṛṣṭiparyāpannena*),[42] the term most commonly used in the Mahāyāna literature to refer to non-Buddhists. The story, in other words, has become a parable, not just about the merit of giving to religious institutions, but about the relative worthlessness of giving to anyone other than the Buddha. The *Kāraṇḍavyūha*, it seems, reflects a situation in which Mahāyāna Buddhists were in competition with other sects for religious patronage.

However, despite this radical reworking of the myth, the sūtra cannot do away entirely with the idea of Bali's failure to provide the third stride of land, so fundamental is this to the original story. Shortly before the second of Bali's laments about his failure to put his gift in the right place, he confesses to

Viṣṇu that the third pace is not to be found.[43] Next, the god says that where he places him, there he will stay.[44] It is this statement, not the promise to give the three paces, that now appears to be the measure of Bali's integrity. He promises to do what the god commands, and then, being asked if he keeps the truth, says that he keeps the truth.[45] The same clumsiness that seemed to be a feature of the sūtra's adaptation of the story of Sukuṇḍala is also apparent here. The narrative has become slightly muddled. It just does not make sense that no sooner has Bali confessed to the evil of one act—the failure to give the third pace—then he is seen, once again, to be decrying the fact that he has erred in doing something else entirely different, namely, putting his gift in the wrong place.[46]

The question remains, however, as to whether our findings represent sufficient evidence to identify a specific purāṇa as a "source" for the sūtra, as Régamey seems to have hoped. One of the problems, here, as Rocher points out, is that the purāṇas, in general, are not monolithic texts, composed and written down at one particular time. Rather, they are composite works, made up of numerous independent sections. These, originating from different places and from different historical periods, may have been circulated quite separately from one another before eventually being gathered together in the same work. Moreover, the mode of their circulation would almost always have been oral, not textual. As Rocher writes: "The principal reason why purāṇic—and epic—stories can be treated with such a high degree of freedom is that, fundamentally, they do not belong in books."[47] Any similarities between the *Kāraṇḍavyūha* and an individual purāṇa is likely only to indicate that the sūtra was influenced by an oral tradition lying behind the purāṇa (or part of the purāṇa) and not that it was actually borrowing from a written document.

Nonetheless, it still seems legitimate to posit, tentatively, a link between the *Kāraṇḍavyūha Sūtra* and the *Skanda Purāṇa*. The evidence for this, as we have seen, is the use of the same verse couplet about the *liṅga* and the similar treatments given to the *vāmana-avatāra* in the two works. The earliest manuscript of the *Skanda* has been dated, on palæographic grounds, to sometime before the middle of the seventh century C.E.[48] However, the dating of the written text is not really an issue here. Even if this represents the date of the "first edition" of the purāṇa, it is still perfectly possible, indeed likely, that elements of the purāṇa derive from much earlier times.

With regard to the couplet, it is, to say the least, unfortunate that Régamey was unable to give a precise reference for this verse in the *Skanda Purāṇa*, having come across it not in any edition of the text itself, but in a modern anthology of Indian religious scriptures compiled by Alain Daniélou. Daniélou notes only that it appears in the *Skanda Purāṇa*.[49] The task of pinpointing the two lines is made somewhat difficult, not only because of the vast size of this purāṇa, but also because it exists in several different editions. Like Régamey,

I, too, have failed to discover the exact location of the couplet. I have, however, found a number of similar verses.

The purāṇa contains numerous statements about the universal practice of worshipping the *liṅga* as Śiva. For instance: "Those who continuously worship Śiva in the form of *liṅga*, whether they be women or *śūdras* or *cāṇḍālas* or other low-caste people, do attain Śiva, the destroyer of miseries."[50] But, discussion of the *liṅga* in the purāṇas is, of course, by no means limited to the *Skanda Purāṇa* alone. It appears, to a greater or lesser degree, in all the Śaivite purāṇas and in some Vaiṣṇavite ones, too. Nonetheless, my own brief survey of several of these other Śaivite works would suggest that statements like the verse couplet of the *Kāraṇḍavyūha*—in which the *liṅga* is defined in terms of a specific ability to absorb all things into itself—are rare. In the course of my search of other Śaivite purāṇas, I found none like this. The *Skanda Purāṇa*, on the other hand, contains at least two passages of this kind. Thus: "The whole range of the three worlds was pervaded in the form of *liṅga* by the great lord. It is called *liṅga* by all the *Suras* and *Asuras* because it absorbs the world within it. *Devas* with Brahmā and Viṣṇu at their head do not know its limits and extremities."[51] And, closer still to the etymological definition of the *Kāraṇḍavyūha*: "Since the entire universe became *līna* (merged) in the *liṅga* of the great *Ātman* (it came to be called so). Learned men say that it is called *liṅga* because of *layana* (merging of the universe)."[52] The common use of this distinctive view of the Śaivite *liṅga* is, surely, a slight indication that the sūtra and the purāṇa may be connected.

As we have already observed, among the many different presentations of the *vāmana-avatāra*, the versions found in the *Bhāgavata Purāṇa*, the *Skanda Purāṇa* and the *Kāraṇḍavyūha Sūtra* are unusual in the degree to which the story is used to promote the virtue of giving to religious cults. However, if either of these two purāṇas—or the oral traditions from which they derive—is to be posited as having any bearing on the way in which the *Kāraṇḍayūha* took up the myth, the *Skanda Purāṇa* is by far the more likely candidate. This is because, as we shall see, the interface between the Buddhist and the purāṇic traditions reflected in the text of the *Kāraṇḍavyūha* is, essentially, a meeting between Buddhism and Śaivism. On those grounds, it is unlikely that the sūtra would have been drawing on a tradition associated with the Vaiṣṇavite *Bhāgavata Purāṇa*. It is possible, though, that the sūtra may have taken the *Skanda Purāṇa* for its lead in the way a Vaiṣṇavite myth might be adapted to promote the virtue of giving to a non-Vaiṣṇavite cult: in the *Skanda* to the cult of Śiva and in the *Kāraṇḍavyūha* to the cult of the Buddha.

The sūtra is clearly not following the written version of the *Skanda*, at least not the version of the purāṇa that we are familiar with. As well as the similarities, there are also a great many differences between the respective treatments of the *vāmana-avatāra*. The version in the sūtra, for instance, contains a long passage describing the imprisonment by Bali of hundreds of thousands of *kṣatriyas* and their subsequent rescue by Viṣṇu, an episode which is wholly absent from the presentation of the myth found in the purāṇas.[53] This section of the sūtra also contains the description of Viṣṇu appearing in the different forms of a fly, a bee, a wild boar and a man,[54] which, as Régamey writes, reflects another different strand of tradition.[55] Régamey also points out the awkward way in which this section is introduced into the sūtra. The narrative changes abruptly from the first person singular to the third person, as Bali's description of the preparations for his sacrifice trails off and gives way to the story of the *kṣatriyas*.[56] It is very difficult from the present perspective to discern how this little episode adds to the general purpose of the sūtra. The disjointed nature of its place in the narrative suggests that it is a secondary addition to the original, main body of the sūtra, made for a reason that must remain, for the time being, obscure.

Similarly, both the *Bhāgavata* and the *Skanda* contain passages unique to their own particular presentation of the *vāmana-avatāra*. The story of the gambler, for instance, or the episode in which Bali's father, Virocana, cuts off his own head are peculiar, in this context, to the *Skanda Purāṇa*. Likewise, the *Bhāgavata Purāṇa* includes a tale about the two brothers, Hiraṇyakaśipu and Hiraṇyākṣa, not found in any other version of the myth.[57] When the former is killed by Viṣṇu (in his boar incarnation), the latter vows to take revenge, but Viṣṇu hides himself within the warrior's body, with the result that after a long search, Hiraṇyākṣa concludes that his brother's killer must be dead. The rationale of this story, however, is connected to the idea of Virocana's magnanimous nature, a theme, as we have seen, also found in the *Skanda Purāṇa*. The story ends by saying that, in this world, enmity continues as far as death. This, then, is immediately followed by a statement to the effect that Virocana, despite knowing that certain brahmins were really enemy gods in disguise, "still conferred his lease of life upon them."[58]

Such differences serve only to emphasise the final independence of all three texts from one another. They virtually rule out a scenario in which the composers of the *Kāraṇḍavyūha* used a written version of a *Skanda Purāṇa* as a "source." But the similarities between the two works are still, I think, enough to warrant taking seriously the idea that the sūtra was influenced by an oral tradition that contributed to the production of the Śaivite purāṇa. The idea may have to remain, for the time being, a working hypothesis. Nonetheless, the sūtra must have been influenced by at least one strand of the Śaivite purāṇic tradition. For the Buddhist encounter with Śaivism is one of the sūtra's recurrent concerns.

As we have already indicated, Régamey's couplet occurs in a section of the *Kāraṇḍavyūha* in which Śaivite beliefs are beings deliberately disparaged. The doctrine of the *liṅga*, described in the couplet, is said to be the talk of foolish, common people. Furthermore, the context in which this passage occurs takes the form of a speech made by Avalokiteśvara to Śiva (referred to as Maheśvara), in which the bodhisattva says that he (Śiva) will appear in the degenerate *kaliyuga* and be called the *ādideva*, or "primordial god," the creator and author of the world. The beings in that time, Avalokiteśvara adds, will be deprived of the path to awakening.[59] A clear distinction is being made here between Buddhism and Śaivism: Śaivite beliefs are presented as misleading and degenerate.

The predominant response to Śaivism reflected in the sūtra is not, however, one of hostile rejection, but, rather, one of friendly (or condescending) conversion. The Buddhist use of the subjugation myth is one of those features of the sūtra that are more commonly associated with the tantras. There, non-Buddhist deities are usually made to submit to *Buddhadharma* by the use of the superior force of a bodhisattva. For instance, in the conversion of Śiva described in the *Sarvatathāgatatattvasaṃgraha*, the bodhisattva Vajrapāṇi actually kills the god and treads him underfoot, before eventually relenting and bringing him back to life to predict his future attainment of buddhahood.[60] In the *Kāraṇḍavyūha Sūtra*, on the other hand, Śiva appears to surrender himself voluntarily to Avalokiteśvara, a reflection, presumably, of the "peaceful" character of this bodhisattva, in contrast to the "wrathful" character of Vajrapāṇi.

The episode is placed near the end of the *Kāraṇḍavyūha*, after the story of the discovery of *Oṃ Maṇipadme Hūṃ* and immediately before the final section of the sūtra, the teaching on monastic discipline given by Śākyamuni to his disciple Ānanda. Śiva (referred to again as Maheśvara) appears before Avalokiteśvara and, unprompted, prostrates himself and asks for a *vyākaraṇa* of his future buddhahood.[61] Like the conversion story of the *Sarvatathāgatatattvasaṃgraha*, Śiva is then identified as the *tathāgata* Bhasmeśvara, or "Lord of Ashes." This is an allusion to the predeliction of Śiva (and the Śaivite yogin) for smearing his body with ashes and practising his meditations in charnel grounds and cemeteries.[62] Umādevī, Śiva's consort, also appears at this point in the sūtra and is told by Avalokiteśvara that she will become the *tathāgata* Umeśvara.[63]

A similar conversion is also, as we have already seen, part of the sūtra's presentation of the *vāmana-avatāra*. Bali, after confessing his wrongdoing and supplicating Avalokiteśvara, is told that he will become the *tathāgata* Śrī.[64] The conversion of all three figures might be said to express the same essentially triumphalist note: the Buddhist path is the superior path, taken up with enthusiasm by Bali and, even, by Śiva himself. The conversion of Śiva and Umādevī has an additional significance, however. It shows how the power of other deities may be tamed and harnessed to the *Buddhadharma*. The myth accounts for the synthesis of Śaivite principles into the Buddhist system.

The conversion of Śiva is also, it seems, the subject of the short chapter of the *Kāraṇḍavyūha* in which Avalokiteśvara appears in the form of a bee (*bhramararūpa*).[65] The buzzing (*ghuṇaghuṇāyamāṇam*) of this bee is said to produce the sound *namo buddhāya namo dharmāya namaḥ saṃghāya.*[66] As a result, the worms and insects of the sewers of Vārāṇasī bring this formula to mind, destroy the "twenty-peaked false view of individuation" (*viṃśatiśikhara-samudgataṃ satkāyadṛṣṭiśailaṃ*) and are born, in Sukhāvatī, as bodhisattvas called "Sugandhamukha."[67] There, they listen to the *Kāraṇḍavyūha Sūtra* in the presence of Amitābha and, like Bali, Maheśvara and Umādevī, receive *vyākaraṇas* of their future careers on the Buddhist path.[68]

Avalokiteśvara, here, appears in a guise traditionally associated with the purāṇic gods. As the sūtra's own presentation of the *vāmana-avatāra* has already demonstrated, Viṣṇu is known to manifest as a bee.[69] It is also a form sometimes adopted by Śiva, as shown in a long list of the god's epithets in the *Śiva Purāṇa*. He is, variously:

> . . . the sacrifice, the performer of sacrifice, Kāla, the intelligent, the bee, the moving one, the one originating from the hedges of the trees . . .[70]

The sound of the bee is, also, traditionally a sign of the presence of the divine. This is not unconnected to the ancient Indian notion of *ruta-jñāna*, the "understanding (*jñāna*) of the cries (*ruta*)" of animals, a faculty possessed by poets and sages enabling them to discern the spiritual significance of the sounds of the natural world. In Monier Monier-Williams' definition of this term, he singles out three sounds that are particularly associated with this interpretative principle: the neighing of horses, the singing of birds, and the humming of bees.[71] In the introduction to the version of the *vāmana-avatāra* in the *Bhāgavata Purāṇa*, Viṣṇu (here referred to as Hari) is surrounded by bees:

> Irradiated with his special splendid *vanamālā* (wreath of forest flowers) resonant with a swarm of humming bees and with the *kaustubha* gem suspended from his neck, Lord Hari dispelled with his splendour the gloom in the house of Kaśyapa, the Lord of Creation, with his effulgence.[72]

Similarly, as Guy L. Beck explains in his study of the use of sound in Indian religion, the buzzing of a bee is one of the sounds said to be heard in the internal world of the yogin. The *Nādabindu Upaniṣad*, for instance, lists a series of these noises in order of progressive refinement. The sound of the bee (*bhramara*) is the most subtle, coming after the sounds of the ocean (*jaladhi*), the cloud (*jīmūta*), the kettle drum (*bherī*), the waterfall (*nirjhara*), a small drum (*mardala*), a bell (*ghaṇṭā*), a military drum (*kāhala*), a tinkling bell (*kiṅkinī*), the bamboo flute (*vaṃśa*)and the harp (*vīṇā*).[73]

The manifestation of Avalokiteśvara as a bee in the *Kāraṇḍavyūha* conforms, then, to an established Indian convention of the appearance of the divine or supernormal. In the sūtra, the buzzing of the bee is heard by the worms and insects (*kṛmikula*) of Vārāṇasī. In the *Vidyeśvarasaṃhitā* section of the *Śiva Purāṇa*, in the course of a discussion of the significance of the *liṅga*, we read:

> The phallic emblem is of two varieties: the stationary and the mobile. Trees, hedges etc. represent the stationary. Worms, insects etc. represent the mobile. For the stationary one, tending and similar service is recommended. For the mobile one *tarpaṇa* (propitiation) is recommended.[74]

Vārāṇasī, of course, is the great Śaivite city. The bee bodhisattva, therefore, would appear to be exercising his influence on a Śaivite constituency, the worms and insects of the city that are, according to the purāṇa, a "mobile" form of the Śaivite *liṅga*. Śiva, as we have seen above, is worshipped as the *liṅga*. The story, in other words, seems to be a rather picaresque way of showing, once again, that Avalokiteśvara converts Śiva to the Buddhist way.

Viṣṇu is also a presence in the *Kāraṇḍavyūha*, particularly, of course, in the version of the *vāmana-avatāra*. However, as we have seen, the use of that myth in the sūtra may be accounted for by the influence of a Śaivite tradition: the *Skanda Purāṇa* provides a precedent for the way in which the Vaiṣṇavite story may be adapted to a non-Vaiṣṇavite polemic. Similarly, although Viṣṇu is regularly mentioned elsewhere in the sūtra, his name only ever occurs in the context of standard lists of deities that betray, if anything, a slight Śaivite bias, in so far as Śiva (or Maheśvara) is usually named before Viṣṇu (or Nārāyaṇa).

Thus, in the description of the great assembly in the *vihāra* at Jetavana, a group of thirty-two gods is said to be led by Śiva and Viṣṇu (or, as the sūtra says, by Maheśvara and Nārāyaṇa).[75] A description of the qualities of Avalokiteśvara, relayed to Śākyamuni by the merchant Vipaśyin, begins by describing how the sun and moon are born from his eyes, Maheśvara from his brow, Brahmā from his shoulders and Nārāyaṇa from his heart.[76] When the *tathāgata* Śikhin explains that Avalokiteśvara can take on whatever form is suitable to accomplish the conversion of beings, after detailing various Buddhist manifestations (*tathāgata*, *pratyekabuddha*, *arhat* and bodhisattva), the list of other such forms begins with Maheśvara and Nārāyaṇa: to beings to be converted to the true religion by Maheśvara he teaches the *Dharma* in the form of Maheśvara and to beings to be converted to the true religion by Nārāyaṇa he teaches the *Dharma* in the form of Nārāyaṇa.[77] Sarvanīvaraṇaviṣkambhin, or "Preventer of all Obstructions," the bodhisattva who is the chief protagonist and interlocutor of the second part of the sūtra, says of the *dharmabhāṇaka* who grants initiation into the use of *Oṃ Maṇipadme Hūṃ*, that the *tathāgata*s are taught by him and that numerous bodhisattvas worship him, as do various gods, beginning with the triad Brahmā, Viṣṇu and Maheśvara.[78]

The evidence of the text would suggest, then, that the environment in which the sūtra was written was one in which the main purāṇic deity was Śiva. That is not to say, however, that Viṣṇu was absent from this milieu. It seems likely that, although Śiva dominated, Viṣṇu filled a significant supporting role. In the sūtra's version of the *vāmana-avatāra*, for instance, it is an accepted fact that Viṣṇu is a powerful and important deity. A certain element of Vaiṣṇavite religiosity is reflected in the text. More precisely, as Régamey points out, this strand of Vaiṣṇavism is also likely to be one in which some emphasis was given to the manifestation of the deity as Rāma, When, at the beginning of the sūtra, Avalokiteśvara enters hell, Yama asks whether he is a manifestation of Maheśvara, Nārāyaṇa or the *rākṣasa* Rāvaṇa: the last of these three is, of course, the name of the great demon of the *Rāmāyaṇa* who captures and carries off Sītā, Rāma's wife, to the island of Laṅkā.[79]

Similarly, in the presentation of the myth in the *Skanda Purāṇa*, no attempt is made to belittle Viṣṇu. Quite the opposite: his significance is often emphasized. Virocana's self-decapitation, for instance, is accounted for by the powerful effects of worshipping Viṣṇu. It was, we read, "very difficult to do, but by resorting to *bhakti* (devotion) alone of Viṣṇu, it was done by him with his mind devoted to him."[80] Viṣṇu is praised in fulsome terms in the course of the Śaivite purāṇa. Bali, at one point, says: "This Viṣṇu is the lord of the fruits of all karma. Certainly, those people in whose heart Viṣṇu is stationed are the most deserving persons. Everything seen in this world is called holy by his name. This Hari is the lord of the universe . . ."[81] As Jan Gonda comments: "Many purāṇic legends indeed give evidence of the conviction that the great divine powers complement each other and that they are to co-operate for the well-being of the world and mankind."[82]

Gonda illustrates this remark by referring to the legend, also found in the *Skanda Purāṇa*, about the formation of a famous well called "Maṇikarṇikā," or "Earring," in Vārāṇasī.[83] The well is said to have been dug by Viṣṇu with his discus and filled with the perspiration from the god's body. However, it is said to have received its name when Śiva, seeing in the well the radiance of a hundred million suns, began praising Viṣṇu and offered to give him whatever he might ask. When Viṣṇu replied that his only desire was that the other god should always live there with him, Śiva shook with delight, with the result that an ornament from Śiva's ear, a *maṇikarṇikā*, dropped into the well.

This is an example of what Gonda refers to as the "complementary" relationship between the two gods, In addition, Gonda also describes what he calls a "compromise," in which one god temporarily allows the other to hold sway, and "inclusivism," in which one god subsumes the power of other deities into himself. An example of "compromise" is the Vaiṣṇavite tradition that, when in the great Śaivite city of Vārāṇasī, even Vaiṣṇavites worship Śiva the supreme deity. Śiva's ability to liberate anyone who dies within the city is said, in this context, to be a privilege granted to him by Viṣṇu, in the form of Rāma, as a reward for the many aeons spent by Śiva in reciting the mantra of Rāma.[84] An example of "inclusivism" is the story attached to the Śaivite *liṅga* at a place in Vārāṇasī named "Brahmātīrtha," so called because it was said to have been brought to the city by the god Brahmā and installed by Viṣṇu, when the latter god's devotion to Śiva proved to be even greater than the former's.[85]

Perhaps the most compact expression of this syncretistic tendency—and another instance of the "complementary" relationship between the two gods—is found in the notion of Hari-Hara, in which Hari (a synonym of Viṣṇu's) and Hara (a synonym of Śiva) constitute the two halves of a single being. As we shall see, it is the opinion of Lokesh Chandra that this form was linked to the development of the thousand-armed Avalokiteśvara. The earliest known example of a Hari-Hara sculpture, Chandra writes, is an image found in a cave at Bijapur, near Mysore. Unfortunately, this bears an inscription giving it the precise date of 578 C.E.,[86] roughly two hundred years after our estimated date for the *Kāraṇḍavyūha Sūtra*. But there may be earlier examples that have not survived, or are yet to be discovered.

For the moment, though, we must conclude this chapter by saying simply that, just as Régamey suspected, close similarities do exist between the *Kāraṇḍavyūha Sūtra* and the purāṇas. The precise nature of this connection remains obscure. However, it seems reasonable to posit some sort of link between the sūtra and the Śaivite *Skanda Purāṇa*. More generally and less controversially, the sūtra clearly reflects a close interaction with a non-Buddhist religious milieu that is predominantly Śaivite, but one which is also respectful of the Vaiṣṇavite tradition. In the following chapter, we trace in more detail how this purāṇic influence shaped the sūtra's conception of the bodhisattva Avalokiteśvara.

CHAPTER 3

Avalokiteśvara as the Buddhist *Īśvara*

The close connection between the *Kāraṇḍavyūha* and the purāṇic tradition is apparent, once again, in the sūtra's presentation of the central figure of Avalokiteśvara, who boasts many of the attributes of the great purāṇic deities. In brief, Avalokiteśvara takes on the form of an *īśvara*, or "lord."[1] This is a term predominantly associated with Śiva, but which is, nonetheless, also used to refer to Viṣṇu.[2] In this respect, then, its application to the figure of Avalokiteśvara might be said to be wholly in keeping with the dominant Śaivite influence apparent in the sūtra that we remarked upon in the previous chapter.

Viṣṇu, for example, is described as an *īśvara* when he appears in the form of Kṛṣṇa in the *Bhagavadgītā*, a work probably composed some time before the beginning of the first millenium C.E.[3] Two examples follow:

> . . . although I am lord (*īśvaro*) of beings . . .[4]

And

> When the lord (*īśvara*) takes on a body and when he steps up out of it . . .[5]

In the *Śiva Purāṇa*, for instance, Śiva is described as *īśvara* as part of a long eulogy paid to the god:

> . . . the lord of the three worlds, *īśvara*, Hara, the bay-eyed, the cause of the dissolution of the Yugas . . .[6]

The god is also often referred to as *maheśvara*, or great (*maha-*) *īśvara*, a term which is also used as a proper name for the god. In the *Śiva Purāṇa*, again, we read:

> It was Śiva who did everything. There is no doubt in this. It was lord *maheśvara* who deluded your splendid intellect and made you suffer on account of love . . .[7]

And in the Śaivite *Liṅga Purāṇa*:

> Brahmā requested me to grant power to create. He said: "O Mahādeva, O *maheśvara*, grant power unto my sons."[8]

In the *Kāraṇḍavyūha Sūtra*, Avalokiteśvara is addressed as *maheśvara* three times: once by Yama, the lord of death, during the bodhisattva's journey into hell,[9] once by Śiva (who is also, somewhat confusingly, referred to as *maheśvara devaputro* at this point),[10] and once by Umādevī,[11] in the course of their respective conversions.

Intimately connected to the idea of an *īśvara* is the notion of a supreme *puruṣa*, a great "man" or "person" who both pervades the universe and is responsible for its creation. "Thus," according to Gonda, "the term does not signify a creator other than the created, but a principle which is eventually one with it."[12] This is an idea which finds its oldest and most influential expression in the so-called *puruṣasūkta*, or *puruṣa* hymn, of *Ṛgveda*, x, 90. Gonda comments: "This poem—which has perhaps been composed about 1000 B.C.—is in ancient India the first expression of the idea that creation is the self-limitation of the transcendent Person manifesting himself in the realm of our experience."[13] In the *Śiva Purāṇa*, Śiva is referred to as *puruṣa*, along with *īśvara* and *maheśvara* in some of the long lists, found in that work, that record the many different epithets of the god. For example:

> . . . the creator of the universe, the sustainer of the universe, the eternal *puruṣa*, the stable one, the presiding deity of Dharma . . .[14]

Elsewhere in the purāṇa, we read:

> You are a great *puruṣa*, the lord, beyond *sattva*, *rajas* and *tamas*. You are both *saguṇa* and *nirguṇa*. You are a great lord, a cosmic witness, and free from aberration.[15]

In the *Bhagavadgītā*, references to Kṛṣṇa as *puruṣa* are numerous.[16] Both *īśvara* and *puruṣa* are found together, for instance:

> In this way, lord in the highest degree (*parameśvara*), you have described your self; I desire to see your supreme form, greatest of persons (*puruṣottama*).[17]

And

But there is another, higher person (*puruṣa*), called the Supreme Self, the eternal lord (*īśvara*) who, penetrating the three worlds, sustains them.[18]

Viṣṇu is also identifiable as a *puruṣa* in some of the purāṇic versions of the *vāmana-avatāra*. Viṣṇu's *viśva-rūpa*, or "all-pervading form," which the god manifests in order to make his three enormous strides, is often shown to produce different parts of the created order from different parts of the god's body. This is an idea that is classically expressed in the *puruṣasūkta*. In the *Ṛgveda*, we read:

The Brāhman was his mouth,
The arms were made the Prince,
His thighs the common people,
And from his feet the serf was born.

From his mind the moon was born,
And from his eye the sun,
From his mouth Indra and the fire,
From his breath the wind was born.

From his navel arose the atmosphere,
From his head the sky evolved,
From his feet the earth, and from his ear
The cardinal points of the compass:
So did they fashion forth these worlds.[19]

In the *Nārada Purāṇa*, for instance, Viṣṇu is praised in similar fashion:

From whose head the brahmin was born, from both his arms the *kṣatriya* arose, from his thighs the *vaiśya* was born, from his feet the *śūdra* was born. From his mind the moon was born, and from his eyes the sun, from his mouth Agni and Indra, from his breath Vāyu. From his body the *Ṛg*, *Yajus*, and *Sāma Vedas*, whose soul exists in the seven musical notes, whose is the form of the six *vedāṅgas*, I praise him more and more.[20]

The description of Viṣṇu's *viśva-rūpa* in the *Kāraṇḍavyūha* does not present the god as *puruṣa*-creator. Viṣṇu is merely said to be vast in size, bearing the sun and moon on his shoulders (a detail which, perhaps, carries an echo of the vedic hymn), and armed with noose, wheel, bow, javelin, and lance.[21] Instead, it is Avalokiteśvara who is depicted as the great cosmic *puruṣa*.

A passage located near the beginning of the sūtra is, clearly, another improvisation on the vedic hymn. The sun and moon are said to be born from the bodhisattva's eyes, Maheśvara from his brow, Brahmā from his shoulders, Nārāyaṇa from his heart, Sarasvatī from his teeth, the winds from his mouth, the earth from his feet and the sky from his stomach.[22]

The *puruṣasūkta* is also the inspiration for another of the features of the great bodhisattva. For the *puruṣa*, traditionally, has various "thousandfold" bodily characteristics. The vedic hymn begins:

> A thousand heads hath *puruṣa*, a thousand eyes, a thousand feet. On every side pervading earth he fills a space ten fingers wide.[23]

This is true of Śiva. In the *Kūrma Purāṇa*, for instance, we read:

> They saw the lord with a thousand heads, a thousand feet, a thousand shapes, and a thousand arms, with matted hair and with his coronet embellished with the crescent moon.[24]

And in the much earlier Śaivite work, the *Śvetāśvatara Upaniṣad*, Śiva is described as follows:

> A thousand heads (this) person has,
> A thousand eyes, a thousand feet . . .[25]

It is also true of Viṣṇu. In the *Bhagavadgītā*, Kṛṣṇa is said to have a thousand arms:

> O thousand-armed one, whose material form is the universe . . .[26]

Similarly, in the *Kāraṇḍavyūha Sūtra*, in the course of the tour of the worlds contained within the hair pores of Avalokiteśvara, the bodhisattva is suddenly described as appearing in a form with one hundred thousand arms (*śatasahasrabhujaḥ*) and one hundred thousand *koṭi* of eyes (*koṭiśatasahasranetro*).[27] Once again, the same basic "thousandfold" motif is apparent, in a slightly developed form. Similarly, as Chandra points out, a hymn found in the Chinese Buddhist canon which is dedicated, in its colophon, to the thousand-armed, thousand-eyed Avalokiteśvara, actually begins with a salutation to the bodhisattva in which he is described as possessing a thousand feet, a thousand tongues and a thousand heads, as well as the more familiar thousand arms and thousand eyes.[28]

The description of the "thousandfold" form of Avalokiteśvara also contains the most explicit indication in the *Kāraṇḍavyūha* that the bodhisattva is taking on the attributes of Śiva and not of Viṣṇu. We have already seen that Avalokiteśvara, like Śiva, is called *"maheśvara."* Here, the bodhisattva is said to have eleven heads (*ekādaśaśīrṣaḥ*).[29] This imitates a standard form of Śiva, in which the eleven heads correspond to eleven different manifestations of the god.[30] The hairstyle of the bodhisattva also betrays a Śaivite influence. He is twice said to have a head of twisted locks of hair (*jaṭāmukuṭadharo*), once when he appears in the hell realms and once when he appears to the *dharmabhāṇaka*.[31] This is a characteristic of Indian yogins of all sects, but one which is, nonetheless, particularly associated with Śiva and his devotees.[32]

No trace of the thousand-armed, thousand-eyed Avalokiteśvara has been found on Indian soil.[33] Probably the closest related archaeological find to date is a statue of a four-armed Avalokiteśvara found at the caves at Kanheri just north of present-day Mumbai. This image, like the hundred thousand-armed form described in the *Kāraṇḍavyūha Sūtra*, has eleven heads. It has been dated to the time of the Vakataka dynasty of the late fifth and early sixth century C.E.[34] The dearth of Indian artefacts connected to the "thousandfold" form of the bodhisattva is striking. Judging by the enthusiasm with which its iconography and associated practices were eventually transmitted to the Chinese, it would seem to have been quite popular.

The first of the many images of the thousand-armed Avalokiteśvara to appear in China, for instance, is said to have been painted between 618 and 626 C.E. for the T'ang emperor, by an Indian monk known by the Chinese as Ch'u-to-t'i-p'o.[35] The cave paintings at Tun-huang also include several depictions of this form of the bodhisattva, though the earliest of these was apparently painted over two hundred years later in 836 C.E.[36] The apparent disparity between the amount of Indian and Chinese iconographic evidence connected to this form may, however, be consistent with the scenario that was suggested in chapter 1. Like the *Kāraṇḍavyūha Sūtra* itself, the form and associated doctrine of the "thousandfold" Avalokiteśvara may have originated in Kashmir and subsequently have been taken north, but not south.

According to a survey conducted by Chandra, two different *dhāraṇīs*, extended incantations to the thousand-armed Avalokiteśvara, accompanied the progress of the iconographic form into China. No documents of the original Sanskrit versions of these *dhāraṇīs* are extant. They were first transliterated into Chinese characters over three hundred years before the earliest recorded Chinese translation of the *Kāraṇḍavyūha Sūtra* (983 C.E.). The first of the two *dhāraṇīs*, transliterated by one Chih-t'ung in 653 C.E., praises the bodhisattva in terms of his relationship with Amitābha and the Pure Land of Sukhāvatī, recalling the role adopted by Avalokiteśvara in the Pure Land sūtras. This is an aspect of the bodhisattva which is, as we shall see, by no means forgotten in the presentation of Avalokiteśvara found in the *Kāraṇḍavyūha Sūtra*.

In the context of our continuing discussion of the purāṇic influence on the conception of Avalokiteśvara, the second of these hymns is the more interesting of the two, in so far as it praises the bodhisattva in terms of an invocation to both Śiva and Viṣṇu. Three distinct versions remain. The shortest of these was also the first to be transliterated, between 650 and 661 C.E., by Bhagavaddharma,[37] and later on by the eighth-century translator Amoghavajra (705–774 C.E.).[38] A somewhat longer version of the *dhāraṇī* was transliterated between 731 and 736 C.E. by Vajrabodhi.[39] A longer version still is preserved in Tibetan. This is a translation of a Chinese text (which no longer appears to exist) made by the Chinese translator Fa-ch'eng (known in Tibetan as Chos grub) during the reign of the ninth-century Tibetan king Ral pa can (817–836 C.E.).[40]

The shorter version of the hymn has been reconstituted by Chandra, on the basis of the versions attributed to Bhagavaddharma and Amoghavajra. It begins, according to Chandra's translation:

> Adoration to the Triple Gem. Adoration to *ārya* Avalokiteśvara, bodhisattva, *mahāsattva*, the Great Compassionate One.

The central section reads:

> Thus. *Oṃ*. Oh effulgence, world-transcendent, come oh Hari, the great bodhisattva, descend, descend. Bear in mind my heart-*dhāraṇī*. Accomplish, accomplish the work. Hold fast, hold fast, victor, oh great victor. Hold on, hold on, oh lord of the earth. Move, move, oh my immaculate image. Come, come, thou with the black serpent as thy sacred thread. Destroy every poison. Quick, quick, oh strong being. Quick, quick, oh Hari. Descend, descend, come down, come down, condescend, condescend. Being enlightened enlighten me, oh merciful Nīlakaṇṭha. Gladden my heart by appearing unto me.
>
> To the siddha hail. To the great *siddha* hail. To the lord of *siddha* yogins hail. To Nīlakaṇṭha hail. To the boar-faced one hail. To one with the face of Narasiṃha hail. To one who has a lotus in his hand hail. To the holder of a *cakra* in his hand hail. To one who sports a lotus in his hand hail. To Nīlakaṇṭha the tiger hail. To the mighty Śaṅkara hail.[41]

The presence of Viṣṇu is evoked twice by the vocative Hare and, also, by references to a boar and a man-lion, recalling the god's appearances as an *avatāra* in those forms. There are numerous Śaivite epithets: Nīlakaṇṭha, "the blue throated one" (three times);[42] Śaṅkara, "the beneficent one"; the one who wears a black serpent as a sacred thread; the destroyer of poisons; the *siddha*;

the great *siddha* and the lord of *siddha* yogins. An introductory preamble to the hymn also states that the *dhāraṇī* is associated with Nīlakaṇṭha.[43] The relative status of Śiva and Viṣṇu in the hymn follows a similar pattern to the one identified, at the end of the previous chapter, in the *Kāraṇḍavyūha*. The two gods are repeatedly invoked one after the other, indicating that they stand in a "complementary" relationship to each other. At the same time, though, Śiva is recognizably the superior deity. Chandra decides that the hymn is an offering of veneration to the Hari-Hara form, even though Śiva is not actually invoked here as Hara.[44] In general terms, though, the hymn clearly reflects a similar sort of purāṇic influence—with Śiva dominant and Viṣṇu supporting—as the one reflected in the pages of the sūtra.

Avalokiteśvara's manifestation as a bee, as we have already seen, shows the bodhisattva taking on more of the characteristics of a purāṇic deity. The same, finally, is also true of a description of the bodhisattva that occurs near the end of the *Kāraṇḍavyūha*, at the conclusion of the tour of the worlds said to be contained within the pores of the bodhisattva's skin. The four oceans, Śakyamuni says, emerge from the right big toe of Avalokiteśvara.[45] But the bodhisattva's knees, the Buddha continues, are not immersed in these waters,[46] which fall into the "mouth of the mare" (*vaḍavamukhe*), extinguishing the "heap of ashes" (*bhasmarāśim*).[47]

Several purāṇic motifs are reflected here. The first is the idea that the waters of the earth flow out of the supreme *īśvara*. The second, not unrelated idea, is that the dimensions of the *īśvara* transcend the known limits of the phenomenal world. In the version of the *vāmana-avatāra* presented in the *Skanda Purāṇa*, for instance, Viṣṇu's third step is said to break out of Brahmāṇḍa (literally Brahmā's egg or "*aṇḍa*", one of the names traditionally given to the universe), whereupon the river Ganges is said to arise from Viṣṇu's step and flood the triple world.[48] In both sūtra and purāṇa, then, waters emerge from the foot of the *īśvara* and each *īśvara* is shown to be bigger than the created order itself. Meanwhile, the "mouth of the mare" into which these waters, in the *Kāraṇḍavyūha*, are said to pour, is the name given to an entrance to the lower realms and another standard image used to describe the end of the known world.[49] The "heap of ashes" refers to a subterranean fire believed to be the cause of the waters of the ocean evaporating and turning into rain and snow.[50] That the waters from the toe of Avalokiteśvara extinguish this "heap of ashes" is, I suggest, a repeat allusion to the bodhisattva's ability to put out the fires of hell, described in more detail near the beginning of the sūtra. There, Avalokiteśvara is actually shown to enter the Avīci hell, whereupon the fires of hell are said to be spontaneously extinguished, the infernal cooking vessel is burst asunder and a lotus pond—with lotus flowers the size of chariot wheels—spontaneously appears in the middle of the infernal stove.[51]

It is not surprising to discover, however, that the identification of Avalokiteśvara as an *īśvara* is not wholly unqualified. The idea of a Buddhist *īśvara*, after all, represents the attempt to assimilate an essentially theistic doctrine (the *īśvara* idea) into an essentially nontheistic religious system (Buddhism). The presentation in the sūtra of Avalokiteśvara as the all-pervasive *puruṣa*, for example, tiptoes carefully around what might be considered the Buddhist heresy of depicting the bodhisattva as a creator god in the fullest sense. In the sūtra's version of the *puruṣasūkta* myth, only the gods are seen to emanate from the bodhisattva's body and not the created order itself. Though it might initially appear that the sun and moon are born from Avalokiteśvara's eyes, the Sanskrit words used for "sun" and "moon" actually refer here to the vedic gods of the sun and moon, Āditya and Candra.[52] Similarly, when the sūtra appears to indicate that the winds come from his mouth, the earth from his feet and the sky from his stomach, this is really a reference to the gods of the winds, earth, and sky, respectively Vāyu, Dharaṇī and Varuṇa.[53] This is made explicit in the sentence that follows on immediately afterwards. It reads: "Once these gods were born from the body of noble Avalokiteśvara (*yadaite devā jātā āryāvalokiteśvarasya kāyāt*), then the great bodhisattva Avalokiteśvara spoke to the god Maheśvara."[54]

Avalokiteśvara, thereby, is associated with one of the central tenets of the *īśvara* doctrine—the idea of the cosmic *puruṣa*—without offending Buddhist norms. The sūtra version of the *puruṣasūkta* myth, in the end, reads like a variation on the classic Mahāyāna belief that Avalokiteśvara is able to manifest in different forms according to the needs of different individuals. A statement to this effect—typical of its kind—occurs at one point in the *Kāraṇḍavyūha Sūtra*, when Avalokiteśvara is said to teach the Dharma in whatever way is most suitable to accomplish the conversion of beings.[55] The list of the different forms that the bodhisattva is then said to adopt includes very nearly all the gods he has, earlier, been said to produce from his body. He can appear, it is said, as a *tathāgata*, a *pratyekabuddha*, an *arhat*, a bodhisattva, Maheśvara, Nārāyaṇa, Brahmā, Indra, the gods of the sun, the moon, fire, the sky, and the wind (Āditya, Candra, Agni, Varuṇa, Vāyu), a *nāga*, Vighnapati (the lord of obstacles), a *yakṣa*, Vaiśravaṇa,[56] a king, a king's soldier, a mother and a father.[57] Only Sarasvatī and Dharaṇī, from the *puruṣasūkta*-derived section of the sūtra, are missing.

That the sūtra is anxious to distance itself from the doctrine of a creator god is also apparent in a passage that we examined briefly in the previous chapter. This is the speech, which immediately follows the sūtra's version of the *puruṣasūkta*, in which the bodhisattva attacks Śiva and the doctrine of the *liṅga*. Maheśvara, the bodhisattva says, will appear in the *kaliyuga* in a world of perverted beings, and will be called the primordial god (*ādideva*), the creator and author of the world (*ākhyāyase sraṣṭāraṃ kartāram*).[58] Régamey writes that these remarks imply that, from the Buddhist point of view, the heresy is not the belief in a primordial god, but the belief that this primordial god is Maheśvara rather than Avalokiteśvara.[59] I disagree. In view of the circumscribed presentation of Avalokiteśvara as cosmic *puruṣa* that has gone before, it seems much more likely that the sūtra is deliberately attacking the purāṇic doctrine of a primordial creator god, per se.

As Régamey goes on to say, the idea of a primordial creator was, undoubtedly, specifically endorsed by at least one part of the Buddhist *Saṃgha*, namely, that section responsible for the composition of the later verse version of the *Kāraṇḍavyūha*. This, as we saw in chapter 1, includes a passage describing the birth of Avalokiteśvara not from an *ādideva*, but from an *ādibuddha*, or "primordial buddha," said to be synonymous with the *svayaṃbhu*, or "self-existent one" and the *ādinātha*, or "primordial lord." Even in the later text, though, this primordial creator is still not identified with Avalokiteśvara himself. The bodhisattva is not the *ādibuddha*, but is produced from the *ādibuddha*. Once again, he is said only to be responsible for the emanation of gods from the different parts of his body and not for the appearance of the created order itself. The point is not, as Régamey seems to think, that the prose *Kāraṇḍavyūha Sūtra* accepts the doctrine of the primordial creator and the verse sūtra builds on that. Rather, the prose *Kāraṇḍavyūha* seems to reflect a Buddhist sensibility that resisted the infiltration of the creator doctrine, while the verse sūtra reflects a sensibility that had, at a later time, come to accept it.[60]

It seems likely, too, that the *Kāraṇḍavyūha Sūtra* deliberately glosses over another important aspect of the *īśvara* doctrine that clashes with standard Buddhist teaching. This is the association of the *īśvara* with the idea of the *ātman*, that is to say the real "self" or "soul" of an individual that is believed to exist independently of, or beyond, the phenomenal dimension of his or her being. This is a doctrine ostensibly at odds with the central Buddhist teaching of *anātman*, or "non-self," the idea that no such *ātman* can be found within an individual because no such entity exists. In the *Śiva Purāṇa*, for instance, we read:

> In his attributeless pure form he is glorified as Śiva, the supreme *ātman* [*paramātman*], *maheśvara*, the supreme Brahman, the undecaying, the endless, and Mahādeva.[61]

And in the *Skanda Purāṇa*:

> Through offering obeisance (bowing down) the individual soul becomes one with Śiva, the Supreme *ātman*.[62]

In the *Bhagavadgītā*, Kṛṣṇa says:

I am the self (*ātmā*), Guḍākeśa, situated in the hearts of all creatures.[63]

However, nowhere in the *Kāraṇḍavyūha Sūtra* is any mention made of this central purāṇic doctrine. At a point where one might expect this term to appear—in the list of attributes ascribed to the one hundred thousand-armed form of Avalokiteśvara—it is conspicuous only by its absence. The bodhisattva, we read, is the great yogin, established in *nirvāṇa*, distinguished, greatly wise, a deliverer of beings, well-born, invisible, wise, in his exposition he casts no shadows on any elements and is not heard or seen by anyone.[64] He is not, however, the *ātman*, or *paramātman*. Once again, it seems, the idea of Avalokiteśvara as a purāṇic-style *īśvara* has been tailored to the requirements of Buddhist orthodoxy.

The terms *ātman* and *paramātman* do, of course, appear elsewhere in the Mahāyāna corpus. In the context of some of the so-called *tathāgatagarbha*, or "buddha nature," sūtras such as the *Mahāparinirvāṇa Sūtra*, the *ātman* terminology is employed to describe the buddha nature itself. Though it remains an issue of some controversy, some scholars have argued that the buddha nature genre, like the *Kāraṇḍavyūha Sūtra*, was strongly influenced by purāṇic doctrinal thinking. In parenthesis, then, it seems worth considering whether the *Kāraṇḍavyūha* might be grouped alongside those buddha nature sūtras, such as the *Laṅkāvatāra Sūtra*, which, assuming they are influenced by purāṇic thought, demonstrate the same careful vigilance in avoiding any use of the purāṇic terms *ātman* and *paramātman*.[65]

The *Kāraṇḍavyūha* faces one further set of considerations in presenting Avalokiteśvara as a Buddhist *īśvara*. In addition to trimming this essentially purāṇic doctrine of elements disagreeable to the Buddhist point of view, the sūtra must also show that the bodhisattva is still recognizably the same figure that appeared in earlier Mahāyāna sūtras. The sūtra, naturally, considers itself as a development of the Mahāyāna and not as a break away from the tradition. Throughout the work, then, Avalokiteśvara is seen to fulfill, not only the role of *īśvara*, but also many of the functions that have previously been associated with him in earlier texts.

There are still some other elements of the presentation of the bodhisattva in the *Kāraṇḍavyūha* that appear to break with all precedent. In some parts of the sūtra, for instance, Avalokiteśvara, it is implied, is greater in stature than the buddhas. In describing the way in which the bodhisattva brings vast numbers of creatures to maturity, Śākyamuni comments that even the *tathāgatas* do not have an illumination (*pratibhānaṃ*) like his.[66] Later, having listened to Śākyamuni's sermon on the merit of Avalokiteśvara, the bodhisattva Ratnapāṇi observes that it is inconceivable, and that he has never seen or heard of such a heap of merit (*puṇyaskandhaḥ*) belonging to the *tathāgatas*, let alone to a bodhisattva.[67] Twice it is said, once by the bodhisattva Ratnapāṇi and once by the bodhisattva Gaganagañja, that the power (*viśaya*) possessed by Avalokiteśvara has never been seen or heard of as belonging to a bodhisattva and that it is not found even among the *tathāgatas*.[68]

This sense of the bodhisattva's superiority over even the buddhas is also maintained in passages connected to the presentation of *Oṃ Maṇipadme Hūṃ*. One of the first things that is said about the six-syllable formula, for instance, is that all the *tathāgatas* have wandered for sixteen *kalpas* for its sake,[69] a claim which is, to some degree, illustrated by the story of the journey made by the *tathāgata* Padmottama in order to obtain the formula.[70] Śākyamuni himself says that, in a previous lifetime, he traversed countless realms in search of the six syllables and served numerous *tathāgatas* without obtaining or hearing the formula.[71]

It would be a mistake, however, to think that these passages reflect a new Mahāyāna doctrine in which the status of buddhahood is deemed inferior to the status of an *īśvara*. They are not unlike descriptions, found elsewhere in the Mahāyāna corpus, of other important Buddhist figures. As Paul Williams has shown, Mañjuśrī, the great bodhisattva of wisdom, is presented in a comparable manner: he is sometimes said to be a buddha and sometimes, even, both the father and mother of innumerable buddhas.[72] The phenomenon of temporarily treating one great bodhisattva as preeminent in this way, apparently at the expense of the prestige of other buddhas and bodhisattvas, is entirely in keeping with Indian religious convention. In the vedic hymns, for instance, whichever god is being praised is always treated, in that instance, as the greatest god of them all.

There is one other aspect of the conception of Avalokiteśvara presented in the *Kāraṇḍavyūha Sūtra* that is not found in accounts of the bodhisattva anywhere else in Mahāyāna literature. This is the idea, described immediately before and immediately after the story of the search for *Oṃ Maṇipadme Hūṃ*, that the hair pores of Avalokiteśvara's body contain different worlds. The bodhisattva Sarvanīvaraṇaviṣkambhin is taken on a tour of these worlds by Śākyamuni. The Buddha then announces that whoever brings to mind the six-syllable formula will be born in these pores, never again to wander in *saṃsāra*, traveling from one pore to the next until *nirvāṇa* is attained.[73] This is the cue for the start of Sarvanīvaraṇaviśkambhin's quest for *Oṃ Maṇipadme Hūṃ* which, as soon as it is accomplished, gives way to another, slightly shorter description of these hair pores.

Avalokiteśvara, here, is clearly taking on the characteristics of another, well-known Mahāyāna figure, namely, Samantabhadra, the great bodhisattva of the *Avataṃsaka Sūtra*, that compendium of texts which appears to have been first translated into Chinese, in its entirety, in the early part of the fifth century.[74] At the end of the *Gaṇḍavyūha Sūtra*, the final work of the *Avataṃsaka* corpus, we read:

> Then Sudhana, contemplating the body of the enlightening being Universally Good [Samantabhadra], saw in each and every pore (*ekaikasmin romavivare*) untold multitudes of buddhalands filled with buddhas. And in each buddhaland he saw the buddhas surrounded by assemblies of enlightening beings. And he saw that all those multitudes of lands had various bases, various forms, various arrays, various perimeters, various clouds covering the skies, various buddhas appearing, various enunciations of cycles of the Teachings.[75]

And, just as the practitioner is said to be born into the body of Avalokiteśvara by use of the six syllables:

> Then Sudhana, edified by the advice and instruction of the enlightening being Universally Good, entered into all the worlds within the body of Universally Good and developed the beings toward maturity.[76]

Avalokiteśvara's body, as described in the *Kāraṇḍavyūha Sūtra* is, perhaps, slightly less amazing than Samantabhadra's. The worlds that Śākyamuni describes contained within the hair pores seem, in general, not actually to be buddhalands. Though they share many of the standard characteristics of buddhalands (they are made of jewels, replete with marvelous trees and lotus ponds), their inhabitants are usually not buddhas, but less exalted beings such as *ṛṣis* and *gandharvas*. Nor does there seem to be more than one land in each of Avalokiteśvara's pores, compared to the "untold multitudes" spoken of in the *Gaṇḍavyūha Sūtra*. Nor does the *Kāraṇḍavyūha* match the *Gaṇḍavyūha*'s claim that the pores interpenetrate each other in an extraordinary way. In the latter work, for instance, we read: "And just as he [Sudhana] saw this in each pore (*ekaikasmin romavivare*), so also in all pores at once . . ."[77] Nonetheless, there can be no doubt that this aspect of the presentation of Avalokiteśvara in the *Kāraṇḍavyūha Sūtra* owes a direct debt to the tradition of the *Avataṃsaka Sūtra*.

To make explicit this connection, Samantabhadra himself appears in the sūtra on three separate occasions. Each time, he is compared with Avalokiteśvara and each time he is shown to be in some way the lesser figure. The first of these appearances occurs in a passage that does, in fact, indicate that at least some of the worlds contained in Avalokiteśvara's body are buddhalands. In order to illustrate the ungraspable nature of the hair pores, it is said that even though Samantabhadra roamed these pores for twelve years, he still did not see them, nor the one hundred buddhas residing in each one of them. Then, a little later on in the sūtra, after the description of the "thousandfold" form of Avalokiteśvara, Samantabhadra is singled out again. If the other self-existent *tathāgatas* do not see this form, Śākyamuni says, what chance is there for Samantabhadra and the other bodhisattvas.[78]

Finally, in a passage that indicates that Avalokiteśvara is to be understood as superceding Samantabhadra as the supreme embodiment of the bodhisattva ideal, the two bodhisattvas have a "*samādhi* contest" (*samādhivigraha*),[79] a kind of duel in which the power of one bodhisattva is pitted against the other. Avalokiteśvara is said to be furnished with hundreds of *samādhis* (*anekaiḥ samādhiśataiḥ samanvāgataḥ*),[80] a characteristic shared by Samantabhadra in the *Avataṃsaka Sūtra*. There, for instance, we read:

> Then the enlightening being Universally Good arose from this concentration; when he did so, he rose from media of oceans of concentrations numerous as atoms in all oceans of worlds.[81]

In the "*samādhi* contest" of the *Kāraṇḍavyūha*, the two bodhisattvas compare seven pairs of *samādhis*,[82] and then reveal their hair pores to one another.[83] Samantabhadra then appears to admit defeat when he congratulates Avalokiteśvara on possessing such brilliancy (*yastvamīdṛśaṃ pratibhānavān*).[84]

The notion of Avalokiteśvara as a being greater than Samantabhadra and greater even than the *tathāgatas* might appear, initially, to outstrip and leave behind the more modest conception of the bodhisattva described in the so-called Pure Land sūtras. There, Avalokiteśvara is, though extremely wondrous, a subordinate, servile figure: an attendant of the Buddha Amitābha. In the longer *Sukhāvatīvyūha Sūtra*, a text translated into Chinese during the second century C.E.,[85] Avalokiteśvara and the bodhisattva Mahāsthāmaprāpta are said to have left the buddhafield of Śākyamuni to be reborn in Sukhāvatī, the "Land of Bliss," Amitābha's buddhafield. There, the light they emanate is said to shine throughout the world.[86] A similar scenario is described in the third of the great Pure Land sūtras, sometimes given the Sanskrit name *Amitāyurbuddhānusmṛti Sūtra* or the *Amitāyurdhyāna Sūtra*.[87] In the text, it is said at one point that Amitāyus (who is Amitābha by a different name)[88] "appeared in the sky with the two great beings, Avalokiteśvara and Mahāsthāmaprāpta, standing in attendance to his left and right."[89] Later, in the same sūtra, we read: "These two bodhisattvas assist Amida[90] Buddha in his work of universal salvation."[91]

However, despite the undoubted aggrandisement of Avalokiteśvara in the *Kāraṇḍavyūha*, the conception of the bodhisattva as a servant of Amitābha is not forgotten. Avalokiteśvara is, for instance, shown to obey the orders of Amitābha. In order to receive the six-syllable formula, the buddha Padmottama first asks for it from Amitābha, who tells Avalokiteśvara to bestow it.[92] Then, on receiving the formula, Padmottama offers Avalokiteśvara a string of pearls. The bodhisattva accepts this gift, before offering it, in turn, to Amitābha. In so doing, the bodhisattva indicates that his ability to bestow the formula depends upon the generosity of the buddha.[93] Near the beginning and near the end of the sūtra, Avalokiteśvara is depicted as a kind of emissary of Amitābha. Appearing in the Jetavana grove, he prostrates himself before a buddha and offers him some lotus flowers that he has brought from Amitābha in Sukhāvatī.[94]

Other traits of Avalokiteśvara, familiar from earlier texts, are also preserved in the *Kāraṇḍavyūha Sūtra*. In the *Gaṇḍavyūha Sūtra*, for instance, the bodhisattva is presented chiefly in terms of the development of his compassion. He is discovered by Sudhana seated on the summit of Mount Potalaka, expounding a doctrine called "'the light of the medium of great love and compassion,' which concerns the salvation of all sentient beings."[95] When asked for instructions on how to learn and carry out the practice of a bodhisattva, Avalokiteśvara describes a practice called "undertaking great compassion without delay."[96] Later, he says: "I have only attained this way of enlightening practice through unhesitating great compassion."[97]

The bodhisattva is frequently linked to the same quality in the course of the *Kāraṇḍavyūha Sūtra*. At the beginning of the text, in the course of coming to the aid of the *pretas* and, a little later, of the *yakṣas* and *rākṣaṣas*, he is said to generate a mind of great compassion (*mahākaruṇācittotpādya*).[98] As he sets off to meet Bali, he is said to have a heart full of great compassion (*mahākaruṇāsaṃpīḍitahṛdayo*).[99] He or she who recites *Oṃ Maṇipadme Hūṃ* is said to become furnished with great compassion (*mahākaruṇayā samanvāgato bhavati*).[100] Upon receiving the formula, Sarvanīvaraṇaviṣkambhin is said to enter several *samādhis*, one of which is called "rejoicing in loving kindness and compassion" (*maitrīkaruṇāmudito nāma samādhiḥ*).[101]

The treatment of Avalokiteśvara in the *Gaṇḍavyūha Sūtra* also includes an account of the bodhisattva's ability to manifest in whatever form is most suitable for particular beings, a trait that, as we have already observed, is also described in the *Kāraṇḍavyūha Sūtra*.[102] In the *Gaṇḍavyūha Sūtra*, Avalokiteśvara says:

> I also develop sentient beings by appearing in various forms: I gladden and develop them by purity of vision of inconceivable forms radiating auras of light, and I take care of them and develop them by speaking to them according to their mentalities, and by showing conduct according to their inclinations, and by magically producing various forms, and by teaching them doctrines commensurate with their various interests, and by inspiring them to begin to accumulate good qualities, by showing them projections according to their mentalities, by appearing to them as

members of their own various races and conditions, and by living together with them.[103]

The fullest exposition of this doctrine, however, occurs in the twenty-fourth chapter[104] of the *Saddharmapuṇḍarīka Sūtra*, a text first translated into Chinese by Dharmarakṣa in 286 C.E.

> In some worlds, young man of good family, the bodhisattva *mahāsattva* Avalokiteśvara preaches the law to creatures in the shape of a buddha; in others he does so in the shape of a bodhisattva. To some beings he shows the law in the shape of *pratyekabuddha*; to others he does so in the shape of a disciple; to others again under that of Brahmā, Indra, or a *gandharva*. To those who are to be converted by a goblin (*yakṣa*), he preaches the law assuming the shape of a goblin; to those who are to be converted by *īśvara*, he preaches the law in the shape of *īśvara* . . .[105]

. . . and so on, with regard to the shape of a *maheśvara*, a *cakravartin*, a *piśāca* (a kind of demon), Kubera (*vaiśravaṇa*, the chief of the yakṣas), Senāpati (the general of an army and a name given to Śiva in the Mahābhārata),[106] a brahmin and the bodhisattva Vajrapāṇi.[107]

Like the *Saddharmapuṇḍarīka*, the *Kāraṇḍavyūha* also prefaces its account of this doctrine with a section describing the benefits of the use of Avalokiteśvara's name. The *Kāraṇḍavyūha* is quite brief here. Happy are they in this world, it is said, who hold in their minds the name (*nāmadheyamanusmaranti*) of Avalokiteśvara.[108] They are liberated from the anguish and suffering of old age, death, disease, grief, and lamentation. They do not experience the sufferings of *saṃsāra*. Dressed in brilliant white, like swans flying as fast as the wind, they go to Sukhāvatī, where they hear the Dharma from the *tathāgata* Amitābha.[109]

The much longer and more detailed presentation of the *Saddharmapuṇḍarīka* is rather different. Rebirth in Sukhāvatī is not, in fact, linked to the use of the name here. Instead, the effects of using the name that are described in chapter twenty-four of the sūtra seem to fall into two broad categories. First, calling upon the bodhisattva or bringing to mind his name is said to save the individual from a wide variety of perilous situations. Second, the practice is said to produce a huge amount of merit. For instance:

> If a man given up to capital punishment implores Avalokiteśvara, young man of good family, the swords of the executioners shall snap asunder. Further, young man of good family, if the whole triple chiliocosm were teeming with goblins and giants, they would by virtue of the name of the

> bodhisattva *mahāsattva* Avalokiteśvara being pronounced lose the faculty of sight in their wicked designs . . .[110]

And:

> He who adores a number of Lords Buddhas equal to sixty-two times the sands of the river Ganges and cherishes their names, and he who adores the Bodhisattva Mahāsattva Avalokiteśvara and cherishes his name, have an equal accumulation of pious merit . . .[111]

The Avalokiteśvara of the *Kāraṇḍavyūha Sūtra,* then, despite his assumption of the role of great Buddhist *īśvara,* is still identifiably the same bodhisattva that appears in earlier Mahāyāna sūtras. How, though, are we to understand, did the bodhisattva become this supreme *īśvara* figure?

The doctrine of the chameleon-like nature of Avalokiteśvara, does not, I think, constitute a wholly satisfactory explanation for this change. It is true that it is explicitly stated, in the relevant passages from the *Saddharmapuṇḍarīka, Gaṇḍavyūha* and *Kāraṇḍavyūha*, that Avalokiteśvara can adopt the shape of an *īśvara*. But these passages almost certainly originate from a time before the bodhisattva had been conceived of as the Buddhist *īśvara*. They refer, surely, to the ability of the bodhisattva to appear, not as a Buddhist *īśvara*, but as a non-Buddhist *īśvara*. Avalokiteśvara, in this context, adopts the temporary disguise of this kind of non-Buddhist being. The *Kāraṇḍavyūha Sūtra* as a whole, though, describes a very different situation. There, the role of *īśvara* is not incidental to Avalokiteśvara's activity. It has become a central, permanent part of his being. Furthermore, he is not Śiva or Viṣṇu, but a separate, distinctively Buddhist *īśvara*.

The bodhisattva's transformation in this regard must be accounted for, rather, by the mechanism described in the subjugation myth. The conversion of Śiva by Avalokiteśvara that is, as we have seen, a feature of the *Kāraṇḍavyūha*, carries with it the implication that through taming Śiva and his power, the bodhisattva is able to take on the characteristics of the god. This absorption of the personalities of different, lesser deities into the being of a single, greater figure is a process described in both Buddhist and non-Buddhist texts. As Robert Mayer writes: "Just as the Hindu conquering deities appropriate the accessories of their victims . . . , so also the Buddhist conquerors appropriate the accessories of their victims . . ."[112] By defeating the Śaivite *īśvara*, Avalokiteśvara is able to manifest as the Buddhist *īśvara*.

The name of Avalokiteśvara might, of course, be taken as an indication that the bodhisattva was regarded as an *īśvara* from the very start. In a part of the later verse version of the *Kāraṇḍavyūha Sūtra*, for instance, "Avalokiteśvara" is said to mean "the lord" (*-īśvara*) who "looks down" (*avalokita-*) "with compassion."[113] This discussion, however, forms part of the epilogue dialogue between Aśoka and his preceptor Upagupta and is wholly absent in the earlier, prose version of the sūtra: an indication that it probably belongs to a relatively late stage of reflection on the nature of the bodhisattva. In actual fact, the original name of the bodhisattva was almost certainly not Avalokiteśvara, but was, instead, Avalokitasvara.[114]

The name Avalokitasvara does not, it is true, appear in any known surviving complete Sanskrit manuscripts. It does, however, feature in a set of early Sanskrit fragments of the *Saddharmapuṇḍarīka Sūtra*, discovered in eastern Turkestan and first commented on by N. D. Mironov in 1927. The documents, Mironov states, can be assigned to the end of the fifth century C.E. on palæographical grounds. There are three fragments of the twenty-fourth chapter where the name of the bodhisattva is spelt Avalokitasvara. "As the name occurs five times on an incomplete leaf," he comments, "the possibility of a clerical error is hardly admissible."[115]

Moreover, with one exception, all the early Chinese translations of the Mahāyāna sūtras (up until the middle of the seventh century) show that the name of the bodhisattva always ended in *-svara*, translated by the Chinese character transliterated as *-yin*. Kuan-yin, the term that remains in popular use to this day, is a translation of Avalokita-svara. The earliest reference to the use of this name, according to a survey conducted by Chandra, is found in a sixth-century commentary on Kumārajīva's separate translation of the twenty-fourth chapter of the *Saddharmapuṇḍarīka Sūtra*. This is rather late. However, Chandra also points out that a translation of the *Vimalakīrtinirdeśa Sūtra* made between 223 and 228 C.E. by Chih Ch'ien, refers to the bodhisattva as K'uei-yin, an alternative Chinese form of the same Sanksrit name. In a translation of the same sūtra made by Kumārajīva in about 400 C.E., the name of the bodhisattva appears as Kuan-shih-yin, another common Chinese rendering of the name, reflecting the Sanskrit Avalokita-loka-svara.

The use of Kuan-shih-yin is widespread. According to Chandra, it appears in: translations of the *Sukhāvatīvyūha Sūtra* and a text called the *Gṛhapati Ugra Paripṛcchā*, made by Saṃghavarman in 252; a text called the *Kuan-shih-yin-ying-yen-chi*, written between 374 and 426; a translation of the *Saddharmapuṇḍarīka Sūtra* made by Kumārajīva in 406; a translation of the *Karuṇāpuṇḍarīka Sūtra* made by Dharmakṣema between 414 and 421; a translation of the *Avataṃsaka Sūtra* made by Buddhabhadra between 418 and 422; another version of the *Kuan-shih-yin-ying-yen-chi* produced in 501 and a translation of the *Saddharmapuṇḍarīka Sūtra* made by Jñānagupta and Dharmagupta in 601. In addition, a translation of the *Saddharmapuṇḍarīka Sutra* made by Dharmarakṣa in 286, uses the slight variant Kuang-shih-yin, where *kuang* means "light" or "splendor."[116]

Meanwhile, the earliest known instance of the Sanskrit form Avalokiteśvara, with the *-īśvara* ending, occurs later than all the above references. It is first apparent in the so-called Petrovsky manuscript of the *Saddharmapuṇḍarīka Sūtra* found at Kashgar, which has been dated to the seventh century C.E. Similarly, the Chinese rendering of Avalokiteśvara, Kuan-tzu-tsai, does not seem to occur in any manuscript written before the middle of the same century. Its earliest known appearance occurs in the work of the famous traveling scholar and translator Hsuan Tsang. We find it, for instance, in his translation of the *Mahāprajñāpāramitā Sūtra*, made between 660 and 663. Kuan-tzu-tsai also appears in: a translation of the *Sukhāvatīvyūha Sūtra* made by Bodhiruci between 693 and 713; a translation of the same sūtra made by Fa Hien between 973 and 1001, and a translation of the *Avataṃsaka Sutra* made by Śikṣānanda between 695 and 699.[117]

It is also interesting to note that though Hsuan Tsang was convinced that Avalokiteśvara was the correct form, his Chinese biographers were not. In a note added to the third chapter of his travelogue, the *Si Yu Chi*, or "Buddhist Records of the Western World," written in 646 C.E., Hsuan Tsang asserts that the old Chinese versions of the name—Kuan-shih-yin, corresponding to Avalokitalokasvara, and Kuan-shih-tzu-tsai, corresponding to Avalokitalokeśvara—are wrong, and that the alternative form of Kuan-tzu-tsai, or Avalokiteśvara is correct.[118] Nonetheless, the nineteenth-century English translator of Hsuan Tsang's travelogue, Samuel Beal, remarks: "It is singular, if the expression (Kuan-shih-yin) is erroneous, that Hsuan Tsang, or rather Hwui-lih (the traveler's biographer) uses it constantly in his biography."[119] This shows, presumably, that Kuan-shih-yin was the accepted form in seventh-century China and continued to be used by Hsuan Tsang's biographer, while Kuan-tzu-tsai was the translation of a new form of the bodhisattva's name—Avalokiteśvara—discovered to be in use in India by Hsuan Tsang.

One of Hsuan Tsang's pilgrim predecessors, the Chinese monk Fa Hien, who visited the so-called Western Buddhist kingdoms between 399 and 414 C.E., refers to the bodhisattva as Kuan-shih-yin, once when students of the Mahāyāna are said to make offerings to the bodhisattva (as well as to the Prajñāpāramitā and to Mañjuśrī) and once when, in very rough seas, he is said to "think with all his heart" of the bodhisattva.[120] This suggests that the name Avalokiteśvara was still not much used in India during the first part of the fifth century and that it only became popular over the course of the following two hundred years, after which time it was noticed by Hsuan Tsang. It is possible, though, that the name Avalokiteśvara was, in fact, already in use in India during the time of Fa Hien's travels and that the Chinese pilgrim simply stuck to the older and (what was to him) the more familiar form in his travelogue.

Another early example of the dilemma over which of these titles to use—Kuan-tzu-tsai or Kuan-shih-yin—occurs in a commentary on the *Avataṃsaka*

Sūtra, the *Ta Fang Kuang Fo Hua-yen Ching Su,* written between 784 and 787 C.E. It reads: "In the Sanskrit originals themselves two different names of the bodhisattva occur. It is due to this difference in the Sanskrit originals that the Chinese translators of these same originals differ as to the names of the bodhisattva."[121] A Sanskrit-Chinese dictionary, the *Fan-i Ming-Chi,* compiled in 1151 C.E., seems to consider Avalokiteśvara correct, but comments that sūtra texts found north of the Himālayas maintain the use of the *-svara* ending.[122] Once again, this points to a situation in which Avalokiteśvara was a name that emerged in India at a later time, after texts containing the original form of Avalokitasvara had been taken over the Himālayas and translated into Chinese.

There can be no reasonable doubt, then, that the original name of the great bodhisattva ended in *-svara,* denoted by the Chinese -yin, either as in Avalokitasvara, Kuan-yin, or as in Avalokitalokasvara, Kuan-shih-yin. The translation of the last two syllables of these names, *-svara,* is relatively straightforward: it means "sound," "noise," or "voice," being used, for instance to denote the different notes of a musical scale.[123] The first five syllables, *avalokita-*, are slightly more problematic however, being a past participle form of a verb *avalok,* usually translated to mean "to look upon or at, view, behold, see, notice, observe."[124] The natural translation of Avalokitasvara, then, would be something like "the sound that is seen," which makes little obvious sense.

However, in an irregularity of Sanskrit grammar, some past participles can sometimes take an active, rather than a passive sense. In her study of Avalokiteśvara, Marie-Thérèse de Mallmann cites three different scholars who support this view. Eugène Burnouf, commenting on the *Kāraṇḍavyūha Sūtra*, wrote that there was some precedent for such a peculiar usage and that, besides, this would not have been the first time that the Buddhists had stretched the grammatical rules of brahmanical composition.[125] Louis Renou points to the Sanskrit form *hataputra,* meaning "the killer of a son" and not, as one would normally expect, "the son (that has been) killed."[126] Louis de la Vallée Poussin notes another analogous form, *parijita,* which would normally mean "(having been) conquered," but which, in one particular context, seems much more likely to mean "conquering." He also concludes that there are likely to be other instances of the grammatical irregularity.[127]

Avalokitasvara, then, might be translated as "sound viewer," or "sound seer." "Sound perceiver" is, perhaps, a better translation. The significance of this title refers, it seems, to the bodhisattva's ability to respond to the cries of the beings who call upon him in distress. He is the "perceiver" of the "sounds" made by those who need his help, as described in the twenty-fourth chapter of the *Saddharmapuṇḍarīka*. This etymological explanation does, in fact, appear in an early Chinese translation of that sūtra. Śākyamuni responds to a question about the meaning of the great bodhisattva's name in the following way:

> Illustrious youth! Though there were untold millions of creatures in the universe all suffering from miseries incidental to their several conditions, they need only hear this name of Kuan-shih-yin bodhisattva, and with one heart invoke it, and Kuan-shih-yin, immediately perceiving the sounds of the voice so pronounced, shall deliver them all.[128]

Here, the Chinese character transliterated as *-yin* is not only the third syllable of the bodhisattva's name, it is also the character translated here as "sounds." The name of the bodhisattva, in other words, is shown to refer to the activity of "perceiving" (*avalokita-*) "sounds" (*-svara*).

The role of the "sound perceiver," then, might be said to fill the gap between the mundane world and the transcendent realm of the buddhas. According to Tucci, Avalokiteśvara (or Avalokitasvara) was not necessarily intrinsically connected to Amitābha from the very start. Tucci refers to another Mahāyāna text, the *Śrīmahādevīvyākaraṇa*, in which Avalokiteśvara is connected to the activity of Śākyamuni preaching in Sukhāvatī.[129] This link between the bodhisattva and the Buddha is also apparent in the *Kāraṇḍavyūha Sūtra*. Avalokiteśvara is seen to prostrate himself before Śākyamuni on several different occasions: once, as we have already seen, when he appears in the Jetavana *vihāra* bringing lotus flowers from Amitābha[130] and once again, just before the Buddha's final teaching on monastic discipline.[131] Also, when the bodhisattva returns to the Jetavana *vihāra* at both the beginning and the end of the sūtra, he makes a report of his work to Śākyamuni. "Just as the Lord has ordered (*yathājñapto bhagavatā*)," he says at the end, "thus have I established the levels of my activity (*evaṃ ca mayā karmabhūmirniṣpāditā*)." The Buddha then congratulates him.[132] The "sound perceiver," then, acts as an intermediary for both Amitābha and Śākyamuni. On behalf of the two buddhas, he enters the different realms of *saṃsāra* in order to save beings from suffering and, in particular, to lead them to the pure land of Sukhāvatī. His name, as Tucci suggests, may derive from the compassionate gaze of the buddhas—*avalokana*—said, for instance, to have been shown by Śākyamuni before he entered into the human world as the buddha of our own historical period.[133]

It is interesting to note that the Sanskrit edition of the *Saddharmapuṇḍarīka Sūtra* used by H. Kern reads very differently at this point from the Chinese translation quoted above. Śākyamuni's reply, in this version, reads simply:

> All the hundred thousands of myriads of *koṭis* of creatures, young man of good family, who in this world are suffering troubles, will, if they hear the name of the bodhisattva *mahāsattva* Avalokiteśvara, be released from that mass of troubles.[134]

The Sanskrit text clearly reflects a time when the original name of the bodhisattva had been supplanted by the later Avalokiteśvara form. As a result, the explanation of the bodhisattva's name in terms of "sounds" loses its force, because *-svara,* the Sanskrit word for "sound" and the original ending of the name, has been replaced by the *-īśvara* ending, meaning "lord." Mironov comments: "The obvious inappropriateness of the explanation of the name Avalokiteśvara in this passage was early felt. When Avalokitasvara was abandoned and supplanted by Avalokiteśvara, the text . . . was remodelled, viz. the words 'voice,' 'invoke,' preserved in Chinese, were eliminated."[135]

To conclude this investigation into the original name of the bodhisattva, it remains only to show that this was Avalokitasvara, translated in Chinese as Kuan-yin, and not Avalokitalokasvara, as suggested by the popular Chinese form Kuan-shih-yin. First of all, as we have already noted, the name Avalokitasvara is found in the fifth-century Sanskrit fragments of the *Saddharmapuṇḍarīka Sūtra* commented on by Mironov. Second, although Kuan-shih-yin does appear, overall, to be the more popular version of the name in the early Chinese translations, we should remember that a Chinese translation of Avalokitasvara, not as Kuan-yin but as K'uei-yin, does occur in a translation of the *Vimalakīrtinirdeśa Sūtra* made between 223 and 228 C.E.

The Chinese form Kuan-shih-yin, it seems likely, arose due to the influence of a folk etymology of the original Sanskrit name Avalokitasvara. The bodhisattva was, it seems, understood to be the perceiver (*avalokita-*) of the sounds (*-svara*) of the world (*loka*). *Loka,* the Sanskrit word for "world," though in actual fact absent from the name, was nonetheless felt to be "implied," as Chandra puts it, by the third syllable in Avalokitasvara.[136] Unlike the Sanskrit, of course, the Chinese name Kuan-yin carried no trace of this sense, so *shih,* the Chinese character for *loka* was simply added to the name, resulting in the emergence of a new form, the popular Kuan-shih-yin. The Sanskrit equivalent of Kuan-shih-yin, Avalokitalokasvara, however, almost certainly never existed: it has never been found in any Sanskrit manuscript. The same may also be said for Avalokitalokeśvara, the hypothetical Sanskrit equivalent of Kuan-shih-tzu-tsai, another Chinese form of the bodhisattva's name mentioned by Hsuan Tsang.[137]

That Kuan-shih-yin was a Chinese invention is conclusively demonstrated by the contents of the *Fan-i Ming-i Chi* and the *Ta Fang Kuang Fo Hua-yen Ching Su,* the texts A. von Staël-Holstein uses to show that both the *-svara* and *-śvara* endings of the bodhisattva's name were known to the Chinese. Both texts, he writes, "regard Kuan-shih-yin (Avalokitalokasvara) as an exact equivalent of Avalokitasvara, which is of course wrong. The character *shih* (*loka*) is not represented in their transliterations, which transcribe merely the forms Avalokiteśvara and Avalokitasvara."[138] In other words, despite the fact that the Sanskrit versions of these texts clearly used the names Avalokiteśvara and Avalokitasvara, the Chinese translators nevertheless still insisted on using what had become the preferred form of the name, Kuan-shih-yin.

In passing, brief mention should also be made of the fact that the bodhisattva is sometimes referred to by the abbreviated form Avalokita. This name is used, for instance, in the *Bodhicaryāvatāra*, the poetic exposition of the Mahāyāna path attributed to the Indian *ācārya* Śāntideva. The Tibetan name for the bodhisattva, *sPyan ras gzigs*, is also an honorific form of the Sanskrit Avalokita.[139] Chandra suggests, plausibly, that this version of the name became popular during the period in which people were confused about whether to use the original name of the bodhisattva, Avalokitasvara, or the new name, Avalokiteśvara.[140]

Avalokitasvara eventually became Avalokiteśvara, it seems likely, due once again to the force of another folk interpretation of the name, here based upon the identification of the bodhisattva as a *lokeśvara*. This is a generic term meaning, literally, "lord" (*-īśvara*) "of the world" (*loka-*), applied to a wide range of supernormal beings in Indian religious thought. Bearing in mind, then, that very few people would ever have seen the name of the bodhisattva in written form, it is quite understandable that the pronunciation of the *-asvara* ending should have slipped to the homophonic *-eśvara*, thereby producing a name—Avalokiteśvara—that would actually have seemed a more appropriate title for a being understood to be a great *lokeśvara*. Even in written form, the two names may have been easily confused. Meiji Yamada writes: "In fact, if corrupt forms of both Avalokitasvara and Avalokiteśvara had been written in Karoṣṭhī orthography in North-West India, the two forms probably would have been the same."[141] The subsequent identification of the bodhisattva as the Buddhist *īśvara* was, no doubt, facilitated by the use of the new name Avalokiteśvara.[142]

It is beyond the scope of this study to explore the development of the many different forms of Avalokiteśvara. These are represented in schemata such as the arrangement of one hundred and eight manifestations of the bodhisattva that is famously depicted in the Macchandar Vahal temple in Kathmandu[143] and in the group of thirty-three forms of Kuan-yin that is so popular in the Far East.[144] In brief, the appropriation of these different forms can, I think, be accounted for both by the process of subjugation and conversion (when the bodhisattva takes the form of a deity) and by the chameleon-like ability of the bodhisattva (when he takes on the form of a particular human being). The only one of these forms alluded to in the *Kāraṇḍavyūha Sūtra* appears to be Cuṇḍā, a manifestation of the bodhisattva familiar as a member of a scheme of six Kuan-yins that has been preserved in the Japanese and Korean traditions.[145] Shortly after Sarvanīvaraṇaviṣkambhin receives *Oṃ Maṇipadme Hūṃ*, what is now generally agreed to be Cuṇḍā's own concise formula, *Oṃ Cale Cule Cunde Svāhā*, appears as a *dhāraṇī* said to be spoken by seventy-seven families of *tathāgatas*.[146] However, there is no clear indication that Cuṇḍā is actually conceived of, here, as a form of Avalokiteśvara. No further comment is made about the formula and the text reverts immediately to the second part of Śakyamuni's description of the worlds contained within the hair pores of Avalokiteśvara.

In conclusion, then, the *Kāraṇḍavyūha Sūtra* presents Avalokiteśvara as an *īśvara* in the mould of the two great purāṇic deities, but particularly of Śiva. The sūtra shows that the bodhisattva is recognizably the same figure that appears in earlier Mahāyāna literature. The evolution of the conception of the bodhisattva can be traced from his early appearance as Avalokitasvara (the "sound-perceiver" attendant of Amitābha and Śākyamuni), to his appearance under the name of Avalokiteśvara (due to his being identified as a *lokeśvara*), to his eventual manifestation as the supreme Buddhist *īśvara* (due to his subjugation and conversion of the Śaivite *īśvara*). The next chapter, then, will compare the presentations of *Oṃ Maṇipadme Hūṃ* in the *Kāraṇḍavyūha Sūtra* and of *Namaḥ Śivāya* in the purāṇas, examining to what extent the six-syllable formula of the Buddhist *īśvara* can be regarded as analogous to the five-syllable formula of the Śaivite *īśvara*.

CHAPTER 4

Oṃ Maṇipadme Hūṃ and *Namaḥ Śivāya*

A superficial scanning of the *Kāraṇḍavyūha* reveals that the six syllables *Oṃ Maṇipadme Hūṃ* actually only occur twice in the entire text. This is not to say, however, that the presentation of the mantra in the sūtra is incidental to the main thrust of the work. A substantial proportion of the *Kāraṇḍavyūha* is devoted to explaining the significance of the formula. It is, however, referred to throughout the text by the Sanskrit phrase *ṣaḍakṣarī mahāvidyā,* or "the six-syllable great formula," *vidyā,* literally "knowledge," referring in this instance to a particular type of mantra.

The different uses of the term *vidyā* may be divided into three basic categories. The word may refer, first, to a "science," or "field of knowledge." In the vedic tradition, for instance, there are generally said to be four principle *vidyās* of this kind: *trayī,* the science of the triple Veda; *ānvīkṣikī,* the science of logic and metaphysics; *daṇḍanīti,* the science of government and *vārttā,* knowledge of the practical arts, such as agriculture, commerce, and medicine.[1] *Vidyā* may also be used as a synonym for "mantra," which, like the more conventional sciences, is traditionally held to bestow a kind of mental control over different aspects of reality. In the *Aṣṭasāhasrikā,* for example, the term is used derogatorily in this fashion. In a section outlining the qualities of an irreversible bodhisattva, we read: "He [the bodhisattva] does not in any way embark on those spells (*vidyā*), mutterings, herbs, magical formulae, medical incantations, etc., which are the work of women."[2] *Vidyā,* finally, may refer to "knowledge" in the more crucial sense of "insight," "realization," or "enlightenment." In the *Kāraṇḍavyūha,* for instance, one of the titles regularly given to the buddhas is the standard epithet *vidyācaraṇasaṃpannaḥ,* or "accomplished (*saṃpannaḥ*) in knowledge (*vidyā-*) and conduct (*-caraṇa-*),"[3] and Avalokiteśvara himself is addressed at one point as *vidyādhipataye,* or "O lord (*adhipataye*) of knowledge."[4]

At some stage, however, the latter two meanings have coalesced to describe a mantra believed to be capable of bringing about both magical effects and enlightenment itself. In the *Aṣṭasāhasrikā,* in a passage that must be part of a later recension of the text than that which includes the passage quoted immediately above, the Perfection of Wisdom itself is said to be a *vidyā* of this kind: "A great lore (*vidyā*) is this Perfection of Wisdom, a lore without measure, a quite measureless lore, an unsurpassed lore, an unequalled lore, a lore which equals the unequalled."[5] It has protective power: "When they bring to mind and repeat this Perfection of Wisdom, the calamities which threaten them from kings and princes, from king's counsellors and king's ministers will not take place."[6] And it also leads to enlightenment: "For thanks to this lore (*vidyā*), i.e., the Perfection of Wisdom, the buddhas of the past have known full enlightenment. Thanks to it the buddhas of the future will know it. Thanks to it, the buddhas of the present do know it. Thanks to it, I [Śākyamuni] have known it."[7] The formula promoted in the *Hṛdaya Prajñāpāramitā Sūtra—Gate Gate Parāgate Parāsaṃgate Bodhi Svāhā*—is an example of the Perfection of Wisdom as such a *vidyā*.[8] *Oṃ Maṇipadme Hūṃ*, then, as the *ṣaḍakṣarī mahāvidyā*, may be said to be a mantra of this type. Furthermore, as a feminine noun, *vidyā*, when applied to a formula, usually denotes the fact that the formula in question is itself, in some sense, female in gender.[9] This, as we shall see, is a qualification that also applies to *Oṃ Maṇipadme Hūṃ*.

The *ṣaḍakṣarī mahāvidyā* is first properly introduced as the means by which people may be born into the worlds contained within the hair pores of Avalokiteśvara.[10] The bodhisattva Sarvanīvaraṇaviṣkambhin then asks Śākyamuni how he might obtain this formula.[11] Put very briefly, the Buddha's reply consists of a long description of the many extraordinary benefits of reciting the six syllables, together with an account of the search for the formula made by the *tathāgata* Padmottama. Before Padmottama is granted initiation into its use, the text introduces a colored maṇḍala made out of the dust of precious stones.[12] Sarvanīvaraṇaviṣkambhin is next told that he must seek out a suitable *dharmabhāṇaka*: a man who bears the formula in mind (*dhārayati*), speaks it (*vācayati*) and pays proper attention to it (*yoniśaśca manasi kurute*), and who, in addition, lives in the city of Vārāṇasī.[13] The bodhisattva then sets off with a retinue of followers to meet this preceptor. After another sermon on the marvelous qualities of *Oṃ Maṇipadme Hūṃ*, the *dharmabhāṇaka* finally grants initiation into the use of the mantra.[14]

It is only at those two moments in the *Kāraṇḍavyūha*, when first Padmottama and then Sarvanīvaraṇaviṣkambhin receive the formula, that the six syllables "*Oṃ Maṇipadme Hūṃ*" are explicitly spelled out in the text.[15] This economy of use is surely a deliberate ploy to build up a sense that the formula is something of enormous value and that the personal discovery of the actual identity these syllables represents a rare and precious opportunity. The dissemination of the formula may, in fact, be regarded as one of the most important concerns of the *Kāraṇḍavyūha*, as an examination of the overall structure of the work shows. The edition of the text edited by Vaidya, for example, consists of approximately fifty pages of Sanskrit, divided into two parts (*nirvyūhaḥ*) of more or less the same length. The section dealing with *Oṃ Maṇipadme Hūṃ* takes up about nine pages of text and is the central section of the second part of the sūtra.[16]

The first part (*nirvyūhaḥ*) of the *Kāraṇḍavyūha* is predominantly concerned with descriptions of the salvific adventures of the bodhisattva Avalokiteśvara. The sūtra begins, in typical Buddhist style, with a description of the gathering of beings around Śākyamuni Buddha in the Jetavana grove. This assembly is then said to become illuminated by a gorgeous light shining out of the Avīci hell,[17] which the bodhisattva Sarvanīvaraṇaviṣkambhin is told emanates from Avalokiteśvara.[18] There follow descriptions of the great bodhisattva's compassionate visitations to a number of different locations: to hell; to the ghost realm; to the *asuras*; to a place known as the "level made of silver" (*rūpyamayāṃ bhūmyāṃ*) populated by "four-legged beings with the souls of men" (*catuṣpādikāni sattvāni puruṣapudgalāni*); to the level made of iron (*ayomayāṃ bhūmyāṃ*) where Bali is bound; to the *yakṣas*; to the gods; to the *rākṣasīs* of Siṃhala; to the worms and insects of Vārāṇasī and, finally, before returning to the Jetavana grove, to the famine-stricken inhabitants of Magadha.

In between these accounts of Avalokiteśvara's travels, the sūtra also includes sections detailing other attributes of the bodhisattva: the theophany of various gods from different parts of his body; the emergence of different colored light rays from his mouth; the transformation of the Jetavana grove, upon his entrance, into a fragrant, bejewelled paradise akin to the pure lands of the buddhas; the inconceivable amount of merit accrued by the bodhisattva; the enormous benefits of bringing to mind his name and his ability to manifest in numerous different forms.

The second half of the sūtra begins with a fairly lengthy presentation (taking up four pages of Vaidya's edition) of the story of Siṃhala's voyage to the island of *rākṣasīs* and his subsequent rescue by the magical, flying horse Bālāha. There then follows the first part of a tour of the worlds contained within the hair pores of the bodhisattva, which includes the sight of his "thousandfold" form. This is immediately followed by the long section wholly concerned with matters pertaining to *Oṃ Maṇipadme Hūṃ*.[19] Once this is over, the sūtra returns to a second, somewhat shorter description of more of these worlds. Avalokiteśvara then proceeds back to the assembly in the Jetavana grove. Finally, after accounts of the conversion of Maheśvara and Umādevī by the bodhisattva and the "*samādhi*-contest" between Avalokiteśvara and Samantabhadra, the sūtra ends with a teaching on monastic discipline, given by Śākyamuni to his disciple Ānanda.

The *Kāraṇḍavyūha*, then, like the purāṇas, is a composite work consisting of stories, as well as doctrinal and ethical teachings, gathered together and placed within the "casket" (*kāraṇḍa*) of a single book. It seems reasonable to suggest, moreover, that the two sections of the work correspond to two separate stages of recension. Each section, for example, contains a story about the bodhisattva's visit to the island of *rākṣasīs*, the details of which contradict each other. In the first instance, Siṃhala is the name of the island, which is visited by Avalokiteśvara in the guise of an anonymous brahmin.[20] The bodhisattva then overcomes the *rākṣasīs* by preaching the Dharma to them, thereby transforming them into well-behaved Buddhists. In the second half of the sūtra, Siṃhala is both the name of the island and the name of the merchant shipwrecked there,[21] who is not Avalokiteśvara, but the Buddha Śākyamuni in one of his past lives. Rather than overcoming the *rākṣasīs* by his own power, Siṃhala is saved from them by the flying horse Bālāha, who is a manifestation of Avalokiteśvara.

The aim of the first section might be said, in simple terms, to generate devotion towards the figure of the Buddhist *īśvara*, by detailing the various inspiring deeds and qualities of Avalokiteśvara. There is, however, in this half of the sūtra, no instruction about any form of practice related to the bodhisattva, apart that is from a few lines in one short chapter (chapter eight in Vaidya's edition), where the immense benefits of bringing to mind the name of Avalokiteśvara are recounted. However, it does not appear as if the text is giving any great emphasis to this practice (its description occupies a mere nine lines of text),[22] and it seems likely that it is included principally as a necessary part of a recapitulation of the classic presentation of the bodhisattva found in chapter twenty-four of the *Saddharmapuṇḍarīka Sūtra*. As in that work, the value of calling upon Avalokiteśvara is immediately followed by an account of the many different forms the bodhisattva may adopt in order to save different kinds of beings. *Oṃ Maṇipadme Hūṃ* is, in fact, alluded to once in the first part of the sūtra: as part of the *vyākaraṇa* given to him by Avalokiteśvara, Bali is told that the six-syllable formula will be obtained.[23] But the complete isolation of this reference to the mantra makes it not unlikely that it is a later addition to the sūtra's own presentation of the *vāmana-avatāra*.

The principal purpose of the second part of the *Kāraṇḍavyūha* is, I suggest, precisely to fill this gap left by the first section and to promote, in the recitation of *Oṃ Maṇipadme Hūṃ*, a particular practice by which the presence of Avalokiteśvara might be invoked. The great importance of the mantra is, first of all, indicated by the extensive length of its presentation. Although only nine pages are obviously involved with descriptions of the glories of the mantra, it actually seems reasonable to think that all the other elements of this second part of the sūtra spring from the central intention of promulgating the six syllables.

The worlds contained within the hair pores of Avalokiteśvara and the appearance of the "thousandfold" form of the bodhisattva constitute the components of a vision of the bodhisattva brought about through the recitation of

Oṃ Maṇipadme Hūṃ. The ethical teachings at the end of the sūtra and the story of Siṃhala both promote the celibate, monastic ideal, a specific response to the challenge presented to the Mahāyāna establishment by the kind of non-celibate practitioners that originally promoted the doctrine of the Buddhist *īśvara* and his concise formula. The conversion of Maheśvara, finally, together with the fact that the *dharmabhāṇaka* resides in the great Śaivite city of Vārāṇasī, are descriptive of the way in which this doctrine has been taken over from the Śaivite tradition, before being remodeled and absorbed into the categories of the Mahāyāna Buddhist system. How, then, does *Oṃ Maṇipadme Hūṃ*, the six-syllable formula of the Buddhist *īśvara* Avalokiteśvara, compare to the *pañcākṣara*, or "five-syllable" formula *Namaḥ Śivāya* of the Śaivite *īśvara* Śiva?

Our discussion of this issue revolves principally around the presentation of *Namaḥ Śivāya* in the Śaivite *Skanda Purāṇa*, the work which, as we saw, may be linked in some way to the *Kāraṇḍavyūha Sūtra*. In addition to many occasional references to this five-syllable formula, the purāṇa contains one chapter wholly devoted to its description.[24] Our analysis is supplemented, too, by a consultation of the *Śiva Purāṇa*, which includes one chapter on the five-syllable formula and the single syllable *Oṃ* together,[25] and a group of three chapters that discuss the qualities and the correct use of *Namaḥ Śivāya* alone.[26] In addition, passages from the *Liṅga Purāṇa*, which also contains a chapter on the glory of the five-syllable mantra, will be taken into account.[27]

The relevant chapter in the *Skanda Purāṇa* begins with an introductory passage paying homage to Śiva. The sages then demand to hear of the greatness of the god's mantras.[28] The *sūta* replies that the performance of the repeated utterance of formulae (*japayajñā*) "is proclaimed as greater than all the *yajñās* of meritorious nature and cause of excellent welfare."[29] Next, *Namaḥ Śivāya* is first introduced, not in its normal five-syllable form, but in the common, variant six-syllable form *Oṃ Namaḥ Śivāya*. This is said to be "the great means of securing prosperity," "of divine nature," and "the greatest of all mantras."[30] The chapter immediately reverts to descriptions of the formula in its more familiar form. *Namaḥ Śivāya*, it is said, is "the bestower of salvation on those who repeatedly mutter it." It is "resorted to by all excellent sages desirous of supernatural powers." Even Brahmā, we read, is unable to describe its greatness. The *śrutis* are said to "reach the ultimate principle therein and became fully satisfied." Śiva "revels" in it. It was "evolved out of all the Upaniṣads." By means of the formula, "all the sages attained the Supreme Brahman, free from all ailments." It is "of the nature of Supreme Brahman." It is the "primordial mantra" uttered by Śiva himself, who desired "the welfare of all embodied ones fettered by the noose of worldly existence."[31]

Once the formula is "fixed in the heart," to what avail, the *sūta* asks, are the many other mantras, holy places, penances, and sacrifices connected to

Śiva? As long as embodied beings do not utter the formula "even once," then they will continue to "move round and round in the terrible mundane world infested with miseries." It is "the supreme king of the kings of all the mantras," "the crest-jewel of all the Vedāntas," "the storehouse of all spiritual knowledge," "the illuminating lamp on the path of salvation," "the submarine fire unto the ocean of ignorance," and "the forest fire of great woods of heinous sins." It is, therefore, "the bestower of everything."[32]

Its use is openly available to women, *śūdras* and men of mixed social class and birth, and involves neither special initiation, nor *homa*, consecration, water-libation, special occasion, nor special process of instruction. It is "ever pure." It can destroy great sins and grant salvation. It should be acquired, the purāṇa then says, from an excellent preceptor, who is described as free from impurities, quiescent, well-behaved, of few words, free from lust and anger, with control over the sense organs and possessed of good conduct. If then repeated in a sacred place, the formula immediately brings inordinate or supernatural power. Six holy places are then listed which are conducive to the attainment of such powers: Prayāga, Puṣkara, the "charming" Kedāra, Setubandha, Gokarṇa and Naimiṣāraṇya.[33]

There then follows what is said to be an ancient anecdote "conducive to auspiciousness to those who listen to it once or on many occasions." This concerns the marriage between a king called "Dāśārha" of the Yadu dynasty of Mathurā and a princess called "Kalāvatī", the beautiful daughter of the king of Kāśī. On their wedding night, despite Dāśārha's repeated entreaties, Kalāvatī is disinclined to join him in bed until, eventually, the king attempts to take her by force. Kalāvatī, however, orders the king not to touch her, telling him that she is "under a vow of observance." "You do know what is Dharma and what is Adharma," she says, "Do not be rash with me."[34]

"Sexual union increases pleasure, if both husband and wife are equally keen and desirous," she continues. She and the king, she says, will only sleep together when love has been aroused in her. No man, she says, should lustfully approach a woman who is either displeased, sickly, pregnant, observing a religious fast or a vow, in her monthly course, or who is "not keen in love-sport." A loving husband who wants to enjoy the delights of a woman, she concludes, should only approach her "after fondling and pleasing her, after a great deal of coaxing and cajoling, and after looking into her requirements with sympathy and smoothness."[35]

The king ignores this rebuke, however, and presses himself upon Kalāvatī, only to discover that her body is red hot, scorching him and causing him to cast her off in great fright. Struck with wonder, he then listens as she tells him that, during her childhood, an eminent sage imparted to her the five-syllable formula of Śiva. By reciting this mantra, her body became free of sins and impurities, to the extent that she can no longer be touched by sinful people. The king, she reminds him, habitually consorts with whores and other liquor-drinking women, fails to take a daily bath, repeats the mantra without purity of mind and body and does not propitiate Īśāna (Śiva). "How can you be fit to touch me?" she asks.[36]

The king then implores his wife to initiate him into the practice of the five-syllable formula in order that, after purifying himself of all sins, he may eventually be fit to sleep with her. The queen tells him he must approach the preceptor Garga for this initiation. They then go together to Garga, who takes them to the banks of the river Kālindī. There, the king is told to fast and to bathe in the holy waters, to sit facing the east and to bow at the feet of Śiva. The preceptor then places his hand on the king's head and imparts the mantra. Immediately, thousands of crows fly out of the king's body, screaming and falling to the earth, where they are burnt to ashes.[37]

These crows, the preceptor explains, are the king's innumerable sins accumulated over thousands of lifetimes. Now that his soul has become sanctified, he is told, he may go and "sport about" with his wife as he pleases. The delighted couple take leave of the preceptor and, "shining lustrously," return to their palace. The king then embraces the queen, whose body, by now, is said to be cool "like sandalpaste." Dāśārha, finally, is said to achieve exquisite satisfaction "like a penurious wretch after acquiring wealth." By way of a conclusion, the story and the chapter as a whole ends by observing that the five-syllable formula is "an ornamental jewel unto the entire range of Vedas, Upaniṣads, purāṇas and other scriptural texts" and "spells destruction of sins."[38]

In many obvious respects, this presentation is clearly very different from the way in which *Oṃ Maṇipadme Hūṃ* is written about in the *Kāraṇḍavyūha*. At the same time, however, it is not very difficult to discern that both the purāṇas and the sūtra are promoting a similar type of religious phenomenon. The Śaivite formula is *pañcākṣara*, "five syllables," while the Buddhist formula is *ṣaḍakṣara*, "six syllables." Although *Namaḥ Śivāya* seems, in general, to be referred to as a mantra, it is also, like the Buddhist six syllables, described as a *vidyā*.[39] Both formulae are, furthermore, said to be the *hṛdaya*, or "heart" of the *īśvara*: *Oṃ Maṇipadme Hūṃ*, in the *Kāraṇḍavyūha*, is repeatedly referred to as the *paramahṛdaya*, or "innermost heart";[40] *Namaḥ Śivāya*, in the *Liṅga Purāṇa*, as *hṛdaya* (This mantra . . . is my heart . . .)[41] and in the *Śiva Purāṇa* as *mahāhṛdaya*, or "great heart" (This Śaiva mantra is my great heart).[42]

Both the Śaivite and the Buddhist formulae are also promoted as sui generis means of attaining liberation. In the *Skanda Purāṇa*, for instance, *Namaḥ Śivāya* is "the bestower of salvation on those who repeatedly mutter it." It is the bestower of everything, the means by which "the ultimate principle" is reached and the Supreme Brahman is attained. Similarly, in the *Śiva Purāṇa*, we read: "(But) he who worships me even once with devotion repeating the five-syllabled mantra, attains my region through the weightiness of the mantra alone."[43] And in the *Liṅga Purāṇa*: "It is the excellent knowledge leading to salvation."[44]

Oṃ Maṇipadme Hūṃ, meanwhile, is said early on in the sūtra's presentation, to bring about liberation (*mokṣa*). Whoever knows (*jānāti*) this *paramahṛdaya*, we read, knows liberation (*mokṣaṃ jānāti*).[45] A little later, it is said that whoever is given solace by *Oṃ Maṇipadme Hūṃ* is said to become an irreversible bodhisattva and, before long, a fully enlightened buddha.[46] The formula is the incomparable teaching on supreme enlightenment and *nirvāṇa*.[47] Bringing it to mind leads to the destruction of all evil and the attainment of enlightenment.[48] Reciting it brings sublime liberation.[49] Without *Namaḥ Śivāya*, the *Skanda Purāṇa* says, beings will "move round and round in the terrible mundane world infested with miseries." *Oṃ Maṇipadme Hūṃ*, likewise, is said to be the cause of the destruction of rebirth in the five realms of *saṃsāra*, leading to the drying up of the hellish *kleśas* and also to the end of the animal realms.[50]

Both *Namaḥ Śivāya* and *Oṃ Maṇipadme Hūṃ* are presented, in the same somewhat paradoxical manner, as formulae whose use may be enjoyed by almost everyone, regardless of any distinctions of class or gender, but which are yet, at the same time, extraordinarily difficult to come by. Similarly, though at one moment various complicated ritual processes appear to be absolutely necessary for effecting initiation into the use of these formulae, at another such procedures appear to be entirely dispensable. In the *Skanda Purāṇa*, for instance, *Namaḥ Śivāya* is said, on the one hand, to be recited by women, *śūdras* and men of mixed caste and birth: categories that would have been excluded from participation in many other Indian religious practices. Its use, moreover, is said to involve no special initiation, *homa* (sacrifice), consecration, water libation, occasion nor special process of instruction. On the other hand, though, in the story of Dāśārha and his bride, the king pleads with his wife to grant him the five-syllable mantra, as if initiation into its use was something rather extraordinary. Although his preceptor Garga is said to grant him use of the formula by the simple expedient of placing his hand on the king's head, Dāśārha is also said, somewhat in contradiction of the earlier spirit of the text, to undergo a series of fairly rigorous preparatory practices before this moment is reached. He fasts, bathes in the sacred river Kālindī, sits facing the east, and bows to the feet of Śiva.

The same pattern is apparent in the *Śiva Purāṇa*. At some points, the text stresses the democratic nature of the practice of reciting *Namaḥ Śivāya*. We read: "A person steady in the *japa* of the five-syllabled mantra is released from the cage of sins whether he be a *śūdra*, base-born, fool or a learned man."[51] And later: "Since this mantra functions without references to castes, the defects found in the other mantras are not found in this mantra."[52] Yet, a little earlier in the purāṇa, a preliminary procedure is described which would surely deter any but the most determined devotee. The initiant, we read, is required to propitiate his preceptor mentally, verbally, physically, and monetarily. If he is affluent he should give him horses, elephants, chariots, ornaments, grains, and riches. Next, he should serve the preceptor for a year. On an auspicious day and in an auspicious place, he should bathe the preceptor and dress him in considerable finery. The preceptor will then repeat the mantra "with due accents," make the disciple repeat it, and, finally, declare everything to be auspicious. "Thus," it is said, "the preceptor shall impart the mantra and allow him to practise it."[53] Elsewhere, as Rocher has pointed out,[54] it is said that the secret of the formula is known by Śiva alone (*rahasyaṃ śivamantrasya śivo jānāti nāparaḥ*).[55] It is imparted by Śiva himself: to Brahmā and Viṣṇu,[56] and to others, such as the *sūta*.[57]

Likewise, in the *Kāraṇḍavyūha Sūtra*, the use of *Oṃ Maṇipadme Hūṃ* is also shown to cut across social and religious class barriers. Either a son or a daughter of noble family (*kulaputro vā kuladuhitā vā*) is said to be able to enter the maṇḍala of the six-syllable formula.[58] Either a son or a daughter of noble family who recites the formula is said to achieve an indestructible lustre.[59] No mention is made of any restrictions concerning matters of social class with regard to the use of the formula (as is only to be expected in a Buddhist text). When Sarvanīvaraṇaviṣkambhin sets out for Vārāṇasī in order to find his preceptor, he is said to gather around him a retinue of many different types: bodhisattvas, householders, renunciants, boys and girls.[60] Most strikingly, in the course of instructions attributed to Avalokiteśvara about the preparation of the maṇḍala connected to *Oṃ Maṇipadme Hūṃ*, initiation into the use of the mantra is said not to be restricted to followers of the Mahāyāna alone, but to be available to Buddhists of any persuasion. The text reads:

> *athavā śraddhādhimuktakasya dātavyā / athavā*
> *mahāyānaśraddhād himuktakasya dātavyā /*
> *na ca tīrthikasya dātavyā/*[61]

The formula, in other words, is to be given (*dātavyā*) either (*athavā*) to one who has exhibited faith (*śraddhādhimuktakasya*), or (*athavā*) to one who has exhibited faith in the Mahāyāna (*mahāyānaśraddha-*). *Oṃ Maṇipadme Hūṃ*, it seems, may be used by adherents of both the Mahāyāna, or "great vehicle," and the contrasting Hīnayāna, or "lesser vehicle." The text here provides valuable support for the view that the original distinction between these two vehicles was based not in their use of different practices, but in different motivations: different visions of the ultimate goal of the Buddhist endeavor. Whereas in the Mahāyāna, the practitioner is said to set out with the aim of becoming a buddha in order to help bring about the buddhahood of all sentient beings, the Hīnayāna Buddhist sets out with the more limited aim of achieving only his or her own liberation. The *Kāraṇḍavyūha* indicates, at this point, that Buddhists of both persuasion lived together in the same communities and engaged in the same forms of practice, including, it seems, the recitation of *Oṃ Maṇipadme Hūṃ*.

The passage, then, is not concerned with the putative division between these two different classes of Buddhist, but with maintaining a division between Buddhist and non-Buddhists. Though the formula may be given to Mahāyāna or non-Mahāyāna Buddhists, we read, it is not to be given (*na dātavyā*) to the *tīrthika* (*tīrthikasya*), or non-Buddhist. The important implication of this statement, surely, is that there were occasions when these *tīrthikas* did apply for initiation into the use of the *Oṃ Maṇipadme Hūṃ*. This, in turn, is an indication that this Buddhist practice may not have been very obviously different from non-Buddhist practices. It may, for instance, have been perceived as a simple variant of the non-Buddhist, Śaivite formula *Namaḥ Śivāya*. The original proponents of worship of the Buddhist *īśvara* by means of his concise formula may not, it seems, have appeared very different from worshippers of Śiva. The *Kāraṇḍavyūha*, however, is at pains to stress the Buddhist identity and application of the six-syllable formula. Nonetheless, within those parameters, *Oṃ Maṇipadme Hūṃ* is promoted as a universal practice, available to all Buddhists.

At the same time, the formula appears to be something that is almost impossibly secret and elusive. Sarvanīvaraṇaviṣkambhin's first enquiries about the formula, for instance, are met with the reply that it is difficult to obtain and that it is not known by the *tathāgata*s, let alone by bodhisattvas.[62] Yogins and *tathāgata*s know it to be difficult to obtain and unfathomable, let alone bodhisattvas.[63] As the *tathāgata*s have wandered for sixteen *kalpas* for its sake, who knows when the bodhisattvas will know it?[64] Such warnings are immediately illustrated by the tale of the *tathāgata* Padmottama's arduous search for the formula and, then, by the search of Sarvanīvaraṇaviṣkambhin himself. Just as *Namaḥ Śivāya* is said to come from Śiva, so, too, in the *Kāraṇḍavyūha Sūtra*, is *Oṃ Maṇipadme Hūṃ* shown to be the gift of Avalokiteśvara, first when the bodhisattva (prompted by Amitābha) bestows the formula on Padmottama[65] and second when, according to the preceptor in Vārāṇasī, Avalokiteśvara grants it to Sarvanīvaraṇaviṣkambhin.[66] Finally, initiation into the use of *Oṃ Maṇipadme Hūṃ* is said to be dependent on the extremely costly construction of a special maṇḍala. Avalokiteśvara is reported as saying that the formula should not be given to one who has not seen the maṇḍala.[67] This diagram, we then read, should be four-cornered and about the size of five hands, containing a depiction of the buddha Amitābha made out of the powder of sapphires, rubies, emeralds, quartz, gold, and silver.[68]

However, it quickly becomes apparent that this represents an ideal situation. A few sentences later on in the text, Amitābha tells Avalokiteśvara that if someone is unable to afford these precious substances, colored dyes and flowers may be used instead.[69] If even these are unavailable, the maṇḍala may simply be meditated upon by the preceptor for a month before he gives instruction on the mantra and the relevant *mudrās*.[70] The initiant, in other words, does not actually need to see the maṇḍala at all, relying, instead, on the previous visualization practice of his preceptor. Indeed, when Sarvanīvaraṇaviṣkambhin eventually comes to receive the formula, no mention is made of the use of any maṇḍala: the *dharmabhāṇaka* simply gazes into the sky, where he sees Avalokiteśvara, and tells Sarvanīvaraṇaviṣkambhin that he has been granted the formula by the great bodhisattva.

Both sūtra and purāṇa, then, suggest that *Oṃ Maṇipadme Hūṃ* and *Namaḥ Śivāya* were promoted as popular practices, available to one and all. Nonetheless, by virtue of the fact that their use was deemed to be dependent upon the good will or grace of the Buddhist or the Śaivite *īśvara*, these formulae are presented as rare and wondrous treasures, a conceit occasionally reinforced by the performance of elaborate initiation rituals. The necessity of a qualified preceptor is consistently stressed. King Dāśārha approaches the guru Garga. The bodhisattva Sarvanīvaraṇaviṣkambhin has to seek out the *dharmabhāṇaka* of Vārāṇasī. Similarly, in the *Śiva Purāṇa*, we read: "A *japa* without the behest of the preceptor, holy rites, faith and the prescribed fees is fruitless though the behest might have been secured."[71] And, in the same work: "O brahmins, the devotee shall take instruction from his preceptor, sit comfortably on the ground cleaned well, and start the *japa*."[72] Initiation into the use of either formula might be a more or less extravagant affair, it seems reasonable to suppose, according to the economic resources of the initiants, to the occasion and to the whim of the preceptor.

But perhaps the most arresting of all the similarities between *Oṃ Maṇipadme Hūṃ* and *Namaḥ Śivāya* is the way in which both sūtra and purāṇa appear to reflect a common understanding of the two formulae as forms of the *praṇava*. This term, derived from the verb *praṇu*, meaning "to hum," or "reverberate," describes what Gonda refers to as a "numinous primeval sound."[73] This is a phenomenon which is, of course, most famously expressed in the form of the mantra *Oṃ*, the single syllable that is the subject of so much speculation in the Vedas and the Upaniṣads. In the *Taittirīya Upaniṣad*, for instance, we read: "*Oṃ* is Brahman. *Oṃ* is the whole universe."[74] And in the *Māṇḍūkya Upaniṣad*: "What was and is and is yet to be, / All of it is *Oṃ*; / And whatever else the three times transcends, / That too is *Oṃ*."[75]

In the *Śiva Purāṇa*, as Rocher observes, *Namaḥ Śivāya* is explicitly identified as a form of the *praṇava*. In the course of its discussion of the five-syllable mantra, the purāṇa, first of all, lists a number of different folk etymologies for this term. It is the best of boats (*nava*) for crossing the ocean of worldly existence (*pra*, as in *prakṛti*, the created order). It is that which produces no (*na*) diffusiveness (*pra*) for you (*va*). It is the ideal (*pra*) guide (*na*) to *mokṣa,* or "liberation," for you (*va*). It is the ideal way (*pra*) to provide new (*nava*) wisdom. The *praṇava* also, the purāṇa goes on to explain, has both a subtle (*sūkṣma*) and a gross (*sthūla*) form. The former is *ekākṣara,* made up of "one syllable" and the latter is *pañcākṣara,* made up of "five syllables." We read: "The subtle one is of a single syllable where the constituent five syllables are not differentiated clearly (*avyakta*). The gross one is of five syllables where all the constituent syllables are manifest (*vyakta*)."[76] The subtle *praṇava* and the gross *praṇava* are, then, *Oṃ* and *Namaḥ Śivāya*.

This conception of *Namaḥ Śivāya* as a form of the *praṇava* illuminates many aspects of its presentation. Just as *Oṃ* is also believed to be the means for attaining all one's goals, for instance, so, too, is *Namaḥ Śivāya*. In the *Kaṭha Upaniṣad,* for instance, *Oṃ* is described as follows: "Who so this imperishable (*akṣara*) comes to know, what he desires is his."[77] Similarly, in the *Śiva Purāṇa*: "A man can achieve everything by means of the *japa* of the five-syllabled mantra."[78]

Oṃ is also regarded as both the essence and source of all religious teachings and practices. In the course of the discussion of *Oṃ* found in the *Śvetāśvatara Upaniṣad,* for instance, we read: "Hymns, sacrifices, rites and ordinances, / What was and what is yet to be, / (All) that the Vedas proclaim, / All this does he who is possessed of creative power emit / From that (same syllable) . . ."[79] Similarly, in the *Skanda Purāṇa, Namaḥ Śivāya* is: "evolved out of all the Upaniṣads," "the supreme king of all the mantras," "the crest-jewel of all the *vedāntas,*" "the storehouse of all spiritual knowledge," and "an ornamental jewel unto the entire range of Vedas, Upaniṣads, purāṇas, and other scriptural texts."[80] The *Śiva Purāṇa* states of *Namaḥ Śivāya*: "Then all the Vedas, scriptures etc. are stationed in the five-syllabled mantra."[81] And again: "This five-syllabled lore is present in all Upaniṣads."[82] And in the *Liṅga Purāṇa*: "At that time the Vedas and scriptures are stationed in the five-syllabled mantra."[83]

Like *Namaḥ Śivāya, Oṃ Maṇipadme Hūṃ* is also said to have the qualities characteristic of a *praṇava*. We have already seen how the six syllables are repeatedly said, in the *Kāraṇḍavyūha,* to be self-sufficient means of achieving many different kinds of religious goals. The Buddhist formula is also presented, in the sūtra, as the condensed expression of all religious teachings. Whoever writes *Oṃ Maṇipadme Hūṃ,* we read, is said to have written "the eighty-four thousand *dharmas*" (*caturaśītidharmaskandhasahasrāṇi*), shorthand for the idea of the complete Buddhist literary corpus.[84] The formula is also, a little later on, said to be the means by which "the twelvefold wheel of *Dharma* is turned" (*dvādaśākāraṃ dharmarandhracakramāvartayeyam*), referring to another well-known phrase used to denote the entirety of all Buddhist teaching.[85] It is, elsewhere, said to be the indestructible instruction on all wisdom.[86]

The idea of *Namaḥ Śivāya* as both the essence and source of all things is conveyed in terms of a simple, though nonetheless evocative image. The formula is repeatedly described as the seed of a banyan tree. In the *Śiva Purāṇa,* for instance, in the course of a discussion of the six-syllable *Oṃ Namaḥ Śivāya,* we read: "The first mantra consisting of six syllables is the seed of all lores. It is very subtle but serves a great purpose. It shall be known like the seed of the banyan tree."[87] Likewise, in the *Liṅga Purāṇa* presentation of *Namaḥ Śivāya*: "It is very subtle and its meaning is great; it is like the seed of the holy banyan tree."[88]

The use of this image appears also to be another aspect of the presentation of *Namaḥ Śivāya* derived from a conception of the formula as a form of the *praṇava.* It is evocative of similar images found in the Upaniṣads to describe *Oṃ.* In the *Jaiminīya Upaniṣad Brāhmaṇa,*[89] for instance, increasingly refined levels of the created order are described as the *rasa,* the "juice" or "sap," first of the Vedas and then of the levels of creation that have already emerged. Thus, *pṛthi,* "the earth" is said to be the *rasa* of the *Ṛg Veda* and *agni,* "fire," the *rasa* of *pṛthi.* Eventually, however, the creator god Prajāpati is said to reach a syllable from which he is unable to take the sap, implying that he has now reached the very essence of all reality. This is *Oṃ* (*athaikasyaivākṣarasya rasaṃ nāśaknod ādātum Oṃ ity etasyaiva*).[90] *Oṃ,* the *sūkṣma praṇava,* is the *rasa* of the cosmic fruit. *Namaḥ Śivāya,* the *sthūla praṇava,* is the essential seed of a banyan tree.

A similar sort of image—also derived from nature—is used to describe *Oṃ Maṇipadme Hūṃ.* The Buddhist formula, in the *Kāraṇḍavyūha Sūtra,* is said to be like a grain of rice. As such, the formula is both the regenerative seed (like the banyan seed *Namaḥ Śivāya*) and also the essential, nourishing part of the plant (like the *rasa Oṃ*). This conception of *Oṃ Maṇipadme Hūṃ* is not just mentioned in passing, but is developed over the course of several lines of the text. The six-syllable formula, we read, is "the grain of rice of the Mahāyāna" (*taṇḍulavatsāraṃ mahāyānasya*). It is, once more, the condensed expression of Buddhist teaching: its recitation is the equivalent of the singing of many Mahāyāna sūtras and the teaching of a great variety of texts. It is a sui generis means of achieving the great religious goals: its simple recitation brings sublime liberation (*japitamātreṇa śivaṃ mokṣam*).

To obtain the formula, the sūtra explains, is to possess the pith (*sāram*), just as one obtains the pith of rice grains, by taking them home, filling jars with them, drying them in the sun, threshing them, and leaving them for four years. All other yogas are like chaff (*tuṣasadṛśāḥ*). The six-syllable formula is like the rice grain.[91] *Oṃ Maṇipadme Hūṃ,* here again, appears deliberately to be presented as a kind of Buddhist *praṇava.* The use of this type of imagery, in parenthesis, represents another link between the *Kāraṇḍavyūha Sūtra* and the buddha nature sūtras of the Mahāyāna. The kernel of grain inside the husk and the seed within a fruit, for instance, are, respectively, the third and sixth of nine similes used to describe the *tathāgatagarbha* in the *Mahāyānottaratantraśāstra*.[92]

The six-syllable Buddhist formula is also, like the Śaivite formula, personified as a female deity. In the *Śiva Purāṇa*, for instance, *Namaḥ Śivāya* is described as follows:

> It is the goddess, my own expression coming out of my mouth at first. The goddess having the splendour of molten gold, plump, lifted-up breasts, four arms, three arees [?], and the crescent moon as the crest-jewel. Her hands are as tender as lotuses. She is gentle with the gesture of boon and protection; she is possessed of all characteristics. She is bedecked in ornaments. She is seated on a white lotus. Her tresses are blue and curly. She has five colours with beaming discs, viz., yellow, black, smoky, golden and red.[93]

Oṃ Maṇipadme Hūṃ, or *ṣaḍakṣarī mahāvidyā* as the formula is dubbed, also appears as a goddess in the maṇḍala presented in the *Kāraṇḍavyūha Sūtra*. She has four arms, is "autumn yellow" in color (*śaratkāṇḍagauravarṇā*), is decorated with many ornaments, holds a lotus (*padmaṃ*) in her outer left hand and a string of prayer beads in her outer right, with her two inner hands joined in the *mudrā* of *sarvarājendrā*.[94] The latter, which probably means "the lord of all kings" is identified by some scholars with the *añjalimudrā*, the gesture of holding the two hands in front of one's chest, fingertips pointing upwards, with the palms together, though slightly cupped.[95] This description of the personified formula in the maṇḍala, however, represents the limit of sūtra's presentation of *Oṃ Maṇipadme Hūṃ* as a female person.

In the Śaivite text, on the other hand, the personification of *Namaḥ Śivāya* as a goddess is part and parcel of a wider presentation of the formula as an expression of Śiva's *śakti*. The latter term, of course, refers to the creative dimension of the deity, perceived sometimes as inherent to the god's own nature, but often as his female partner—separate from him, though nonetheless joined to him in the intimate union of their marriage.[96] Thus, in the discussion of the five syllables in the *Śiva Purāṇa*, we read: "Protected by my *śakti* they do not perish."[97] Elsewhere in the purāṇa, it is explained: "The mantra is of the nature of Śiva."[98] And a little later on: "The presence of the goddess continues to be felt as long as the mantra continues to be repeated."[99]

The relationship between Śiva and the goddess was also, in some sense, to be acted out in the actual physical relationship between a practitioner and his (or her) consort. In another description given in the *Śiva Purāṇa* of the procedure for gaining initiation into the use of *Namaḥ Śivāya*, the aspiring devotee is required to bring together five, well-established practitioners, each of whom represents a different form of the deity. The first of these five acts as the preceptor. The wife of this individual, it is said, should be regarded as the god's female partner. Thus:

> For the sake of the worship he shall invite five great devotees of Śiva along with their wives. One of those shall be an excellent preceptor who shall be assigned the *Sāmba* form, another will represent *Īśāna*, the third will represent the *Aghora* aspect of Śiva, the fourth will represent the *Vāma* aspect of Śiva and the fifth will represent the *Sadyojata* aspect of Śiva.[100]

And then:

> The preceptor's wife must be considered as the great goddess. The wives of the other devotees *Īśāna* and the rest shall be duly worshipped and honoured . . .[101]

The idea that the engagement of a practitioner with *Namaḥ Śivāya* and his (or her) engagement with a sexual partner may, in some sense, be seen as equivalent, in so far as both are means of reenacting the union of Śiva and *śakti* is, surely, exactly what is expressed in the *Skanda Purāṇa*'s story of king Dāśārha and queen Kalāvatī. There, the two themes, first, of a man's approach towards sexual union with his wife and, second, of his attempts to engage successfully with the practice of reciting the five-syllable mantra are woven together into one seamless whole. Queen Kalāvatī may be understood, simultaneously, as a woman, as a personification of *Namaḥ Śivāya* and as a goddess.[102]

Such a doctrine is, inevitably, going to pose a challenge to any religious community rooted in celibate, monastic discipline, no matter how much stress is given to a symbolic, nonliteral interpretation of the teaching. This was the problem, it seems likely, that confronted that section of the Mahāyāna Buddhist establishment responsible for the creation of the *Kāraṇḍavyūha*. The previous chapter has, I think, demonstrated beyond reasonable doubt that the figure of Avalokiteśvara in the sūtra has taken on many of the attributes of Śiva. This chapter, similarly, has shown that the six-syllable Buddhist formula *Oṃ Maṇipadme Hūṃ* represents an adaptation of the five-syllable Śaivite formula *Namaḥ Śivāya*. Both are concise *vidyās*, the *hṛdayas* of their respective *īśvaras*, sui generis means of attaining liberation, universally available, though of rare value and somewhat secret. Both are also, it has been argued, conceived of as forms of *praṇava*. Their close similarity, it seems, even led non-Buddhists to seek initiation into use of the Buddhist formula. The *Kāraṇḍavyūha*, however, contains nothing remotely like the story of king Dāśārha.

The next chapter, then, will explore the way in which the sūtra describes a secondary stage of the Buddhist appropriation of this Śaivite doctrine and mode of practice, integrating the use of the concise formula of Avalokiteśvara into the orthodox doctrinal and ethical categories of the Mahāyāna mainstream. As we shall see, the basis for the use of the concise formula is no longer the tantric *śakti* idea. Instead, *Oṃ Maṇipadme Hūṃ* is linked, primarily, to a scheme borrowed from the *bhakti* side of the purāṇic tradition, which is reconfigured in the terms of the Mahāyāna. This scheme, in turn, is linked to the central Mahāyāna religious goal of rebirth in the Buddhist pure land of Sukhāvatī.

CHAPTER 5

Oṃ Maṇipadme Hūṃ and the *Mahāyāna*

The *Kāraṇḍavyūha Sūtra* is clearly written from the point of view of a monastic establishment governed by a rule of celibacy. It is striking, for instance, that while the practice of reciting the Śaivite formula *Namaḥ Śivāya* is illustrated by a story about the consummation of the marriage between a king and his young bride, the presentation of the use of the Buddhist mantra *Oṃ Maṇipadme Hūṃ* is prefaced by the tale of a shipwrecked sailor and his narrow escape from the seductive allure of a collection of attractive women, who, he is made aware, are really a band of man-eating demonesses. Women are seen as goddesses in the purāṇa, but as monsters in the sūtra.

The legend of the mariner Siṃhala is placed at the beginning of the second part of the *Kāraṇḍavyūha*,[1] immediately after a passage describing the many different *samādhis* achieved by the bodhisattva Avalokiteśvara.[2] After a storm at sea, so the story goes, Siṃhala and his five hundred companions are washed up on the shore of a desert island and greeted by a host of beautiful women, who ask the sailors to become their husbands. The men agree and begin to enjoy a pleasurable married existence. One night, however, Siṃhala discovers that these women are, in fact, *rākṣasīs*, female monsters, who, after an initial period of amorous indulgence, are in the habit of transferring their lovers to the confines of a walled compound, where these unfortunate men are kept imprisoned until, eventually, they are cannibalized. Siṃhala, though, manages to find his way back to the safety of the mainland by climbing aboard the back of the magical flying horse Bālāha. His shipmates, however, all perish, because, while on the flying horse, they ignore the orders of Bālāha to keep their eyes shut and not to look back at the island. Seeing their *rākṣasī* wives weeping and wailing, they fall back into the sea and are promptly eaten.

After the story has been told, the Buddha Śākyamuni reveals that it was he himself who experienced suffering in a former life as the bodhisattva caravan leader (Siṃhala) and who was liberated from the fear of death by Avalokiteśvara, who was Bālāha, the king of horses. It is impossible, Śākyamuni continues, to calculate the amount of merit accrued by Avalokiteśvara. He will, instead, he says, give a brief discourse on the individual hair pores of the great bodhisattva. A description of the different lands contained within these pores ensues. Śākyamuni then says that those who bring to mind the six-syllable formula will be born in these very hair pores, never again to wander in *saṃsāra*, traveling from one pore to another until they achieve the state of *nirvāṇa*. This is then the cue for the beginning of the long section describing the qualities of *Oṃ Maṇipadme Hūṃ* and its discovery by the bodhisattva Sarvanīvaraṇaviṣkambhin.

The story of Siṃhala is being used here not simply as an incidental warning about the spiritual dangers of becoming involved with sex and marriage. It must be seen, rather, as part of a general policy of the *Kāraṇḍavyūha* to advocate, not just the virtue of celibacy, but, more specifically, the actual ordination of individuals into the Buddhist monastic life. This interest is explicitly expressed at the end of the sūtra when, after the section dealing with *Oṃ Maṇipadme Hūṃ*, the conversion of Maheśvara and Umādevī and the *samādhi* contest between Avalokiteśvara and Samantabhadra, Śākyamuni's disciple Ānanda—who was a monk—appears and asks to be given a teaching on moral conduct (*śikṣāsaṃvaram*).[3] The Buddha's discourse lists a number of conditions prerequisite to monastic ordination, a series of punishments to be expected by those who abuse the rules of the *Saṃgha* and the rewards promised to those who do manage to uphold the moral precepts.[4] It begins with the instruction that those wishing to enter the monastery should first of all look carefully at a suitable cell and declare it to be clean: free of any bones or filth.[5]

This promotion of the process of monastic ordination is also, I think, detectable within the sūtra's version of the story of Siṃhala. As Siegfried Lienhard has pointed out, the legend, as it has come down to us in a variety of different forms, may be divided up into three different sections. The first ends with the safe return of Siṃhala to his native country, the second describes his coronation there, and the third shows how he then goes on to wage a successful war against the demonesses of the island. The *Kāraṇḍavyūha*, like the Pāli *Valāhassajātaka*, a Prakrit Jain, and a Khotanese Buddhist presentation of the story, contains only the first part of the story; the Lokottaravādin Mahāsaṃghika work, the *Mahāvastu*, contains a version which includes the first two parts; the Mūlasarvāstivādin *Divyāvadāna*, meanwhile, actually only articulates the last two, stating simply, after describing the embarkation of the mariners, that there then follows the *rākṣasī sūtra*, assuming the reader's familiarity with the events that take place on the island and passing straight on to Siṃhala's return home.[6]

What is peculiar about the presentation of the story in the *Kāraṇḍavyūha* and absent in the versions found in the *Valāhassajātaka*, the *Mahāvastu*, and the *Divyāvadāna*, is the description, first, of certain procedures acted out by Siṃhala prior to his flight to safety on the back of the flying horse and, second, of the reaction of his parents when he returns. The preparations for his escape are said to take place over the course of two days. To begin with, Siṃhala is brought an array of many different offerings by his own *rākṣasī* wife. After eating these, he lets out a sigh, saying that the men of Jambudvīpa delight in their own country. Asked by his hostess why this is so, when the island they are on is so well-provided with food, water, clothes, gardens, and lotus pools, Siṃhala remains silent. This is how the first day passes.[7] On the second day, he makes a succession of different offerings and finalizes his affairs.[8] On the third day, he sets out at dawn with his companions.[9] They convene outside the town and Siṃhala tells them that noone must ever look back at the island of Siṃhala.[10] They find the horse Bālāha, who eats a herb called "All White" (*taṃ sarvaśvetānāmauṣadhīmāsvādayati*), turns around on "the place of golden sand" (*āsvādayitvā suvarṇavālukāsthale āvartanaṃ karoti*), stretches out his body (*śarīraṃ pracchoḍayati*) and shakes the island (*siṃhaladvīpaṃ calati*).[11] He asks three times the question: "Who is going to the other side?" (*kaḥ pāragāmī*).[12] He then gives the warning that no one should look back at the island or open their eyes when he stretches out his body.[13]

There seem to be good reasons for identifying this sequence as an allegorical description of the steps involved in an initiation of some sort, comprising, as it does, a final valedictory meal (served by the female *rākṣasī*), a declaration of intent to leave an old form of life (on the island of Siṃhala) for a new one (on Jambudvīpa), preparatory rituals (on the second day) and a dawn ceremony involving certain other rituals (the precise significance of the eating of the herb, the place of the golden sand, the turning around, the stretching of the body, and the shaking of the body remains obscure). The threefold repetition of Bālāha's question is somewhat reminiscent of the standard threefold declaration of "going for refuge" to Buddha, *Dharma* and *Saṃgha*. This impression is supported by an earlier incident in the story, when Siṃhala first describes the horse Bālāha to his comrades: having explained the danger they are all in, he asks them whom they have refuge in (*asmākaṃ gatiḥ śaraṇaṃ parāyaṇaṃ*).[14]

That the initiation rite in question is, in fact, a form of the ordination ceremony is strongly suggested by the events that take place at the end of the story. There, Siṃhala's parents appear to show their approval of their son's heroic actions, while also absolving him of the need to perform the filial duty of looking after them financially in their old age, actions entirely appropriate to the occasion of a married couple's witnessing the entry of a son or daughter into monastic life. On his return from the island, the parents embrace Siṃhala tearfully[15] and say that, since he is still alive, they have no need of money.[16] Nonetheless, they continue, he is their support in old age (*jarākāle yaṣṭibhūto*), in the darkness he shows them the path (*andhakāre mārgasyopadarśakaḥ*), at the time of death he gives them the "sacred cake" (*maraṇakāle piṇḍadātā*), he offers protection to the dead (*mṛtasya sanāthīkaraṇīyam*) and, like a cooling wind, he is a giver of delight.[17] Though a monk is unable to provide for his parents materially, the sūtra seems to suggest, they should nonetheless be happy that he will be able to take care of them spiritually.

Not content with promoting ordination, the *Kāraṇḍavyūha* is, also, it seems, intent on redressing certain aspects of corruption in the monastery. For the sūtra appears to reflect a situation in which these celibate institutions had been infiltrated not only by practitioners that were simply badly behaved, but also, more damagingly perhaps, by practitioners who were, in fact, accompanied by sexual partners. After specifying the need to find a suitable cell, Śākyamuni states that neither ordination (*nopasaṃpādayitavyam*) nor the "motion" (*na ca jñaptirdātavyā*)[18] should be given by mendicants of bad moral character (*duḥśīlena bhikṣuṇā*), an ambiguous definition, but one which, in the context, immediately suggests those who are unable to keep the vow of celibacy.[19]

"Why?" (*kiṃ bahunā*) the sūtra asks. The answer is that a cell should not be made by these mendicants of bad moral character, let alone the "fourth proposal" (*bhikṣavo duḥśīlena bhikṣuṇā nānāvāsaṃ na kartavyam, prageva jñapticaturtham*).[20] They do not obey the rules (*śāsanadūṣakāḥ*).[21] These mendicants of bad moral character should not be given a cell among the moral and the venerable (*duḥśīlānāṃ bhikṣūṇāṃ śīlavatāṃ dakṣiṇīyāṇāṃ madhye āvāso na dātavyaḥ*), but outside the *vihāra* (*teṣāṃ bahirvihāre āvāso dātavyaḥ*). No *saṃgha* food should be given them (*saṃghālāpo na dātavyaḥ*).[22] They are neither worthy of the rank of the *saṃgha* (*na ca teṣāṃ sāṃghikī bhūmimarhati*), nor are there any genuine monks among them (*na ca teṣāṃ kiṃcidbhikṣubhāvaṃ saṃvidyate*).[23]

The Buddha then lists the unpleasant rebirths awaiting those who misbehave in various different ways: those who "misuse the teeth-cleaning wood" (*dantakāṣṭhamasatparibhogena paribhuñjante*) of the community will be born among the creatures of the sea;[24] those who "misuse the rice and grains" (*tilataṇḍulakodravakulatthadhānyādīnasatparibhogena paribhuñjante*) of the community will be reborn in the city of *pretas* (where they will endure various misfortunes and tortures associated with their unsatiable hunger and thirst);[25] those who "misuse the food and drink" (*annapānāderanyāyena paribhogaṃ kurvanti*) of the community will be reborn (hideously deformed) in low-caste families,[26] and those who "misuse the rank of the *Saṃgha*" (*sāṃghikīṃ bhūmimasatparibhogena paribhuñjante*) will be reborn in hell, where they will live for twelve *kalpas*, before being reborn as blind beggars back in the the land of Jambudvīpa.[27]

At the head of this succession of warnings, however, is the announcement that rebirth in the form of the creatures that live among the filth of

Vārāṇasī is the fate awaiting those who hold the title of householder in the monastery (*ye vihāre gṛhisaṃjñāṃ dhārayiṣyanti*), who are surrounded by sons and daughters (*te dārakadārikāparivṛtā bhaviṣyanti*), who misuse their cells by filling them with high seats and comfortable beds (*te sāṃghikaṃ mañcapīthaṃ vaṃśikopabimbopadhānakaṃ śayanāsanaṃ asatparibhogena paribhokṣyante*), and who "make excrement and urine on the customs of the *Saṃgha*" (*ye ca sāṃghikopacāre uccāraṃ prasrāvaṃ kurvanti*).[28]

It is, one might say, ironic that, of all the characters that appear in the pages of the *Kāraṇḍavyūha Sūtra,* the one that conforms most closely to this type of reviled married practitioner also happens to be one of the most highly revered personages in the whole work. The *dharmabhāṇaka,* the preceptor from Vārāṇasī whom Sarvanīvaraṇaviṣkambhin is told to seek out in order to receive the six-syllable formula, is described as being without moral code or moral behaviour (*śīlavipannaḥ ācaravipanno*), surrounded by wives and children (*bhāryāputraduhitṛbhiḥ parivṛtaḥ*), wearing a robe covered in urine and excrement (*kāṣāyoccāraprasrāvaparipūrṇāḥ*) and being non-celibate (*asaṃvṛtteryāpathaḥ*).[29] Yet, he should be seen, we are told, as the same as a *tathāgata* (*dharmabhāṇakastathāgatasamo drṣṭavyaḥ*), as like a heap of merit (*pūṇyakūṭa iva*), like all the sacred bathing places of the Ganges (*sarvatīrthī gaṅgeva*), like one who does not speak lies (*avitathavādīva*), like one who speaks the truth (*bhūtavādīva*), like a heap of jewels (*ratnarāśiriva*), like a boon-giver and a wish-fulfilling jewel (*varadaścintāmaṇiriva*), like a *Dharma*-king (*dharmarāja iva*), and like a rescuer of the world (*jagaduttāraṇa iva draṣṭavyaḥ*).[30] The unkempt family man, in this instance, escapes censor. It is not his behaviour or modus vivendi as such, it seems, that is being condemned. Indeed, as a *dharmabhāṇaka,* he is clearly to be treated with the utmost respect. It is only, we may deduce, when such a practitioner makes his home in the monastery that he is criticized, for at that point he becomes guilty of the serious offense of defiling the moral code of the monastic way of life.

The description of this *dharmabhāṇaka* goes beyond the normal configuration of a Mahāyāna preacher. The difficulty of seeing through a dubious exterior to the true, inner nature of such a teacher was not, to be sure, a problem that was without precedent. In as early a Mahāyāna text as the *Aṣṭasāhasrikā Prajñāpāramitā Sūtra,* for instance, the bodhisattva Sadāprarudita is advised that his teacher's apparent involvement with the phenomenal world is merely a display of his *upāya,* or "skillful means." "For there is always Māra, the Evil One," he is told, "who may suggest that your teacher tends, enjoys and honours things that can be seen, heard, smelled, tasted or touched, when in actual fact he does so from skill in means, and has really risen above them. You should therefore not lose confidence in him . . ."[31] The idea, meanwhile, that a layman (and not a monk) might fulfill the role of preacher is also to be found in earlier Mahāyāna literature. In the chapter from the *Saddharmapuṇḍarīka Sūtra* devoted wholly to the figure of the *dharmabhāṇaka*, we read: " Again, Bhaiṣajyarāja, if some creature vicious, wicked and cruel-minded should in the (current) age speak something injurious in the face of the *tathāgata*, and if some should utter a single harsh word, founded or unfounded, to those irreproachable preachers of the law (*dharmabhāṇakānām*) and keepers of this *sūtrānta* (*asya sūtrāntasya dhārakānāṃ*), whether lay devotees (*gṛhasthānāṃ vā*), or clergymen (*pravrajitānāṃ vā*), I declare that the latter sin is the graver."[32]

Nevertheless, in his ownership of many wives and children, his shabby bearing and the emphasis given to the amorality of his manner, the *dharmabhāṇaka* of the *Kāraṇḍavyūha* is no ordinary Mahāyāna preacher. He is, surely, representative of another type of practitioner. The sketch given in the sūtra of his unconventional demeanor is evocative of nothing more than the figure of the antinomian tantric yogin, epitomised by the great *mahāsiddhas*, the "great (*mahā-*) accomplished ones (*-siddhas*)" championed by both the Buddhist and the Śaivite traditions.[33] Furthermore, quite apart from his outward appearance, the ability of the *Kāraṇḍavyūha's dharmabhāṇaka* to grant initiation into the use of *Oṃ Maṇipadme Hūṃ* suggests that he is, in fact—true to the nature of such yogins—more of a "guru" than a "preacher," more involved with the transmission of tantric practices than with the elucidation of the sūtras. Indeed, on one of the occasions Sarvanīvaraṇaviṣkambhin asks to be given the six-syllable formula, he addresses the preceptor as "guru" (*evaṃ gururdadasve me ṣaḍakṣarīṃ mahavidyārājñīṃ . . .*).[34]

The tantric affiliations of *Oṃ Maṇipadme Hūṃ* are more clearly apparent in the sūtra in the connection that is made between the formula and the idea of the *vidyādhara*, the "holder (*-dhara*) of *vidyā*." In the course of Śākyamuni's first discourse to Sarvanīvaraṇaviṣkambhin on the qualities of the six syllables, it is said that he or she who recites the formula will become indestructible (*akṣayapratibhāno*), purified by esoteric wisdom (*jñānarāśiviśuddho*), furnished with great compasssion (*mahākaruṇayā samanvāgato*) and will, every day, fully accomplish the six perfections (*dine dine ṣaṭpāramitāḥ paripūrayati*).[35] Next, it is said, he will recieve the *abhiṣeka*, or "consecration," of the *vidyādhara-cakravartin* (*vidyādharacakravartyabhiṣekaṃ pratilabhate*), or the "emperor (*cakravartin*) of *vidyādharas*."[36]

A *vidyādhara* also appears in the maṇḍala connected to the formula. The central figure of the diagram, which is said to be four-cornered (*nimittaṃ caturasraṃ*) and about the size of five hands (*pañcahastapramāṇaṃ sāmantakena*) is the Buddha Amitābha (*madhye maṇḍalasyāmitābhaṃ likhet*), made out of the powder of sapphires, rubies, emeralds, quartz, gold, and silver (*indranīlacūrṇaṃ padmarāgacūrṇaṃ marakatacūrṇaṃ sphāṭikacūrṇaṃ suvarṇarūpyacūrṇāny amitabhasya tathāgatasya kāye saṃyojayitavyāni*).[37]

On his right is a bodhisattva called "Mahāmaṇidhara," or "holder (*-dhara*) of the great jewel (*mahāmaṇi-*)," or "the great (*mahā-*) holder of the jewel (*-maṇidhara*)."[38] On his left is the six-syllable formula, described, as we saw in the previous chapter, in the form of a goddess.[39] The *vidyādhara* stands at her feet (*tasyāḥ ṣaḍakṣarimahāvidyāyāḥ pādamūle vidyādharaṃ pratisthāpayitavyam*), holding a spoon of smoking incense in his right hand (*dakṣiṇahaste dhūpaka-ṭacchukaṃ kartavyaṃ dhūmāyamānam*) and a basket of various ornaments in his left (*vāmahaste nānāvidhālaṃkāraparipūrṇaṃ piṭakaṃ kartavyam*).[40] (To complete the description, at the four doors of the maṇḍala stand four great kings (*mahārājāḥ*) holding various weapons and at its four corners stand four jars full of precious stones.)[41]

Comparatively little in the way of critical scholarship has been produced on the subject of the *vidyādhara*. In brief, therefore, the term seems to refer, originally, to a being who may, at one time, have been an ordinary man, but who, through his own exertions, has transcended his limitations to become something much more than a man: a magician, wizard or genie, perhaps, possessed of supernatural powers which, the tradition says, enable him to demonstrate miraculous behavior, such as the ability to fly. The term *vidyā*, as we have seen, may describe both a mantra and enlightenment itself. A *vidyādhara*, then, literally a "holder (*-dhara*) of *vidyā*," is one who is both adept in the use of esoteric formulae and who is, to some degree at least, enlightened. The *vidyādhara* is not a uniquely Buddhist phenomeonon. Together with his feminine counterpart the *vidyādharī*, he is the hero of countless folktales told in regions as far flung as Nepal, Persia and the Tamil world of South India. The most famous collection of such stories is probably the *Bṛhatkathā*, a Kashmiri Śaivite work dated to sometime towards the end of the first millennium C.E.[42]

In the early Mahāyāna Buddhist texts, the *vidyādhara* is mentioned only obliquely. In the *Ratnaguṇasaṃcayagāthā*, the bodhisattva who "does not come to a standing place in the suchness of the *Dharma*-element" is said to "become as one who, like a cloud, stands in the sky without anywhere to stand on," and "as a sorcerer (*vidyādhara*) who, like a bird, rides on the wind which offers him no support."[43] The implication is not, I think, that the bodhisattva is a *vidyādhara*. The text simply means to say that the state of coursing in the Perfection of Wisdom may be understood as analogous to the experience of flying through the sky, which is, according to the stories, one of the things that the *vidyādhara* is, literally, able to do.

The *vidyādhara*, however, is much more prominent in the literature of Buddhist tantra, where, in some texts at least, "*vidyādhara*-hood" is presented as one of the main goals of tantric religious endeavor. In seventh-century India, the Chinese pilgrim I-Tsing remarks upon a large collection of texts devoted to tantric ritual, one hundred thousand stanzas long, known as the *vidyādharapiṭaka*, or the "basket (*-piṭaka*) of the *vidyādharas*," in contrast to the sūtra collection of the *bodhisattvapiṭaka*, or "basket of bodhisattvas."[44] In Tāranātha's *History of Buddhism in India*, tantric practitioners are explicity referred to as *vidyādharas* and are said to attain the *siddhi* of the *vidyādhara*. We read: "Not that the esoteric *yoga* and *anuttara* tantras were not prevalent among the fortunate people before their time. Shortly after the spread of the Mahāyāna doctrine, there were a hundred thousand *vidyādharas*,"[45] and, "People of the earlier generations had the capacity of keeping the secret. Therefore, nobody could know them as practising the *guhya-* (secret) *mantra* so long as they did not attain the *vidyādhara-siddhi*."[46] In the *Mañjuśrīmūlakalpa*, a work which, as we saw in chapter one, like the *Kāraṇḍavyūha*, straddles the divide between sūtra and tantra, the *vidyādhara* appears both as a human magician and as part of the extraordinary retinue of the great bodhisattva Vajrapāṇi.[47] Like the *Kāraṇḍavyūha*, this text also advertises the possibility of becoming a *vidyādhara-cakravartin*.[48]

The *vidyādhara* is also to be found in the purāṇas. There, he is often mentioned in the same breath as the *mahāsiddha* (or *siddha*). Passages taken from the presentations of the *vāmana-avatāra* found, respectively, in the Vaiṣṇavite *Bhāgavata Purāṇa* and the Śaivite *Padma Purāṇa*, for instance, depict these two types of beings as hovering together, in attendance of the supreme deity, in the company of other rarefied beings. The former passage, in translation, reads: "Hosts of *siddhas* and *vidyādharas*, along with *kimpuruṣas* and *kinnaras* (beings which are half man-half animal), *cāraṇas* (celestial singers), *yakṣas* (semidivine beings) and *rakṣas* (guardians), *suparṇas* (eagles), best of serpents, and the attendants of gods sang and danced. Highly extolling the Lord, they showered flowers on the hermitage of Aditi and its premises."[49] The latter reads: "The group of *gandharvas* (spirit beings) sang with notes full of emotion; and the groups of heavenly damsels, mingling with their lords, and full of emotions, danced there (i. e. in the heaven). In the same way, groups of *vidyādharas* and *siddhas* wandered in (i.e. being seated in) aeroplanes."[50]

The fact, then, that a *vidyādhara* is found at the base of the maṇḍala employed in the initiation into the use of *Oṃ Maṇipadme Hūṃ* and that recitation of the formula is said to lead to the *abhiṣeka* of the *vidyādhara-cakravartin* strongly suggests that the concise formula of the Buddhist *īśvara* is a practice derived, originally, from tantric-style religious circles. It also confirms the impression, derived from his unconventional appearance, that the *dharmabhāṇaka* responsible for conferring this initiation may be understood as a tantric-style yogin.

As we have already seen, the use made of the *vāmana-avatāra* in the *Kāraṇḍavyūha Sūtra* reflects a situation in which Buddhists were having to compete with non-Buddhists for lay patronage: Bali is continually advised of the benefits of filling the alms bowl of a bodhisattva or a *tathāgata* and, also, of the dangers of not doing so, until eventually, the whole story is turned around so that Bali's great crime is not, as is usually the case, the failure to keep his promise, but instead, the fact that he has made his offering to the wrong being (*kukṣetre mayā dānaṃ dattaṃ*). The same competitive sentiment is expressed in another passage in the sūtra, in which the *dharmabhāṇaka* makes a list of those who have become consecrated in various different places (*nānāsthāneṣu dīkṣante*), into various religious orders (*mokṣārtheṣu nānāpaṭeṣu dīkṣante*) and into the cult of different *maheśvaras* (*divasanirīkṣakā maheśvareṣu dīkṣante*). These other practitioners, the Buddhist *dharmabhāṇaka* concludes, will not achieve liberation and there will be no end to the eternal round of their births and rebirths.[51]

We have, also, previously remarked upon the instruction given in relation to the maṇḍala connected to *Oṃ Maṇipadme Hūṃ*, to the effect that it may be given to Mahāyāna or non-Mahāyāna Buddhists, but not to *tīrthikas*. This, it was argued, was expressive of an inclusivist aspect of the practice of reciting the formula, showing that *Oṃ Maṇipadme Hūṃ* might be used by any Buddhist, regardless of their status. The stricture against *tīrthikas*, moreover, indicates that some non-Buddhists were applying for initiation into the use of the Buddhist formula and had to be stopped. The corollary of this, presumably, is that, one of the reasons why a non-Buddhist practitioner might have thought there was nothing wrong in taking a Buddhist initiation was because, superficially at least, the appearance and practices of Buddhist and non-Buddhist tantric circles were quite alike.

To recap, then, the *Kāraṇḍavyūha* is written from the point of view of a Mahāyāna monastic establishment entering into an uneasy alliance with the religious circles gravitating around the charismatic presence of tantric yogins. The sūtra reacts to what it sees as the deplorable infiltration of the monasteries by these non-celibate, married practitioners by deliberately advocating the process of ordination into the monastic life and by reasserting the core ethical values of monastic life. Yet, at the same time, the central teaching of the sūtra—the worship of an *īśvara* by means of a concise formula—is one that, as the depiction of the *dharmabhāṇaka* indicates, has itself been derived from these very yogins. The spiritual impetus gathering behind the tantric methods employed by these characters was, presumably, simply too strong to be ignored by the monastics. The central problem faced by the sūtra, therefore, was to show how this new form of practice—the use of *Oṃ Maṇipadme Hūṃ*—could be understood in terms of the conventions of the Mahāyāna monastic tradition. First of all, it had to be seen as distinct from similar practices found in circles of non-Buddhist tantrics living close by. Second, it had to be described within the orthodox doctrinal categories of the Mahāyāna. Third, its expression should not offend the monastic moral code. The practice of reciting

Oṃ Maṇipadme Hūṃ, then, might be seen to enrich the Mahāyāna monastic way without in any way compromising the integrity of the tradition.

We have already observed how the sūtra accomplishes this task in its presentation of the Buddhist *īśvara*. Avalokiteśvara is an *īśvara* in the mould of the Śaivite deity. Yet, he is very clearly distinguished from Śiva. The verse couplet outlining the central Śaivite doctrine of the *liṅga* is dismissed as that which is spoken by the "common people" (*īdṛśapṛthagjaneṣu sattveṣu sāṃkathyaṃ*), at a time when beings are "deprived of the path to awakening" (*bodhimārgeṇa viprahīṇā*).[52] Maheśvara (Śiva) and his consort Umādevī subjugate themselves to Avalokiteśvara in the conversion sequence at the end of the sūtra.[53] Avalokiteśvara is never identified with the *ātman* and, although he is depicted as a supreme *puruṣa*, he is never portrayed as the creator of the universe. He is, moreover, recognizably the same figure that is described in earlier Mahāyāna sūtras. He is still the servant of Amitābha and Śākyamuni, as supremely compassionate and as capable of taking on whatever form is most suitable for the conversion of different individuals.

In addition, on a number of different occasions, Avalokiteśvara is explicitly shown to be different not only from Maheśvara, but also from the gods in general. The first instance of this occurs when, at the beginning of the sūtra, the bodhisattva's entry into hell is reported to Yama, the lord of death. Yama asks himself which god this might be (*kasya punardevasyāyaṃ prabhāvaḥ*): Maheśvara, Nārāyaṇa, one of the other gods, or the great *rākṣasa*, or "demon," Rāvaṇa.[54] He looks around hell and sees a great number of gods and asks himself which one of these it could be.[55] He looks around again, though, and sees Avalokiteśvara, "the great bodhisattva" (*bodhisattvaṃ mahāsattvameva paśyati sma*).[56] Then, when Avalokiteśvara, in the shape of a beggar, visits the brahmin, he is specifically asked whether he is a man or a god (*athavā tvaṃ devo 'si, manuṣyo 'si vā*).[57] In reply, he says that he is not a god, but a man that has become a bodhisattva (*na devaḥ, api tu mānuṣo 'haṃ bodhisattvabhūtaḥ*), feeling compassion for the wretched and miserable and pointing out the path to awakening.[58] Lastly, when Avalokiteśvara produces showers of food and clothing to put an end to the famine in Magadha, the people ask which god could be responsible for this miraculous deed (*kasya devasyāyaṃ prabhāvaḥ*).[59] At this juncture, an old man appears and tells them that this could be the work of no god, but only of Avalokiteśvara (*na yuṣmākamanyadevasya kasyacidīdṛśaḥ prabhāvo bhavati nirahitādavalokiteśvarasya*).[60] Although evidently an *īśvara*, Avalokiteśvara, the sūtra shows, may still be coherently understood as the same Avalokiteśvara (or Avalokitasvara) that appears in other Mahāyāna works, as different from and superior to Maheśvara, and as a bodhisattva not a god.

A similar analysis may be made of the presentation of *Oṃ Maṇipadme Hūṃ* in the *Kāraṇḍavyūha*. The sūtra, for instance, as we saw in the previous chapter, seems to inherit a conception of the concise formula as a kind of *praṇava*: the depiction of the six syllables as a means of attaining all religious goals and as the essence and source of all religious teaching, as well as the image of the "rice grain" used to describe the formula all point to this conclusion. However, unlike the *Śiva Purāṇa*, which explicitly identifies *Namaḥ Śivāya* as the *praṇava* (albeit a *sthūla*, or "gross," form, in comparison with the *sūkṣma*, or "subtle" *Oṃ*), there is no mention of the word *praṇava* in the sūtra. This is not necessarily a deliberate omission: *Namaḥ Śivāya* appears not to be referred to as the *praṇava* in the *Skanda Purāṇa*. However, the fact remains that the idea of the *praṇava* is not part of orthodox Mahāyāna doctrine. What the *Kāraṇḍavyūha Sūtra* does, though, in order to integrate this Buddhist *praṇava* into the Mahāyāna system, is to present the formula in the same terms used to describe the Perfection of Wisdom in the earlier Perfection of Wisdom sūtras. *Oṃ Maṇipadme Hūṃ*, the sūtra implies, has taken the place of the Perfection of Wisdom as the supreme principle of the Mahāyāna.

The constant repetition of the term *ṣaḍakṣarī mahāvidyā*, the "six-syllable great formula," is, to begin with, reminiscent of the continual stress on the word *prajñāpāramitā*, "Perfection of Wisdom," in those early sūtras. A little more tellingly, though, *Oṃ Maṇipadme Hūṃ*, just like the Perfection of Wisdom, is praised as the cause of greater merit than practices connected with *stūpas*. In the *Kāraṇḍavyūha*, Śākyamuni tells Sarvanīvaraṇaviṣkambhin that the fruit of making *stūpas*, made of gold and jewels, for as many *tathāgatas* as there are dust particles and "depositing relics in them each day" (*ekadine dhātvāvaropaṇaṃ kuryāt*), is equivalent only to the fruit of a single syllable of the great six-syllable formula.[61] This has much the same ring to it as passages from the *Aṣṭasāhasrikā*, such as:

> Greater would be the merit of the devotee of the Perfection of Wisdom compared not only with that of a person who would build many *koṭis* of *stūpas* made of the seven precious things, enshrining the relics of the *tathāgata*. It would be greater than the merit of one who would completely fill the entire Jambudvīpa with such *stūpas*.[62]

The recitation of *Oṃ Maṇipadme Hūṃ* is also said to lead, automatically, to the accomplishment of the six perfections, a claim that echoes earlier statements to the effect that the accomplishment of the Perfection of Wisdom somehow entails the accomplishment of the other five perfections. In the *Kāraṇḍavyūha*, we read that those who recite the formula will daily accomplish the six perfections,[63] and, at another point in the sūtra, that a single recitation of the formula accomplishes the six perfections.[64] In the *Aṣṭasāhasrikā*:

> It is therefore because it has dedicated the wholesome roots to all-knowledge that the Perfection of Wisdom controls, guides and leads the five perfections. The five perfections are in this manner contained in the Perfection of Wisdom, and the term "Perfection of Wisdom" is just a synonym for the fulfilment of the six perfections. In consequence, when the Perfection of Wisdom is proclaimed, all the six perfections are proclaimed.[65]

The same pattern is also detectable in the narrative structure of the *Kāraṇḍavyūha Sūtra*, where the description of the search for *Oṃ Maṇipadme Hūṃ* shares many of the traits of the discovery of the Perfection of Wisdom by the bodhisattva Sadāprarudita, as told in the *Aṣṭasāhasrikā*.[66] The latter story is the paradigm example of what Stephan Beyer has dubbed the Mahāyāna "vision quest," a narrative form consisting of three essential stages: an aspiring *Dharma*-practitioner has a visionary experience; he or she is then inspired to go on a "quest"; finally, the practitioner experiences another vision, sometimes a repetition of the initial experience, which represents either the end of the path, or a stage of irreversible attainment some way along the path.[67]

Beyer detects the presence of this underlying structure in a number of different sūtras. The whole of the *Gaṇḍavyūha Sūtra*, for example, may be seen as one long "vision quest," in which the main protagonist, the boy Sudhana, travels from one spiritual adviser to the next before finally experiencing the vision of the tower of Maitreya. Short tales such as the story of Sudatta, in chapter nine of the *Pratyutpannabuddhasaṃmukhāvasthitasamādhi Sūtra*, Beyer remarks, "manifest the same basic themes."[68] Sudatta is taught the *samādhi* of the sūtra's title, "the *samādhi* of the bodhisattva who stands face-to-face with the buddhas of the present," by the *tathāgata* Kṣemarāja, an event which eventually leads to a time when, after a kind of long journey in which he is aided by two other buddhas, the *tathāgatas* Vidyuddeva and Raśmirāja, he becomes fully awakened.[69]

Beyer also draws attention to the structure of the *Amitāyurbuddhānusmṛti Sūtra*,[70] where queen Vaidehī, imprisoned by her son, is first granted a vision of buddhalands by Śākyamuni Buddha. She then states her particular desire to be reborn in the land of Sukhāvatī, is taught several different meditations and is, eventually, said to see Sukhāvatī and gain insight into the non-origination of all existence. Similarly, in the *Sukhāvatīvyūha Sūtra*, the monk Dharmākara is first granted an experience of the buddhafields of billions of buddhas through the teaching of a *tathāgata*. Making numerous vows to create the most perfect buddhafield himself, he practices the bodhisattva path until he himself, as the Buddha Amitābha, teaches the *Dharma* in the pure land of Sukhāvatī.[71] Both the monk and the queen, Beyer writes, "learn to do for themselves what was given them in the first episode."[72] Finally, in the *Saddharmapuṇḍarīka Sūtra*, the bodhisattva Sadāparibhūta, instead of seeing a vision, hears the verses of the *Saddharmapuṇḍarīka Sūtra* on his deathbed. This event prolongs his life and enables him to preach the sūtra to vast quantities of beings, so that, when his days really do come to an end, he meets thousands of buddhas to whom he also preaches the sūtra. Eventually, like Dharmākara, he reaches the level of buddhahood, as the Buddha Śākyamuni.[73]

However, each of these examples differs in some significant way from the story of Sadāprarudita in the *Aṣṭāsahasrikā*. In the *Gaṇḍavyūha*, for instance, the vision of Maitreya that Sudhana experiences at the end of the sūtra is not anticipated in any way at the beginnning of the text, when, before setting out on his journey, he is merely given a wide-ranging *Dharma*-teaching by Mañjuśrī.[74] Apart from Sadāprarudita's, though, Sudhana's "quest" is the only one that actually involves travel, in the normal sense of that word. In the *Pratyutpanna Sūtra*, Sudatta's journey does not take place across space and time, but over the course of a series of different rebirths, first as a god and then as a brahmin. Moreover, his progress is described not as the re-creation of a visionary experience after a fallow period of searching, but as a continuous development of the *samādhi* he has been taught at the outset. Queen Vaidehī's "quest" simply involves listening to a series of teachings describing different meditations, Dharmākara's the practice of the conduct of a bodhisattva (in particular, the making of a series of powerful vows) and Sadāparibhūta's the preaching of the *Saddharmapuṇḍarīka Sūtra*. The latter's initial experience is, also, not something that he tries to recreate, but is, instead, the means by which he is able to attain sufficient merit in order that he may eventually achieve buddhahood.

Bearing in mind all the differences between these various "vision quest" narratives, it is striking how closely the story of Sarvanīvaraṇaviṣkambhin's search follows the basic structure of Sadāprarudita's odyssey. Both stories begin by showing that the respective objects of these quests—the Perfection of Wisdom in one and *Oṃ Maṇipadme Hūṃ* in the other—are means of achieving *samādhis* and visionary experience. In the *Aṣṭasāhasrikā*, Sadāprarudita, standing in a remote forest, is told by a *tathāgata* about the marvelous qualities of the town of Gandhavatī, which is a bejewelled and fragrant place, full of lotus ponds and pleasure palaces, where the bodhisattva Dharmodgata demonstrates the Perfection of Wisdom. Sadāprarudita becomes jubilant and, without going anywhere, hears Dharmodgata demonstrating the Perfection of Wisdom. As a result, he enters various different *samādhis* and sees countless buddhas in the ten directions teaching the Perfection of Wisdom to bodhisattvas.[75]

Sarvanīvaraṇaviṣkambhin's journey is given a similar preliminary context. The second part of the *Kāraṇḍavyūha Sūtra* opens with a short section in which Śākyamuni states that Avalokiteśvara has attained an immeasurable number of *samādhis* and is furnished with *samādhis*, listing sixty-two of them.[76] There are, the Buddha adds, hundreds of thousands of *samādhis* in each of the bodhisattva's hair pores (*tasyaikakaromavivare samādhiśatasahasrāṇi santi*).[77] Then, after the story of Siṃhala, Śākyamuni describes the worlds contained within the hair pores of Avalokiteśvara's body. Those who "bring to mind the name" of the six-syllable formula, the Buddha says, will be reborn in those hair pores,[78] implying, presumably, that they will also experience the *samādhis* contained in those pores. Sarvanīvaraṇaviṣkambhin's search then begins.[79] Like Sadāprarudita, he is inspired by an initial period of visionary experience (although Sadāprarudita actually enjoys these experiences himself, while Sarvanīvaraṇaviṣkambhin is only told about them). In both cases, the motivation for each bodhisattva's "quest" is the re-creation of these (first- or second-hand) experiences.

Like Sadāprarudita, Sarvanīvaraṇaviṣkambhin is described as going on an actual journey: the one travels to the magical city of Gandhavatī, while the other goes to the more worldly city of Vārāṇasī. Both bodhisattvas have to seek out a particular individual in order to receive their respective teachings: the former the bodhisattva Dharmodgata and the latter the *dharmabhāṇaka*. Both stories also end in the recapitulation of the initial experiences. In the *Aṣṭasāhasrikā*, Sadāprarudita is said to enter different *samādhis* and see visions of the *tathāgatas* as soon as he hears the Perfection of Wisdom expounded by Dharmodgata.[80] In the *Kāraṇḍavyūha*, when Sarvanīvaraṇaviṣkambhin receives *Oṃ Maṇipadme Hūṃ*, the earth trembles in "six uncommon ways" (*ṣaḍvikāraṃ pṛthivī prakampitā*) and the bodhisattva is said to obtain *samādhis* (*ime samādhayaḥ sarvanīvaraṇaviṣkambhinaḥ pratilabdhāḥ*), seven of which are listed.[81] Then, after a brief interlude, the sūtra returns abruptly to further descriptions of the lands contained in the hair pores of Avalokiteśvara's body.[82]

A final parallel presents itself in the fact that both stories include the motif of self-mutilation. Sadāprarudita is asked by the god Śakra, disguised as a young man, to give him his heart, blood, and the marrow of his bones because, the deity says, they are needed by his father for a sacrifice. Full of joy, the bodhisattva draws blood by piercing his right arm with a sword, cuts flesh from his thigh, and strides up to a wall in order to break one of his bones.[83] Later, he draws blood once again, in order to sprinkle the ground and prevent dust clouds rising up in the place where Dharmodgata is about to teach.[84] Sarvanīvaraṇaviṣkambhin, meanwhile, offers to use his own skin, blood, and bones if no bark, ink, or reeds can be found with which to write the six-syllable formula.[85] The motif of self-mutilation is also, of course, to be found in other Mahāyāna sūtras: in the *Saddharmapuṇḍarīka Sūtra*, for instance, the bodhisattva Bhaiṣajyarāja recounts how, in a previous life, he burned his own body as an offering,[86] and, at the end of the *Gaṇḍavyūha Sūtra*, Samantabhadra recalls how he gave away different parts of his body to beggars.[87] But, among all the "vision quest" narratives we have considered, it is only found in the stories of Sadāprarudita and Sarvanīvaraṇaviṣkambhin.

The *Kāraṇḍavyūha* is not suggesting that *Oṃ Maṇipadme Hūṃ* makes the Perfection of Wisdom redundant. In the Dhvajāgra hair pore of Avalokiteśvara's body, groups of *tathāgatas* are said to teach the six perfections—including, of course, the Perfection of Wisdom—to the people of Jambudvīpa.[88] Similarly, *śūnyatā*, or "emptiness," the central doctrine of the Perfection of Wisdom sūtras, is specifically said to be contemplated by the bodhisattvas who inhabit the Mahoṣadhīḥ pore of Avalokiteśvara's body.[89] The sūtra is, however, quite explicit in showing that the formula is not simply equivalent, in some way, to the Perfection of Wisdom, but is, also, in some way, superior to it. Before *Oṃ Maṇipadme Hūṃ* is granted to Sarvanīvaraṇaviṣkambhin, he is told by the *dharmabhāṇaka* that all the *tathāgatas* are born from the Perfection of Wisdom and that the Perfection of Wisdom is the mother of all the *tathāgatas*.[90] This, of course, is a straightforward reiteration of a traditional Mahāyāna doctrine also found in the *Aṣṭasāhasrikā*.[91] But the *dharmabhāṇaka* goes on: if she (the Perfection of Wisdom) makes obeisance with hands clasped to the great six-syllable formula, then so much more will the *tathāgatas*, *arhats*, *samyaksaṃbuddhas*, and multitudes of bodhisattvas.[92] *Oṃ Maṇipadme Hūṃ*, the *dharmabhāṇaka* implies, is, in some sense, greater than the Perfection of Wisdom and greater than the *tathāgatas*, *arhats*, *samyaksaṃbuddhas*, and bodhisattvas.

This sentiment might, I suppose, be taken as another expression of the convention, remarked upon in chapter 3, by which the bodhisattva Avalokiteśvara, the chief subject of the sūtra, may—like Mañjuśrī elsewhere in the Mahāyāna—be presented as greater even than the buddhas. But this explanation would fail to address the issue of why the sūtra goes to such great lengths to show that the formula is also, in some way, the equivalent of the Perfection of Wisdom. Far more satisfactory, surely, is the interpretation that this passage is informed by a tacit recognition of *Oṃ Maṇipadme Hūṃ* as a form of the *praṇava*. Indeed, it is immediately followed by the presentation of the formula as the "rice grain of the Mahāyāna" (*taṇḍulavatsāraṃ mahāyānasya*),[93] an image which, as we have argued, is redolent precisely of similes used to describe both the "gross" (*sthūla*) and "subtle" (*sūkṣma*) forms of the *praṇava*, respectively *Namaḥ Śivāya* and *Oṃ*. As a form of the *praṇava*, *Oṃ Maṇipadme Hūṃ* is, by definition, second to no one and nothing. As a Buddhist *praṇava*, the formula may be said to supercede the Perfection of Wisdom as the supreme principle of the Mahāyāna. Thus, the Perfection of Wisdom, together with the *tathāgatas*, *arhats*, and *samyaksaṃbuddhas* bow to it, an event which graphically demonstrates the incorporation of the formula into the Mahāyāna. How, though, does the *Kāraṇḍavyūha Sūtra* employ the conventions of the

Mahāyāna tradition to describe the use of this *praṇava* and its corresponding "vision?"

To begin with, in the simple fact that a maṇḍala is used to confer initiation into the use of *Oṃ Maṇipadme Hūṃ*, the sūtra confirms the original tantric-style character of the practice: a maṇḍala is almost a sine qua non of tantric initiation. The maṇḍala's depiction of the six syllables as a goddess is also, as we have seen, consistent with the idea of the concise formula as *śakti*, one of the central doctrinal tenets of tantra. The sūtra, too, specifies that whoever wishes to "enter the maṇḍala" (*maṇḍalaṃ praveṣṭum*) should write out the names of all the various "clans" (*sarvagotrasyāparaṃparasya nāmāni lihitavyāni*), before throwing these names into the diagram (*maṇḍale prathamataraṃ tāni nāmāni prakṣipet*).[94] The throwing of a token into a maṇḍala is, once again, a type of procedure that is entirely typical of the tantric tradition, both Buddhist and Śaivite.[95]

As Snellgrove explains, the word *gotra* is generally used in pre-tantric Mahāyāna texts to describe the different spiritual capacities of beings, arranged according to their different spiritual goals. The *Sandhinirmocana Sūtra*, for instance, employs a threefold arrangement: the *gotra* of the *śrāvaka*, or "disciple," the *gotra* of the *pratyekabuddha*, or "solitary buddha," and the *gotra* of the *tathāgata*, the latter "clan" encompassing the path of the bodhisattva, the being whose motivation is the attainment of buddhahood for the sake of all other sentient beings.[96] In the tantric texts, however, beings of differing spiritual capacities are arranged in terms of the particular *kula*, or "family," to which they belong. Again, the presentation of these *kulas* varies from text to text: perhaps the most well-known are a threefold scheme involving the *tathāgata-kula*, or "buddha family," the *padma-kula*, or "lotus family," and the *vajra-kula*, or "vajra family," as found in some earlier tantric works such as the *Mañjuśrīmūlakalpa* and a fivefold scheme, comprising these last three, together with the *ratna-kula*, or "jewel family," and the *karma-kula*, or "action family," as found in *yoga* tantras such as the *Sarvatathāgatatattvasaṃgraha*.[97] The fact that some parts of the *Mañjuśrīmūlakalpa*, as Snellgrove also points out, includes groupings usually classified as *gotra* (*śrāvakas*, *pratyekabuddhas* etc.) under the *kula* rubric, is another indication of the transitional character of that text, sharing the characteristics of both the sūtra and tantra genres.[98] The same observation might be made about the *Kāraṇḍavyūha* in the way it employs the sūtra-style term *gotra* in association with the use of tantric-style maṇḍala. The throwing of the names into the maṇḍala, then, was presumably a means of determining which class of *gotra* the initiant belonged to.

To continue the main thread of our argument, however, it becomes apparent that, although the exterior form of the maṇḍala is tantric in style, the practice described by the interior arrangement of the diagram is not. For

Avalokiteśvara, the Buddhist *īśvara* that one might expect to be the focus of the diagram, is conspicuous by his absence. Instead, the central figure of the maṇḍala is the Buddha Amitābha. What this immediately suggests is that the use of the *Oṃ Maṇipadme Hūṃ* is being presented, here, not in terms of the union of the lord and his *śakti*—with all the implicit ethical difficulties this doctrine would present to a celibate monastic establishment—but, instead, as a form of practice that leads to what Gregory Schopen has referred to as the Mahāyāna's "generalized religious goal," the achievement of rebirth in the presence of Amitābha in his pure land of Sukhāvatī.[99] Surveying a number of Mahāyāna sūtras, Schopen demonstrates that rebirth in Sukhāvatī is posited as the reward of a wide range of practices and procedures.[100] This approach to the idea of Amitābha's pure land, he calculates, may already have been an established phenomenon by the beginning of the second century C.E.[101] The central presence of Amitābha in the maṇḍala connected to *Oṃ Maṇipadme Hūṃ* suggests that the use of the formula is also being promoted as a practice leading to the same end.

Rebirth in Sukhāvatī is certainly a recurrent theme throughout the *Kāraṇḍavyūha Sūtra*. It is, for example, twice linked to the hearing of the sūtra itself (augmented in the first instance by practices that include turning towards the sūtra, developing faith towards it, understanding it, writing and having it written, memorizing it, reciting it, worshipping it, reflecting on it, decorating it with finery, displaying it, and bowing to it with great joy, respect, and devotion). At the time of death, the text says, those individuals who have listened to the sūtra will be met by twelve *tathāgatas* who will tell them to have no fear for, because they have heard the *Kāraṇḍavyūha*, they will go to Sukhāvatī.[102]

In the story of Avalokiteśvara's appearance in Vārāṇasī in the form of a bee, the traditional threefold homage to Buddha, *Dharma,* and *Saṃgha* is said to lead to rebirth in Sukhāvatī. The worms and insects of the sewer hear the buzzing of the bee as the sound of this homage. As a result, they are said to "bring to mind the name" (*nāmamanusmārayanti*): *namo buddhāya namo dharmāya namaḥ saṃghāya*. Merely by bringing to mind the name of the Buddha (*buddhanāmasmaraṇamātreṇa*), the text then states (referring in shorthand, presumably, to the repetition of the threefold homage), they destroy the "twenty-peaked false view of individuation" (*viṃśatiśikharasamudgataṃ satkāyadṛṣṭiśailaṃ*) and go to Sukhāvatī.[103]

When the bodhisattva enters the city of the *pretas*, the sound of the *Kāraṇḍavyūha* is said to come forth, whereupon the inhabitants of that realm are miraculously established as bodhisattvas in Sukhāvatī.[104] Later, in the course of Avalokiteśvara's encounter with Bali, the bodhisattva's first speech describes how the actions of requesting a *Dharma* teaching from the *tathāgatas* and of daily filling the offering bowl of a *tathāgata* with a daily meal lead to rebirth in Sukhāvatī.[105] Near the end of this section, Avalokiteśvara promises that Bali will go to Sukhāvatī, having been purified of evil by listening to the *Dharma*.[106]

Avalokiteśvara himself visits Sukhāvatī. When Śākyamuni relates how he was told about the qualities of the great bodhisattva by the Buddha Śikhin, he describes how rays of light emerged from the mouth of that *tathāgata*, traveled to all the different worlds in space and then returned to the *tathāgata*, circumambulating him three times, before re-entering his mouth. When asked why this happened, Śikhin replies that he produced this display because Avalokiteśvara was arriving in Sukhāvatī.[107] Upon his arrival, the text continues, various marvelous phenomena, such as wonderful trees and lotus ponds, manifested, and, when the bodhisattva left Sukhāvatī, the whole of creation is said to have trembled in six different ways.[108] Similarly, near the end of the sūtra, Avalokiteśvara is said to produce rays of colored light that appear in the Jetavana grove, that circumambulate Śākyamuni three times and then proceed on to the Avīci hell, which they freeze over.[109] They also produce various wonderful phenomena in the Jetavana grove.[110] Avalokiteśvara is then said to leave Sukhāvatī and appear in the *vihāra*.[111] The *Kāraṇḍavyūha*, it is no exaggeration to say, is pervaded by the idea of Sukhāvatī. The appearance of Amitābha at the center of the maṇḍala is, we may assume, merely another aspect of this recurring theme.

The exact meaning of the maṇḍala, however, depends on how one interprets the figure of the bodhisattva Mahāmaṇidhara, who is said to be positioned on the right of Amitābha. The appearance of the concise formula as a goddess, stationed to the left of the buddha, may, in this context, be regarded as simply a convenient convention that the *Kāraṇḍavyūha Sūtra* inherits and reproduces, without intending to lay any stress on the idea of *Oṃ Maṇipadme Hūṃ* as *śakti*. How else might the formula have been depicted in the maṇḍala, one might ask? Unlike the six-syllable formula, though, no details are given of the color, *mudrā* or any other attributes of Mahāmaṇidhara: his identity and function are not immediately clear to the modern reader.

My belief is, though, that Mahāmaṇidhara is the personification of the central Mahāyāna virtue of *bodhicitta*, the "awakened-" or "awakening mind" of the bodhisattva. The term *maṇidhara* occurs once again in the sūtra, shortly after the description of the maṇḍala, as the first of what are said to be a total of eight hundred *samādhis* that are to be taken hold of by whoever recites *Oṃ Maṇipadme Hūṃ*.[112] In the Tibetan translation, meanwhile, Mahāmaṇidhara (the bodhisattva) and *maṇidhara* (the *samādhi*) both appear as "*nor bu rin po che 'dzin*," the "bearer of a precious jewel."[113] The term *nor bu rin po che*, in turn, is sometimes used to translate the Sanskrit term *cintāmaṇi*,[114] the "wish-fulfilling jewel." *Cintāmaṇi*, finally, is also sometimes used as a simile to describe *bodhicitta*.[115] The sūtra, it seems reasonable to suppose, means to state, firstly in the context of the maṇḍala, that in conjunction with the mind of *bodhicitta*, recitation of *Oṃ Maṇipadme Hūṃ* leads to rebirth in Sukhāvatī and, second, that recitation of *Oṃ Maṇipadme Hūṃ* leads to a *samādhi* characterized by *bodhicitta*.

The word employed most often in the *Kāraṇḍavyūha* to describe the recitation of *Oṃ Maṇipadme Hūṃ* is the widely used Sanskrit term *japa*, meaning literally "mutter." Meritorious are they, the sūtra reads, who are constantly engrossed in reciting (*japābhiyuktā*) the six-syllable formula;[116] any son or daughter of noble family who recites (*japanti*) this six-syllable formula becomes one of indestructible brilliance[117] . . . (a list of other benefits follows, ending) . . . this is the consequence of reciting (*japamānasya*) the formula;[118] the amount of merit of one recitation (*ekajāpasya*) of the formula is incalculable;[119] meritorious are they who recite (*japanti*) the formula;[120] merely to recite it (*japitamātreṇa*) brings sublime liberation and great happiness;[121] by one recitation (*ekajāpena*) the six perfections are accomplished.[122] *Japa* is also used to describe the recitation of the five-syllable formula. The *Śiva Purāṇa* describes various distinct modes of the *japa* of *Namaḥ Śivāya*: *upāṃśu japa* (in a low voice), for instance, is said to be a hundred times as efficient as *vācika japa* (out loud) and *mānasa japa* (mentally) a thousand times as efficient.[123]

Elsewhere in the Mahāyāna, however, there appears to be very little precedent for this connection between the *japa* of a mantra and rebirth in Sukhāvatī.[124] What the *Kāraṇḍavyūha Sūtra* does, though, in order to facilitate the process of integrating *Oṃ Maṇipadme Hūṃ* into the Mahāyāna system, is to indicate that recitation of the formula may also be thought of as a form of *nāmānusmṛti*, the "bringing to mind of a name," an extremely common Mahāyāna practice and one that is, also, often said to have as its end rebirth in Sukhāvatī. Just as the *Kāraṇḍavyūha* is saturated with references to Amitābha's pure land, so, too, is it replete with instances of *nāmānusmṛti*.

Perhaps the most important expression of this type of practice (and the textual basis of one of the most popular Buddhist "pure land" practices to have survived into present times) occurs in the shorter *Sukhāvatīvyūha Sūtra*, where mental concentration on the name (the Sanskrit term used here is *manasikariṣyati*) of the Buddha Amitāyus is said to ensure rebirth in Sukhāvatī.[125] In the *Kāraṇḍavyūha*, however, the use of a name of a buddha is only referred to in passing. In the course of Avalokiteśvara's sermon to Bali about the fate suffered by worldly beings at the time of their death, the failure to "hold fast to the name of a buddha" (*na buddhanāma gṛhītam*) appears as one of a list of sins of omission (together with the failure to make offerings to a *tathāgata*, the failure to listen to *Dharma*-teachings, the failure to take delight in seeing pleasant offerings, and the failure to keep to the left of *stūpas*).[126]

The *Kāraṇḍavyūha Sūtra*, of course, is primarily concerned with developing the cult of Avalokiteśvara. The bringing to mind of the name of the bodhisattva is famously described in chapter twenty-four of the *Sadharmapuṇḍarīka Sūtra*. There, following Kern's translation, "listening to the name" (*nāmadhayaṃ śṛṇuyuḥ*),[127] "keeping the name" (*nāmadheyaṃ dhārayiṣyanti*),[128] "imploring" the bodhisattva (*ākrandaṃ kuryuḥ*),[129] "pronouncing the name" (*nāmadheyagrahaṇena*),[130] "invoking" the bodhisattva (*ākrandet*)[131] with the phrase, "Adoration, adoration be to the giver of safety, to Avalokiteśvara Bodhisattva" (*namo namas tasmai abhayaṃdadāyāvalokiteśvarāya bodhisattvāya mahāsattvāya*), "adoring" the bodhisattva (*namaskāraṃ kṛtvā*),[132] and "bringing to mind" the bodhisattva (*smarato*)[133] are said to lead to protection from a wide range of troubles and tribulations, such as fire, shipwreck, and capital punishment. In addition, "adoring the Bodhisattva Mahāsattva Avalokiteśvara and cherishing his name" (*avalokiteśvarasya bodhisattvasya mahāsattvasya namaskāraṃ kariṣyati nāmadheyaṃ ca dhārayiṣyati*)[134] is said to be the cause of great merit, more, indeed, than is produced by the worship of sixty-two times as many buddhas as there are sands in the Ganges.

The *Kāranḍavyūha Sūtra* extols the use of the name of Avalokiteśvara on four separate occasions. Twice, the benefits it is said to bestow are rather imprecise. Once, in the Ratnakuṇḍala hair pore, the female *gandharvas* who "bring to mind the name" three times in a row (*trikālamanusmaranti*) are said to procure all good things[135] and once, in the Vajramukha pore, the *kinnaras* who "bring to mind the name" (*nāmānusmaranti*) are said to become endowed with all benefits.[136] Twice, however, (where the Sanskrit phrase used in both instances is *nāmadheyamanusmaranti*) the " bringing to mind" of the bodhisattva's name is specifically said to lead to rebirth in Sukhāvatī. The first occasion is when an assembly of *tathāgatas* announce that they who perform this action are happy, are liberated from the anguish of the suffering of old age, death, disease, grief, and lamentation, are free from the sufferings of *saṃsāra* and will, dressed in brilliant white, fly like swans to the realm of Sukhāvatī, where they will hear the *Dharma* from Amitābha.[137] Next, Bali says that this practice liberates those who engage in it from the hell realms, the *preta* realms and from suffering in general, and will lead them eventually to Sukhāvatī, where they will hear the *Dharma* from Amitābha.[138]

The sūtra also promotes the "bringing to mind" of other phrases. As we have already seen, "bringing to mind the name" (*nāmamanusmārayanti*) of the homage, *namo buddhāya namo dharmāya namaḥ saṃghāya*, is said to lead to rebirth in Sukhāvatī. Otherwise, on two separate occasions, the "bringing to mind of the name" of the sūtra (*kāraṇḍavyūhasya mahāyānasūtraratnarājasya nāmamanusmaranti*) is recommended.[139] At one point, Avalokiteśvara advocates this latter practice in conjunction with the "bringing to mind" (*nāmadheyam*) of a single syllable of the *Kāraṇḍavyūha* and the writing of a four-line stanza of the sūtra (*catuṣpādikāmapi gāthāṃ likhāpayiṣyanti*).[140] Finally, the bodhisattvas of the Amṛtabindu hair pore are said to bring to mind the diverse Mahāyāna (*vividhaṃ ca mahāyānamanusmaranti*),[141] referring, presumably, to the use of the titles of the sūtras rather than their contents.[142] Each of these latter passages, though, while listing a wide range of accompanying rewards to these practices, never actually includes rebirth in Sukhāvatī as one of them.

Oṃ Maṇipadme Hūṃ, meanwhile, is twice said to be the object of *nāmānusmṛti* and twice the object of what is surely a functionally equivalent term, *nāmagrahaṇaṃ*. First, at the conclusion of the first part of the guided tour of the pores contained within Avalokiteśvara's body, Sākyamuni states that those who "bring to mind the name" (*nāmānusmaranti*) of his six-syllable formula, will be born in these pores, never again to wander in *saṃsāra*, being seated in one pore after another, until they reach the *bhūmi*, or "level" of *nirvāṇa*.[143] A little later on, Śākyamuni asks the *tathāgata* Padmottama for the six-syllable formula and is told that merely by bringing it to mind (*nāmānusmaraṇamātreṇa*), all evil is destroyed and the enlightenment that is hard to gain is attained (*durlabhāṃ bodhiṃ pratilabhate*).[144] Then, just before Sarvanīvaraṇaviṣkambhin asks the *dharmabhāṇaka* for the six syllables, he is told that it is extraordinary to "grasp" this "name" (*nāmagrahaṇam*). Merely to "grasp the name once" (*ekavāranāmagrahaṇena*), he is told, is equivalent to the action of offering robes, begging bowls, beds, seats, and medicine to the *tathāgatas*.[145]

It is striking, however, that in none of these examples is *Oṃ Maṇipadme Hūṃ* ever explicitly said to lead to rebirth in Sukhāvatī. Instead, the link between the use of the formula and Amitābha's pure land remains implicit and unspoken. For instance, "grasping the name once" (*ekavāranāmagrahaṇena*) of *Oṃ Maṇipadme Hūṃ* is said to be the equivalent of making offerings to the *tathāgatas*. In the sūtra's presentation of the *vāmana-avatāra*, requesting a *Dharma*-teaching and daily filling the offering bowl of a *tathāgata* is said to be rewarded by rebirth in Sukhāvatī. It follows, then, more or less logically, that "grasping the name once" of the formula may also be a cause of rebirth in the pure land. Similarly, it is said that "simply by bringing to mind the name" (*nāmānusmaraṇamātreṇa*) of the formula all evil is destroyed and enlightenment attained. Bali is also told that he will go to Sukhāvatī as a result of the purification of evil. Therefore, "simply by bringing to mind the name" of *Oṃ Maṇipadme Hūṃ* will also, it would seem reasonable to suppose, lead to rebirth in Sukhāvatī.

Furthermore, the way the formula is first properly introduced in the sūtra suggests that its use is to be seen not just as an indeterminate form of the practice of "bringing to mind the name," but, more specifically, as a form of the practice of the "bringing to mind of the name of Avalokiteśvara." In the Vajramukha pore, the last to be visited in the first part of Śākyamuni's tour of these lands, the *kinnaras* are "always bringing to mind the name of

Avalokiteśvara" (*satatakālamavalokiteśvarasya nāmānusmaranti*).[146] Breaking off the tour at this point, the Buddha then says that it is difficult (*durlabhaṃ*) to grasp his name (*tasya nāmagrahaṇam*), where *tasya*, or "his," must refer to Avalokiteśvara.[147] This is immediately followed by the statement that "those who bring to mind the name of his six-syllable formula" (*ye ca tasya ṣaḍakṣarīmahāvidyānāmānusmaranti*) will be born in those pores, where *tasya* must again refer to the bodhisattva.[148] The juxtaposition of these statements is such that it is hard to avoid the conclusion that recitation of *Oṃ Maṇipadme Hūṃ* is to be seen as a variant of the more straightforward "bringing to mind the name" of the bodhisattva. As the latter practice is twice said, in the *Kāraṇḍavyūha Sūtra,* to be the cause of rebirth in Sukhāvatī, this is yet another indication that the use of the formula is implicitly connected to the attainment of that central Mahāyāna goal.

The question remains, then, as to why the *Kāraṇḍavyūha* avoids declaring a direct link between *Oṃ Maṇipadme Hūṃ* and Sukhāvatī, when, doctrinally speaking, this would seem to be an entirely legitimate option. The answer to this would seem to be that the sūtra wishes to communicate a sense that the use of the formula is connected, first and foremost, to the attainment of an alternative religious goal. As we have seen, the "vision" that inspires Sarvanīvaraṇaviṣkambhin's "quest" for the six-syllable formula is not a simple presentation of rebirth in Amitābha's pure land, but the extensive descriptions of the worlds contained within the hair pores of Avalokiteśvara. It is birth into these pores (*teṣu romavivareṣu jāyante*) that is explicitly said to be the result of "bringing to mind the name" of the formula.[149] The tour of Avalokiteśvara's body is, also, the context for the appearance of the hundred thousand-armed form of the bodhisattva, which is inserted, somewhat abruptly, after the pores of Suvarṇa, Kṛṣṇa and Ratnakuṇḍala and before the pores of Amṛtabindu and Vajramukha.[150] Once again, what seems to be going on here is that the sūtra is reproducing another purāṇic doctrine associated with the *īśvara* idea and the use of a concise formula, and recasting it in the accepted terminology of Mahāyāna Buddhism.

Beyer develops his remarks on the "vision quests" by using the *Bhagavadgītā* to posit a connection between the Mahāyāna sūtras and what he refers to as the "visionary theism" of the purāṇic tradition.[151] He identifies what he considers to be a number of striking resemblances in diction and imagery between the *Bhagavadgītā* and the *Saddharmapuṇḍarīka Sūtra*.[152] Both Kṛṣṇa and Śākyamuni, he observes, are referred to as the "father of the world";[153] the "visions" described by both texts include the image of a blazing, stretched-out tongue or mouth;[154] both texts advocate the offering of a single flower,[155] and both texts emphasize the quality of equanimity that is shown towards all beings by their respective lords.[156]

Beyer also points out that the *Bhagavadgītā* employs the words *smṛti* and *anusmṛti*—terms commonly used in the Mahāyāna sūtras—as equivalents of the important purāṇic term *bhakti*, or "devotion," to denote the means by which visionary experience is attained.[157] In a verse from the end of chapter seven, the *īśvara* Kṛṣṇa announces that he is reached through *bhakti*, while at the beginning of chapter eight he says that he is reached through *smṛti*. The former reads: "Those who worship the gods go to the gods, but those who are devoted to me (*madbhaktā*) go to me."[158] The latter: "And whoever dies, remembering me alone (*mām eva smaran*) at the time of death, attains to my state once he is liberated from the body."[159] Chapter eight continues to use *smṛti* (and *anusmṛti*) and *bhakti* alongside each other: ". . . whatever state he calls to mind (*smaran*) as he abandons his body at its end . . ." (verse six); ". . . think of me (*mam anusmara*) at all times and fight . . ." (verse seven), and, ". . . disciplined with the power of yoga and with devotion (*bhaktyā*), having correctly installed his vital breath between the eyebrows, meditates (*anusmared*) . . ." (verses nine and ten).[160]

The *Bhagavadgītā*, furthermore, enjoins the utterance of the single syllable *praṇava Oṃ*, in conjunction with the practice of *anusmṛti*, as a means of achieving religious success: "The man who, abandoning his body, dies pronouncing the one-syllabled Brahman, *Oṃ* (*om ity ekākṣaraṃ brahma vyāharan*), while thinking on me (*mām anusmaran*), attains the highest goal."[161] Beyer suggests a parallel between this and the injunction to repeat the name of the Buddha Amitābha in the *Amitāyurbuddhānusmṛti Sūtra*.[162]

Finally, Beyer compares the central vision of the *Bhagavadgītā*, the theophany of Kṛṣṇa before Arjuna in chapter eleven, with elements of the Mahāyāna approach. He comments on the way in which Kṛṣṇa first grants Arjuna the vision ("By showing favour to you, Arjuna, through my own power I have made manifest this supreme form of mine . . . ")[163] and then tells him that the experience may only be reproduced through *bhakti* ("But by exclusive devotion (*bhaktyā tv*), Arjuna, I can be known (*jñātuṃ*) and seen (*draṣṭuṃ*) thus, as I really am, and entered into (*praveṣṭuṃ*) . . . ").[164] This, Beyer writes, is "strikingly reminiscent," of the way in which queen Vaidehī, in the *Amitāyurbuddhānusmṛti Sūtra*, is taught the various different meditation techniques after first of all receiving, involuntarily, the vision of the buddhafields.[165] He also writes that Arjuna's vision of "blazing light" is analogous to the visions of dazzling, bejewelled buddha lands found in the Mahāyāna sūtras.[166] Had Beyer consulted the *Kāraṇḍavyūha*, however, he would have found a very much more striking set of parallels between the theology of the *Bhagavadgītā* and the "buddhology" of the Mahāyāna. For the central vision of the sūtra appears to be quite a faithful reworking of precisely the kind of theophany that is described in chapter eleven of the *Gītā*.

In the *Bhagavadgītā*, Kṛṣṇa is said to manifest in such a way that he encompasses the whole world: "Now see, Guḍākeśa, here in my body (*dehe*) the entire universe of moving and unmoving things, and whatever else you desire to behold (*draṣṭum icchasi*)."[167] Many divine and semidivine beings live in this body: "O God, I see (*paśyāmi*) in your body the gods and all kinds of beings come together, Lord Brahmā on his lotus seat, all the seers and the divine serpents."[168] This cosmic manifestation of Kṛṣṇa is also synonymous with the thousand-armed form of the deity: "O thousand-armed one (*sahasrabāho*), whose material form is the universe, assume your four-armed shape."[169] Although this form is predominantly something "to see" (*draṣṭum*), it is also something, as noted above, "to enter" (*praveṣṭum*).[170] Emphasis is given to the difficulty of seeing this form: "I rejoice that I have seen (*dṛṣtvā*) what has never before been seen (*adṛṣṭapūrvaṃ*) . . . ,"[171] and, "This form of mine, which you have seen (*dṛṣtvān*), is very hard to see (*sudurdarśam*)."[172] The gods themselves have difficulty seeing it: "Even the gods crave incessantly for a glimpse (*nityaṃ darśanakāṅkṣiṇaḥ*) of this form."[173] Kṛṣṇa originally grants Arjuna a special faculty to enable him to see this vision: "But you will not be able to see (*draṣṭuṃ*) me with your natural eye, so I give you a divine (*divyaṃ*) eye (*cakṣuḥ*) . . ."[174] Later, however, Arjuna is told that he will see Kṛṣṇa through *bhakti*, or devotion alone (*bhaktyā tv*).[175]

The vision of Avalokiteśvara detailed in the *Kāraṇḍavyūha Sūtra* contains nothing, it is true, of one of the most memorable aspects of this vision of Kṛṣṇa: the manifestation of the purāṇic deity is continually shown to be something that is extremely frightening. He is seen to consume the universe in his manifold, fiery mouths and to chew up human beings in his teeth. "Viṣṇu," Arjuna cries, "you lap up all the worlds with your flaming mouths, ubiquitously devouring; your fierce rays engulf the entire universe in brilliance, roasting it."[176] Friend and foe alike, Arjuna reports, "flow into your terrifying fang-distended mouths. Some can be seen lodged between your teeth, their heads crushed to a pulp."[177] The gods praise Kṛṣṇa " in dread" (*bhītāḥ*),[178] "the worlds reel" (*lokāḥ pravyathitās*),[179] Arjuna is "shaken to the core" (*pravyathitāntarātmā*)[180] and "terrified demons scatter to the winds . . . ," (*rakṣāṃsi bhītāni diśo dravanti*)[181] when they see this "terrible form" (*rūpaṃ ghoram*).[182] The Buddhist *īśvara* of the *Kāraṇḍavyūha*, in contrast, is a consistently benign being, characterized as unwaveringly compassionate from the beginning of the sūtra to the end.

This understanding of Kṛṣṇa as a source of terror is, at least in part, derived from an understanding of the deity as the embodiment of time. "I am time (*kālo*) run on," Kṛṣṇa says, "destroyer of the universe, risen here to annihilate worlds. Regardless of you, all these warriors, stationed in opposing ranks, shall cease to exist."[183] In the *Kāraṇḍavyūha*, Avalokiteśvara is also linked to the concept of time, not as a destroyer though, but in terms of the very much less alarming quality of appearing to beings at unforeseeable moments. When Sarvanīvaraṇaviṣkambhin, immediately after the description of the hundred thousand-armed Avalokiteśvara, asks Śākyamuni how he might see (*paśyāmi*) the great bodhisattva, he is told that Avalokiteśvara appears in this realm in order to see, praise and give worship to the Buddha.[184] When Sarvanīvaraṇaviṣkambhin asks if the great bodhisattva is coming, he is told that Avalokiteśvara first arrives (*prathamataramāgacchati*) when he (meaning, presumably, the lesser bodhisattva) is "mature in spirit" (*sattvaparipāko*).[185] When he asks when, in this time (*asmin kāle*), Avalokiteśvara will come, Śākyamuni laughs and laughs (*hasati vyavahasati ca*), and says that the appointed time of his coming (*āgamanakālasamayaḥ*) is unpredictable (*akālaste*).[186]

In many other respects, however, the two visions correspond very closely to one another. Just as Kṛṣṇa's body is said to contain the whole universe, so, too, does Avalokiteśvara: in his hundred thousand-armed form, he is said to have an omnipresent body (*viśvarūpī*)[187] and in the hair pores of his skin he contains whole worlds. Next, like Kṛṣṇa, his body contains divine and semidivine beings, whose ranks also include buddhas and bodhisattvas: the hair pore of Suvarṇa, for instance, is inhabited by *gandharvas*,[188] the hair pore of Vajramukha by *kinnaras*,[189] the hair pore of Indrarāja by bodhisattvas,[190] and the hair pore of Dhvajāgra by *tathāgatas*, who, gathered in their apartments, teach the six perfections to the people of Jambudvīpa.[191]

The Buddhist vision of the cosmic bodhisattva, like the theophany of the *Bhagavadgītā*, is also expressed, in shorthand, in terms of the *puruṣa* with the various "thousand-fold" attributes, derived from the conventions established in the Vedic *puruṣasūkta*.[192] The sūtra switches from the description of the bodhisattva's hair pores, to his appearance in the form of the Vedic *puruṣa* and then back to the description of the hair pores. Having followed the Buddha's account of the worlds contained within the pores of Suvarṇa, Kṛṣṇa and Ratnakuṇḍala, Sarvanīvaraṇaviṣkambhin expresses his desire to go (*gamiṣyāmi*) and see (*draṣṭukāmo*) these hair pores.[193] The Buddha, however, tells him that the pores are ungraspable and untouchable (*agrāhyā asaṃsparśāḥ*), just as the dimension of space is ungraspable and untouchable.[194] The great bodhisattva Samantabhadra, the buddha says, roamed these pores for twelve years, but still the pores and the hundred buddhas residing in each one were not seen by him (*tenāpi na dṛṣṭāni*). What chance, then do other bodhisattvas have?[195] The "hair pore" (*romavivaraṃ*) was not seen (*na dṛṣyate*) by Śākyamuni himself, he explains, despite investigation and exploration (*vikṣamāṇena parimārgayamāṇena*).[196] There then follows the description of Avalokiteśvara as one hundred thousand-armed (*śatasahasrabhujaḥ*) and having one hundred thousand *koṭis* of eyes (*koṭiśatasahasranetro*).[197] The sūtra then returns to descriptions of the hair pores of Amṛtabindu and Vajramukha. It is not that the hundred thousand-armed

Avalokiteśvara somehow appears within his own hair pores, but rather, that this form is another way of describing the cosmic form of the bodhisattva.

Like Kṛṣṇa, the vision of Avalokiteśvara, too, is said to be encountered both by entering into it and by seeing it: Śākyamuni tells Sarvanīvaraṇaviṣkambhin that those who "bring to mind the name" of the six-syllable formula will be "born in" these hair pores (*teṣu romavivareṣu jāyante*),[198] while the people of Jambudvīpa are, after being taught the six perfections by the *tathāgatas* of the Dhvajāgra pore, said to "see" (*paśyanti*) the hair pores of the bodhisattva.[199] The vision of the bodhisattva is also, like the vision of Kṛṣṇa, very elusive. In the description of the hundred thousand-armed form, Avalokiteśvara is said to be neither heard (*na śruto*) nor seen by anyone (*na kenacid dṛśyate*).[200] And while the gods are said to crave a glimpse of Kṛṣṇa, it is clear from Śākyamuni's response to Sarvanīvaraṇaviṣkambhin's wish to go and see the hair pores, that it is equally difficult for the buddhas and bodhisattvas to catch sight of Avalokiteśvara.

Finally, just as Arjuna is first given access to a visionary encounter of Kṛṣṇa through the gift of the "divine eye" and then, immediately afterwards, told that he can re-create this experience through *bhakti*, so, too, is Sarvanīvaraṇaviṣkambhin first given an account of the worlds contained within the hair pores of Avalokiteśvara and of the hundred thousand-armed form of the bodhisattva, and then, immediately afterwards, told that they who "bring to mind the name" (*nāmānusmaranti*) of the six-syllable formula are the ones who will be born in these pores.[201] Though the *bhakti* taught to Arjuna may indeed, as Beyer suggests, be reflected in the meditations given to queen Vaidehī in the *Amitāyurbuddhānusmṛti Sūtra*, it is, at least in one of its forms, very precisely mimicked in the principle practice propagated in the *Kāraṇḍavyūha Sūtra*: the *anusmṛti* of the single-syllable (*ekākṣara*) *praṇava Oṃ* is echoed in the *nāmānusmṛti* of what we have suggested is the six-syllable (*ṣaḍakṣara*) Buddhist *praṇava, Oṃ Maṇipadme Hūṃ*.

This type of vision of the cosmic *īśvara* is not, of course, unique to the *Bhagavadgītā* and the *Kāraṇḍavyūha Sūtra*. Several purāṇas, both Vaiṣṇavite and Śaivite, contain *gītā* sections, most of which, as Rocher points out, are directly modeled on the *Bhagavadgītā*.[202] All the main elements of the theophany of Kṛṣṇa and the "buddhophany" of Avalokiteśvara are also, for instance, reproduced in the theophany of Śiva contained in the *Īśvaragītā* of the *Kūrma Purāṇa*, a Śaivite text considered to have been composed by the beginning of the eighth century C.E.[203] There, like Kṛṣṇa's, Śiva's body encompasses the world and he contains all beings: "All this universe consisting of the mobiles and immobiles has been pervaded by me. All beings exist in me."[204] And like Kṛṣṇa, he is perceived to consume the created order with fire: "They saw the Lord, the creator of the universe dancing and emitting flames of fire and thereby burning (as it were) the entire universe."[205]

In the *Īśvaragītā*, Śiva is once again described in terms of the "thousand-fold" form of the *puruṣasūkta*: "They saw the lord with a thousand (i.e. innumerable) heads, a thousand feet, a thousand shapes, and a thousand arms . . ."[206] While he contains all beings, he is, also, the object of "seeing" and "knowing," though again, this aspect of the deity is very elusive: "The sages, the *pitṛs* (celestial forefathers) and the heaven-dwellers do not see me. Nor do the others of well-known prowess such as Brahmā, the Manus, and Śakra (the king of gods) know me,"[207] and, "All the worlds, god Brahmā, the grand-sire of the world, do not perceive me."[208] He cannot be encountered without the practice of *bhakti*: "Without ardent and excellent devotion it is impossible to know me."[209] Like the *Bhagavadgītā*, the *Īśvaragītā* also advertises the use of the single-syllable *praṇāva Oṃ*: "The syllable *Oṃ*, the seed of liberation, is your (expressive) symbol."[210] Unlike the *Bhagavadgītā* or the *Kāraṇḍavyūha Sūtra*, however, the *Īśvaragītā* integrates the *śakti* doctrine into this essentially *bhakti*-derived scheme. For instance: "What need there is of prolixity, the entire universe is constituted of my potency (*śakti*)."[211]

In conclusion, then, although, in its depiction of the *dharmabhāṇaka*, its use of the *vidyādhara* idea and its description of the maṇḍala, the *Kāraṇḍavyūha* appears to acknowledge the tantric-style origins of the concise formula of the Buddhist *īśvara*, it presents the practice primarily within a scheme borrowed from the *bhakti* side of the purāṇic tradition. The sūtra is, as we have shown, informed by the need to reassert the central values of monasticism in the face, it seems, of the infiltration of celibate communities by married tantric-style practitioners. The decision to describe the use of the six-syllable formula as a tool of *bhakti* and not, as would appear to have been a possibility, in terms of the tantric-style idea of an engagement with the *śakti* of the *īśvara*, may have been motivated by a desire to avoid the sexual associations of the latter doctrine that would, almost inevitably, have proven problematic to the rule of celibacy.

This purāṇic scheme is integrated into the Mahāyāna system through a number of ingenious ploys. As we have seen, the six-syllable formula—a form of the *praṇava*—is shown, in the *Kāraṇḍavyūha*, to take the place of the Perfection of Wisdom as the supreme principle of the Mahāyāna. The formula is co-opted into a Mahāyāna scheme that is dominated by the idea of rebirth in Sukhāvatī, the pure land of Amitābha. The connection between the formula and Sukhāvatī is most powerfully expressed in the central position given to Amitābha in the maṇḍala described in the sūtra. The sense of this connection is maintained, however, throughout the *Kāraṇḍavyūha*: rebirth in Sukhāvatī is a constant refrain; use of the formula is said to bring about a variety of effects which are, elsewhere in the sūtra, themselves said to lead to rebirth in Sukhāvatī; *japa*, or "muttering," of the formula is recast as a form of the Mahāyāna activity of "bringing to mind the name" (*nāmānusmṛti*) or "taking hold of the name" (*nāmagrahaṇaṃ*), and, implicitly, as a form of "bringing to mind the name" of Avalokiteśvara, a set of practices strongly linked to the Sukhāvatī idea.

But the use of the formula is, as we have observed, never explicitly said to lead to rebirth in Sukhāvatī. This, it was suggested, was a deliberate omission on the part of the sūtra, made in order to be true to the fact that the formula was originally associated with the "entry into" or "seeing of" the vision of the cosmic *īśvara*. The primacy of this association is communicated in the structure of the sūtra: the account of Sarvanīvaraṇaviṣkambhin's initiation into the use of the formula is, basically, told in the form of a quest for a means of experiencing this vision. The first instructions on the use of the formula make no mention of rebirth in Sukhāvatī, but state, instead, that "bringing to mind the name" leads to birth in the hair pores of this cosmic figure.

This purāṇic vision is itself reconfigured by the Mahāyāna. The idea of the all-encompassing size of the body of the *īśvara* is recast in terms of the vision of the *Avataṃsaka Sūtra*: Avalokiteśvara takes on the characteristics of the bodhisattva Samantabhadra, a being so vast that even the hair pores of his skin contain worlds. In the end, however, even this vision feeds back into the central religious goal of rebirth in Sukhāvatī. Immediately after the description of the characteristics and attributes of the hundred thousand-armed form of Avalokiteśvara and just before the return to the account of the worlds contained within the hair pores of the bodhisattva, Śākyamuni makes the following remarks. This inconceivable one (*acintyo 'yaṃ*), he says, referring to the hundred thousand-armed Avalokiteśvara, manifests miracles and brings to maturity countless numbers of bodhisattvas, whom he stands on the path of *Dharma*. Having established them thus, he leads them to the realm of Sukhāvatī, where, in the presence of Amitābha, he teaches them *Dharma*.[212] This passage encapsulates the syncretistic polemic that lies at the heart of the *Kāraṇḍavyūha Sūtra*: the experience of seeing (or entering) the cosmic *īśvara* is to be understood as inseparable from the experience of rebirth in the pure land of the buddha. As we shall see in the next chapter, the unity of these two ideas is reflected in the meaning of *Oṃ Maṇipadme Hūṃ*.

CHAPTER 6

The Meaning of *Oṃ Maṇipadme Hūṃ*

An enquiry into the meaning of any mantra can quickly become a very complicated business. Mantric utterance involves the use of syllables, words, phrases, and sometimes even whole sentences that is, in a number of different ways, quite distinct from ordinary speech. Questions about what we mean by the meaning of mantras and, even, whether mantras have any meaning at all have held Indian thinkers in thrall for many centuries. In recent times, these meditations have been augmented by the work of scholars attempting to test mantras against the rubric of modern linguistic theory.[1] Such considerations now constitute a philosophical and philological jungle of quite considerable proportions which, unfortunately, it is beyond the scope of this study to explore. In the simplest possible terms, then, the following discussion of the "meaning" of *Oṃ Maṇipadme Hūṃ* is essentially concerned with the semantic content of the middle four syllables of the formula: how, in other words, the short Sanskrit compound *maṇipadme* should be correctly parsed and translated into English. It will be the contention of this chapter that the same syncretistic process that has been shown to inform the creation of the *Kāraṇḍavyūha Sūtra* as a whole is also evident, in microcosm, in the form of those four syllables. The "meaning" of *Oṃ Maṇipadme Hūṃ* may, in this way, be seen to be linked to the historical origins of the formula.

Nevertheless, to concentrate exclusively on this slight semantic point would be to present a very narrow and potentially very misleading view of the true significance of *Oṃ Maṇipadme Hūṃ*. Etymologically, as Gonda points out, Sanskrit words in *-tra* (like the Indo-European -tro) often signify instruments of some sort. Thus, *śrotram*, or "ear," is the instrument of hearing and *jñātram*, or "intellect," is the instrument of knowing. *Mantra*, similarly, is an instrument (*-tra*) of the mind (*man-*), being derived from the same root as *manas-*, denoting "mind" in the very broadest sense, encompassing the activity, not only of thought, but also of the emotions, the imagination, and the spiritual faculty of a human being.[2] A mantra, in brief, is a tool for doing something with this mind. What is really important, therefore, about phenomena such as *Oṃ Maṇipadme Hūṃ* is not their meaning, but their function. As

Gonda remarks: "A mantra is always a source of activity, it is always a potential means of achieving a special effect."[3]

In the words of a contemporary Tibetan lama, "A mantra is a series of syllables whose power resides in its sound, through the repeated pronouncing of which one can obtain control of a given form of energy."[4] In the case of *Oṃ Maṇipadme Hūṃ*, this energy is conceived of as the power of Avalokiteśvara. As we have seen, the formula is repeatedly referred to as the *paramahṛdaya*, or "innermost heart," of the bodhisattva. Gonda comments: "The essence of a mantra is the presence of the deity: only that mantra in which the *devatā* has revealed his or her particular aspects can reveal that aspect. The deity is believed to appear from the mantra when it is correctly pronounced. It is indeed true that the term mantra, because of the power considered to be inherent in formulated inspired thoughts and uttered words, also implied that the 'formula' was a means of wielding supranormal power."[5] According to this point of view, then, *Oṃ Maṇipadme Hūṃ* might be said to be a means both of entering into the presence of Avalokiteśvara and of appropriating some of the bodhisattva's power.

The implications of such a belief are, of course, spelled out at great length in the *Kāraṇḍavyūha*. Entry into the presence of Avalokiteśvara is, it seems to me, described in three different ways in the sūtra. First of all, those who bring to mind the six-syllable formula are said to be born in the pores of the bodhisattva's body.[6] Second, as we have argued, birth into these pores is conceived of as synonymous with the elusive "seeing" (*darśana*) of the bodhisattva in his "thousand-fold" form. That *Oṃ Maṇipadme Hūṃ* is connected to the attainment of many different *samādhis* may also, I think, be understood as a third expression of the same idea. Avalokiteśvara himself is said to possess an immeasurable number of *samādhis*, unattainable even by the *tathāgatas*.[7] There are hundreds of thousands of *samādhis* in each of his pores.[8] To enter into one of these mental absorptions, then, may surely be considered equivalent to entering into the being of the bodhisattva himself. Sarvanīvaraṇaviṣkambhin is first told by Śākyamuni that recitation of *Oṃ Maṇipadme Hūṃ* leads to the attainment of eight hundred *samādhis*.[9] Then, as soon as he has been given the formula and has begun to take it up (*udgṛhītumārabdhaḥ*),[10] Sarvanīvaraṇaviṣkambhin is said to obtain seven *samādhis*.[11]

As we have also seen, one of the chief characteristics of Avalokiteśvara is his great compassion. One would, as a result, expect the appropriation of the power of the bodhisattva to be connected with an increase of this quality. It is fitting, then, that one of the *samādhis* said to be attained by Sarvanīvaraṇaviṣ kambhin after taking up *Oṃ Maṇipadme Hūṃ* is the *samādhi* called "rejoicing in loving kindness and compassion" (*maitrīkaruṇāmudito nāma samādhiḥ*).[12] Similarly, we may recall, he or she who recites *Oṃ Maṇipadme*

Hūṃ is said to become furnished with great compassion (*mahākaruṇayā samanvāgato bhavati*).[13]

Avalokiteśvara is also identified as the repository of huge amounts of *puṇya*, or "merit." In the course of the *Kāraṇḍavyūha*, Śākyamuni gives two long sermons on the amount of merit accrued by the great bodhisattva. The first of these takes up the whole of the seventh chapter of the first part of the sūtra,[14] and the second occurs near the end of the text, when Avalokiteśvara has returned to the Jetavana *vihāra*.[15] (His *samādhis*, incidentally, are described as the greatest collection of his merit.)[16] Concomitantly, the recitation of the bodhisattva's six-syllable formula is said to result in the accumulation of immeasurable merit, also described, at great length, in similar fashion.[17] Though, for instance, it is said to be possible to count each drop of water in the oceans, it is said to be impossible to calculate the amount of merit accrued by Avalokiteśvara.[18] Likewise, though it is said to be possible to calculate the number of grains of sand in the oceans, it is said to be impossible to calculate the amount of merit accrued by one recitation (*ekajāpasya*) of the six-syllable formula.[19] Once again, the use of *Oṃ Maṇipadme Hūṃ* is shown to be a means of taking on some of the power of the great bodhisattva.

Another way of taking hold of the power of a supranormal being is said to be to call upon his or her name, a belief not merely confined to the Indian religious traditions.[20] Appropriately enough, the presentation of *Oṃ Maṇipadme Hūṃ* in the *Kāraṇḍavyūha* would seem to imply that the six-syllable formula is also to be regarded as a form of the name of Avalokiteśvara. Recitation of the formula, we have observed, though chiefly referred to by the word *japa*, is, in addition, frequently described by other terms—*nāmānusmṛti*, *nāmadheyamanusmṛti*, *nāmagrahaṇa*—that denote the bringing to mind of a name.

The presentation of *Oṃ Maṇipadme Hūṃ* in the *Kāraṇḍavyūha Sūtra* is certainly consistent with one aspect of the classic presentation, found in the *Saddharmapuṇḍarīka Sūtra*, of the use of the actual name of Avalokiteśvara. In the latter work, the use of the bodhisattva's name, like the use of the six-syllable formula, is also connected to the accumulation of huge amounts of merit. However, there does seem to be one significant difference between the effect of using the mantra and the effect of using the actual name. For a particular stress is laid, in the *Saddharmapuṇḍarīka*, on the association of the latter with the protective power of the bodhisattva. Calling upon the name, for instance, is said to effect miraculous rescue from such very palpable dangers as falling into fire, shipwreck, capital punishment, and imprisonment.[21]

In contrast, *Oṃ Maṇipadme Hūṃ* is only described as an instrument of protection in passing, in much less emphatic and dramatic terms. The comparable Śaivite formula *Namaḥ Śivāya* is explicitly said to have protective power. "In the age of Kali," we read, "there is no greater protective factor than the five-syllabled mantra to a fallen or a low-person devoid of good conduct."[22] Meanwhile, one who wears the Buddhist formula on the body or around the neck is said, for instance, to be known as having a body made of *vajra* (*vajrakāyaśarīra*).[23] He or she who recites the formula is said to become one of indestructible brilliance (*akṣayapratibhāna*).[24] The *Kāraṇḍavyūha* does, of course, attribute various interventionary powers to Avalokiteśvara in the course of the narrative sections of the sūtra. The bodhisattva, for example, is said to have saved the people of Magadha from famine.[25] *Oṃ Maṇipadme Hūṃ*, then, as the *paramahṛdaya* of the bodhisattva, might implicitly be believed to be a means of activating such miraculous saving power. Nonetheless, it remains true that the sūtra contains no express presentation of *Oṃ Maṇipadme Hūṃ* as a protective device.

- *Oṃ Maṇipadme Hūṃ*, then, is both the *paramahṛdaya*, or "innermost heart," of Avalokiteśvara and a form of the *nāma*, or "name," of the bodhisattva. It is also, as we have seen, a *mahāvidyā*, a mantra capable of bringing about the "great knowledge" of enlightenment itself, or perhaps, in this context, a means of acquiring, or entering into, the enlightened mind of the great bodhisattva. He who knows the formula, it is said, knows liberation (*mokṣaṃ jānāti*).[26] One who wears the formula on the body or around the neck is said to be known as the ultimate in the wisdom of the *tathāgatas*.[27] Merely to bring it to mind is to destroy all evil and to attain extraordinary enlightenment (*bodhiṃ*).[28]

- *Oṃ Maṇipadme Hūṃ*, finally, we have argued, is to be regarded as a kind of Buddhist *praṇava*. It is the "rice grain" of the Mahāyāna (*taṇḍulavatsāraṃ mahāyānasya*),[29] that which is both the nourishing essence of the whole plant and, also, the seed from which the whole plant springs. Merely to recite it is to bring sublime liberation (*śivaṃ mokṣam*).[30] It is, moreover, the indestructible instruction on all wisdom (*sarvajñānasya akṣayaṃ nirdeśaṃ*).[31] To write it is equivalent to writing the eighty-four thousand parts of the *Dharma*.[32] It is that by which the twelve-fold wheel of *Dharma* is turned.[33] It is the equivalent of many Mahāyāna sūtras being sung and of a great variety of Buddhist texts being taught.[34] The six syllables of *Oṃ Maṇipadme Hūṃ* are believed to contain, in some sense, all the teachings of the Mahāyāna.

One method of explicating this aspect of the formula has been to make each of its syllables stand for one of the elements of a variety of six-part doctrinal schemes. In this way, the recitation of the formula may be said to become imbued with the force and effect of a number of different *Dharma*-teachings. This convention has played a prominent part in the transmission of the formula by contemporary Tibetan lamas. The six syllables, for instance, are commonly said to correspond to the six *pāramitās*, or "perfections" and the six realms of *saṃsāra*, recitation of the formula leading, respectively, to the accomplishment of the former and liberation from the latter.[35] The same strategy is also found in some of the purāṇic presentations of *Namaḥ Śivāya*. In the *Śiva Purāṇa*, for instance, those five syllables are related to the five elements (ether, air, fire, water, and earth) and to the five senses (hearing, touch, sight, taste, and smell).[36] A more complex set of correspondences is presented in the *Liṅga Purāṇa*, where each syllable of *Namaḥ Śivāya* is associated with a color, a point of the compass (the fifth point being upwards), a deity, a poetic metre, and a sage.[37]

It is somewhat surprising, then, to discover that this treatment is not part of the presentation of *Oṃ Maṇipadme Hūṃ* set out in the *Kāraṇḍavyūha*. Use of the six syllables is, in fact, thrice linked, in the sūtra, to the six *pāramitās*. He or she who recites the formula is said to accomplish the six perfections daily.[38] One of the *samādhis* said to be attained through recitation of the formula is called "the *samādhi* that points out of the six perfections" (*ṣaṭpāramitānirdeśo nāma samādhiḥ*).[39] Finally, a single recitation of the formula is said to accomplish the six perfections.[40] However, in none of these instances is there any sign that each syllable of the formula is believed to correspond to one of the six perfections. Rather, it is the recitation of the one formula that is said to achieve the one overall effect of accomplishing the six perfections. The *Kāraṇḍavyūha* is, moreover, completely ignorant of the idea of linking each of the six syllables to one of the six realms of saṃsāric existence. On the contrary, the sūtra employs a different conception of *saṃsāra* and describes *Oṃ Maṇipadme Hūṃ* as bringing about the destruction of rebirth in five such realms (*unmūlanaṃ saṃsārasya pañcagatikasya*).[41] The popular use of different correspondence schemes to fill out an understanding of the six-syllable formula would appear, therefore, to postdate the *Kāraṇḍavyūha*.

What we have referred to as the "meaning" of *Oṃ Maṇipadme Hūṃ* should, I think, be understood to be of comparable import to these correspondence schemes. That is to say, the precise semantics of the syllables *maṇipadme* should not be regarded as defining the limits of the significance of the formula. Instead, like each correspondence scheme, the "meaning" of *Oṃ Maṇipadme Hūṃ* should be viewed as a means of bringing out an aspect of the multifaceted significance of the formula, as another conceptual expression of the energy believed to be harnessed by the formula and, consequently, as another means by which the practitioner may develop his or her appreciation of this energy. The "meaning" of *Oṃ Maṇipadme Hūṃ* represents a means by which the intellect may be involved in the integration of the individual with the energy of Avalokiteśvara through the use of the mantra.

The power of a mantra is said to lie in its sound. The purely sonic or musical dimension of Avalokiteśvara's formula should not, then, go overlooked. Indeed, it is surely not insignificant that the arrangement of the six syllables "om-ma-ni-pa-dme-hum" does yield a naturally pleasing reverberation when recited. The sounds of the syllables "om" and "hum," at the beginning and end of the formula, tend to merge together into a continuous hum, while the four middle syllables bring a certain liveliness and movement to this single tone. In addition, the fact that the second syllable "-ma-" begins with a nasal consonant, just as the first syllable "om-" consists in the nasalization of a vowel (*anusvara*), facilitates the easy flow of this recitation. The Vedic mantras were said to be *sutaṣṭa*, or "well-fashioned," in the hearts of the *ṛṣis*.[42] When *Oṃ Maṇipadme Hūṃ* was first wrought within the inspired mind of a Buddhist *vidyādhara*, the sound of the compound *maṇipadme*, as well as its meaning, is likely to have contributed to its inclusion in the formula.

For such a little phrase, *maṇipadme* has provoked a great many different interpretations, a symptom largely of the ambiguities of the Sanskrit language. It has been popularly understood to refer to "the jewel (*maṇi-*) in the lotus (*-padme*)," a phrase that has been taken, predominantly, as symbolic of the conjunction of the Buddhist coefficients of wisdom and compassion, of the union of male and female,[43] and the appearance of a buddha (or bodhisattva) in the mind (or heart).[44] But though *padme* may be correctly parsed as a masculine or neuter locative (the noun may be either gender), there appears to be no grammatical precedent for reading *maṇi* here as the nominative form, which would normally be *maṇiḥ*. According to the laws of classical Sanskrit, *maṇi-* is the stem form, making *maṇipadme* a compound noun.

The possible readings of such a compound are, once again, numerous. It has been parsed as a nominative neuter *dvandva*, or "co-ordinative," compound, meaning "jewel and lotus," where the formula is understood to be an expression of a corresponding arrangement of buddhas, in which *Oṃ*, *Maṇi*, *Padme*, and *Hūṃ* are each linked to individual buddhas.[45] There are, it seems to me, three major drawbacks to this interpretation. In order to connect the formula to an orthodox fivefold scheme of buddhas, it becomes necessary to lengthen the formula by the arbitrary addition of the extra syllable *Hrīḥ* (the associated *bīja*, or "seed syllable," which is traditionally used as a symbol of the potentiality of Avalokiteśvara or that from which the bodhisattva may manifest). It is also odd that some of these buddhas should be represented by a single syllable and some of them by a noun. Finally, it depicts the formula not as a particularly "well fashioned" device, but rather, as something clumsily and convolutedly contrived.

A more promising approach might appear to consist in treating *maṇipadme* as a *bahuvrīhi*, or "exocentric," compound, in which, as in the English expressions "redhead," or "paperback," the characteristics of a person or object can also be used as means of referring to the person or thing itself. *Maṇipadme*, here, could describe a "jewel-lotus" (a "lotus made of jewels") or a "jewel and lotus," in the sense of someone or something who is, in some way, a "jewel-lotus" or a "jewel and lotus." Interpretations of this sort have tended to view the compound as a vocative, directed towards a person who has the attributes of a "jewel and a lotus." This, occasionally, has been understood to be a means of addressing Avalokiteśvara himself.[46] However, that would be to treat *maṇipadme* as a masculine vocative, an extremely heterodox reading.[47] In classical Sanskrit, the *-e* ending denotes the vocative only of nominal stems of all genders ending in *-i* or of feminine stems ending in *-ā*. *Maṇipadme* might, then, be a mode of address to a female person Maṇipadmā, who bears the attributes of a "jewel and lotus" or, even possibly, a "jewel-lotus." Who, then, might that person be?

Maṇipadmā, it is argued, is the name of a female partner of Avalokiteśvara. She might, it seems, be the personification of the six-syllable formula itself, which is, as we have seen, presented as a female deity in the maṇḍala of the *Kāraṇḍavyūha Sūtra*. But two important objections prevent this idea from being particularly compelling. First of all, the attributes of the personified formula in the sūtra are not a jewel and a lotus, but a string of prayer beads (*akṣamālā*) and a lotus (*padmaṃ*).[48] Second, although the comparable Śaivite formula *Namaḥ Śivāya* is also personified as a female deity or *śakti* in the purāṇas, those five syllables include no sense of feminine gender. Despite its embodiment in female form, *Namaḥ Śivāya* remains, semantically, an address to the deity himself in the masculine dative.

A positive identification of Maṇipadmā has never, in fact, been made. The name does not appear among the female bodhisattvas sometimes said to accompany Avalokiteśvara. In the second chapter of the *Mañjuśrīmūlakalpa*, for instance, these are listed as Pāṇḍaravāsinī, Tārā, Bhrukuṭi, Uṣṇīṣarājā, Prajñāpāramitā, together with the female *tathāgatā* Locanā.[49] It is, of course, conceivable that Maṇipadmā might be a covert pseudonym for one such figure, but there seems to be no good reason for why this should be the case.[50] Maṇipadmā, finally, has been understood to be the unseen female counterpart of a manifestation of Avalokiteśvara called Maṇipadma Lokeśvara, who is found, for example, among the one hundred and eight forms of the bodhisattva illustrated in the Macchandar Vahal temple in Kathmandu.[51] In support of this hypothesis,[52] it might be pointed out that the attributes of this form are the same as those of the personified formula in the *Kāraṇḍavyūha*. Maṇipadma is four armed, his two principle hands joined together at the chest, with the other two holding a lotus and a string of prayer beads.

The problem with this account of the original "meaning" of *Oṃ Maṇipadme Hūṃ* is that the conception of the figure of Maṇipadma Lokeśvara, far from being an influence on the *Kāraṇḍavyūha* and the six-syllable formula promoted therein, appears actually to represent a doctrinal development that has been derived from the sūtra. The attributes of Maṇipadma Lokeśvara are identical to another figure in the Macchandar Vahal known as Ṣaḍakṣarī

Lokeśvara, the "six-syllable" lord.[53] In the Indian *Sādhanamāla*, the colophon of one of the four *sādhanas* devoted to the worship of this Ṣaḍakṣarī Lokeśvara explicitly acknowledges a debt to the *Kāraṇḍavyūha*. The practice is described as: *kāraṇḍavyūhāmnāyena racitaṃ sādhanaṃ*, "a *sādhana* produced (*racitaṃ*) from the sacred tradition (*āmnāyena*) of the *Kāraṇḍavyūha*."[54] Similarly, one of the Avalokiteśvara *sādhanas* contained in the Peking *bsTan 'gyur* is called the *"Kāraṇḍa-vyūha-āmnāya-kṛta-ṣaḍakṣarī-sādhana*," the "six-syllable *sādhana* made (*kṛta*) from the sacred tradition of the *Kāraṇḍavyūha*." Here, the form of the bodhisattva is only very slightly different. Four-armed, he holds a rosary in his right hand (*phyag gyas na bgrang 'phreng bsnams pa*) and a lotus and jewel in his left (*phyag gyon na padma dang nor bus rnam par brgyan pa*), while his other two hands are joined together at the heart (*phyag gnyis thal mo sbyar ba / rgyal ba'i dbang po kun gyi phyag thugs kar gnas po'i*).[55]

These *sādhanas*, then, would appear to have extrapolated a single iconographic form of Avalokiteśvara from the figures described in the sūtra's maṇḍala. The Indian version has simply changed the gender of the personified formula. The Tibetan version has either, I suggest, amalgamated the attributes of the personified formula with the defining characteristic of the bodhisattva Mahāmaṇidhara, "the holder of the great jewel," who sits opposite the personified six-syllable in the configuration detailed by the sūtra, or simply assumed, from the first part of the name Maṇipadma, that the *lokeśvara* should be holding a jewel.[56] The appearance of Maṇipadma is, it seems likely, a consequence of the prior appearance of the personified *Oṃ Maṇipadme Hūṃ*. The original formulation of *Oṃ Maṇipadme Hūṃ* could not, in that case, be said to have been dependent on Maṇipadma Lokeśvara. The intrinsic "meaning" of the formula remains unexplained.

The promotion of *Oṃ Maṇipadme Hūṃ* is, we have argued, one of the chief practical concerns of the *Kāraṇḍavyūha*. The doctrinal agenda of the sūtra, moreover, is dominated by the syncretism of the purāṇic *īśvara* idea with the orthodox categories of the Mahāyāna and, in particular, with the goal of birth into the pure land of Sukhāvatī. It seems reasonable, then, to ask whether or not the concise formula of the Buddhist *īśvara* Avalokiteśvara, a phenomenon whose basic six-syllable form represents a simple adaptation of the purāṇic five-syllable formula, might also reflect something of the Mahāyāna Buddhist conceptual scheme in its "meaning." Might not the original "meaning" of *maṇipadme* be illuminated by a reading of the Mahāyāna sūtras?

The image of the lotus is found throughout Indian religion. The Mahāyāna is no exception to this rule and uses the flower in many different ways, so that it eventually becomes a symbol that is immediately redolent of a network of interconnected doctrines. The instances of this application are far, far too numerous to be listed exhaustively, but a brief presentation may convey some of its impact. The lotus is, perhaps most fundamentally, expressive of the idea of purity, due to the way in which the flower emerges pristine from out of even the muddiest and murkiest of waters. In the long *Sukhāvatīvyūha Sūtra*, for instance, those born in the pure land are said to be "like the lotus" (*padmasadṛśāḥ*), because they remain untainted everywhere in the world.[57] In the *Saddharmapuṇḍarīka Sūtra*, the followers of Śākyamuni are said to be "untainted as the lotus (*padumaṃ*) is by water."[58] The buddhas themselves, in the same work, are compared to "a great multitude of lotuses" (*padmarāṣiḥ*).[59] In the *Gaṇḍavyūha Sūtra*, bodhisattvas are said to be "supreme lotuses of humanity" (*paramapuruṣapuṇḍarīkā*).[60]

The lotus is a symbol of spiritual fruition. In the *Gaṇḍavyūha Sūtra*, for instance, the monk Sāgaramegha meditates on the ocean. "While I was engaged in these thoughts," he says, "an enormous lotus (*mahāpadmaṃ*) from the bottom of the ocean appeared before me."[61] "That great lotus (*mahāpadmaṃ*)," he explains, "is born from the transcendental roots of goodness of the enlightened . . . is produced by pure deeds . . ." and so on.[62] Later, it is said of the bodhisattva Sudhana that, "the lotuses of his mind (*cittapauṇḍarīko*) opened like a blooming lotus pond (*kamalākaraḥ*) by the instructions of spriritual benefactors."[63] In the *Saddharmapuṇḍarīka*, the bodhisattva Gadgadasvara plunges into a meditation so deep that there spontaneously appear "eighty-four hundred thousand myriads of *koṭis* of lotuses" (*-padma-*).[64]

The lotus is, also, a prominent feature of the pure lands. Sukhāvatī, we read in the long *Sukhāvatīvyūha Sūtra*, is "carpeted in every direction with lotus flowers (*padmaiḥ*)."[65] Furthermore, "above in the open sky there are . . . lotus ponds scattered with blue water lilies, lotuses, white water lilies, and white lotuses . . . (*nānāratnapadmotapalakumudapuṇḍarīkākīrṇāni*)."[66] These lotuses, moreover, like so many of the features of the pure land are made out of jewels. The carpet of lotus flowers is "made of the seven precious substances" (*saptaratnamayai*).[67] The lotus flowers of the ponds are "all made of many kind of jewels" (*nānāratnapadma-*).[68] Similarly, the lotus flower seen by Sāgaramegha is said to be "adorned with a million pure jewels (*-maṇiratna*) in orderly arrays, containing a million radiant jewels (*-maṇiratna-*), blazing with the great splendor of a million dazzling jewels (*-maṇiratna-*), shining endlessly with a million jewels (*-maṇiratna-*) from various sources, adorned with a million jewels (*-maṇiratna-*) symbolic of earth arrayed all around . . . blazing with the light of an endless array of a million wish-fulfilling jewels (*-cintārājamaṇiratna*)."[69] The dazzling and irradiant "jewel-lotus" is, in short, a standard feature of the Mahāyāna vision.

In this vision, buddhas and bodhisattva are often to be seen seated upon these flowers. As Sāgaramegha says: "Also I saw an embodiment of buddha clearly manifest sitting cross-legged on that great lotus (*mahāpadmaṃ . . . paryaṅkaparisphuṭaṃ*)."[70] Elsewhere in the *Gaṇḍavyūha*, Sudhana sees the bodhisattva king Anala sitting on a throne "in a lotus calyx made of magic gems" (*vaśirājamaṇiratnamayapadmagarbhe*).[71] King Mahāprabha appears upon a *Dharma*-throne "in the shape of the calyx of a lotus made of wish-fulfilling gems" (*cintārājamaṇiratnapadmagarbhe mahādharmāsane*).[72] Sudhana himself is said to have "sat on a lotus seat of jewels" (*sarvaratnagarbhapadmāsananiṣaṇṇaḥ*) at the end of the sūtra.[73] He then sees the bodhisattva Samantabhadra sitting "on a lion seat in the calyx of a great jewel lotus" (*mahāratna padmagarbhe siṃhāsane*),[74] and later on, seated "on a jewel lotus calyx lion seat" (*mahāratnapadmagarbhasiṃhāsane*).[75] In the *Saddharmapuṇḍarīka*, the bodhisattva Mañjuśrī is seen seated "on a centifolious lotus" (*sahasrapatre padme*) that is as large as a carriage yoked with four horses.[76] When Mañjuśrī speaks, thousands of lotuses spontaneously rise from the bottom of the sea. "On those lotuses (*teṣu ca padmeṣu*)," we read, "were seated many thousands of bodhisattvas . . ."[77]

The lotus is also generative. Spontaneous birth from a lotus is a mark, once again, of great purity. In the *Gaṇḍavyūha*, for instance, a beautiful courtesan is said to be "born from a lotus" (*padmodbhaveyaṃ*), her body "undefiled like a lotus" (*nirmalapadmagarbhaḥ*).[78] The king of a prosperous and peaceful city is said to be spontaneously born "in the calyx of a lotus" (*padmagarbhe*).[79] Sudhana sees the bodhisattva Maitreya "being born in a lotus calyx (*padmagarbhagataṃ*)."[80] In the carpet of lotus flowers described in the longer *Sukhāvatīvyūha Sūtra*, it is said that "from each jewel lotus (*ratnapadmāt*) issue in every direction thirty-six million rays of light. And from the tip of each of these rays emerge thirty-six hundred thousand million buddhas . . ."[81]

All these different connotations may be said to inform what is perhaps the most central usage of the symbol of the lotus in the Mahāyāna, the doctrine that the mode of entry into the pure lands of the buddhas is to appear seated in such a flower. In the *Vimalakīrtinirdeśa Sūtra*, for instance, when Śakyamuni transforms this world into a buddhafield by touching the ground with his big toe, everyone in his assembly is said to be filled with wonder, "each perceiving himself seated on a throne of jewelled lotuses (*ratnapadmavyūhāsana*)."[82] The *Saddharmapuṇḍarīka* states: "And in the buddhafield where he is to be born, he shall appear by metamorphosis on a lotus of seven precious substances (*saptaratnamaye padme*), face-to-face with the *tathāgata*."[83]

This is the mode of entry into Sukhāvatī. A woman who hears the chapter from the *Saddharmapuṇḍarīka Sūtra* on the bodhisattva Bhaiṣajyarāja is said to be reborn (as a man) in Sukhāvatī in front of the Buddha Amitāyus. We read: "There will he (who was formerly a female) appear seated on a throne consisting of the interior of a lotus (*padmagarbhe*) . . ."[84] The vow made by the bodhisattva Samantabhadra at the end of the *Gaṇḍavyūha*, includes the aspiration to be appear before Amitāyus. "Let me abide in the circle of that buddha," he says, "born in a beautiful lotus (*padmavare*)."[85] In the longer *Sukhāvatīvyūha Sūtra,* some human beings in Sukhāvatī "dwell inside the closed calyxes of immense lotus flowers (*padmeṣu*)," while some "appear sitting cross-legged on the lotus flowers (*padmeṣu*)." The former, it is explained, have planted the roots of merit to be born in the pure land but still entertain doubts, while the latter have also planted these roots but are entirely free of such a handicap.[86]

The symbol of the lotus continues to appear throughout the *Kāraṇḍavyūha Sūtra.* Avalokiteśvara himself is repeatedly described in terms of his "lotus" qualities. Yama greets the bodhisattva with the title *padmaśriye,* "the one who has the auspiciousness of the lotus."[87] Bali calls him *śubhapadmahasta,* "the one who holds the beautiful lotus," and *padmaśriyālaṃkṛtaśuddhakāya,* "the one whose beautiful body is adorned with the auspiciousness of the lotus."[88] The *dharmabhāṇaka* also sees (*paśyati*) the bodhisattva as *śubhapadmahastaṃ* and *padmaśriyālaṃkṛtaṃ.*[89] Maheśvara praises (*namo*) him as *padmaśriye, śubhapadmahastāya, padmadharāya,* "the one who holds a lotus," *padmāsanāya,* "the one who is seated on a lotus," and *padmapriyāya,* "the one who is beloved of the lotus,"[90] while Umādevī uses the expression, "the one who has the auspiciousness of a beautiful lotus" to call upon the bodhisattva.[91]

The lotus is a common feature of the worlds contained within the pores of Avalokiteśvara and in the realms that are purified by the bodhisattva's presence. There are said to be "lotus pools" (*puṣkariṇya*) in each of the Kṛṣṇa, Amṛtabindu and Vajramukha pores.[92] When, for instance, the light rays coming from Avalokiteśvara in the Avīci hell transform the Jetavana *vihāra,* "hundreds of thousand of lotus ponds" (*puṣkarinīśatasahasrāṇi*) are said to manifest.[93] In the Avīci hell itself, the bodhisattva's power leads to the appearance of a "lotus pool" (*puṣkariṇī*) in the middle of the infernal cooking stove, together with "lotuses" (*padmāni*) the size of chariot wheels.[94] When Avalokiteśvara arrives before Śākyamuni in the first part of the sūtra, a "rain of lotuses" (*padmavarṣaḥ*) falls.[95] Then, as at the end of the sūtra, he presents the buddha with "lotuses" (*padmāni*) originally given to the bodhisattva by Amitābha.[96]

Finally, on two separate occasions, the *Kāraṇḍavyūha* describes the goal of reaching Sukhāvatī in terms of being born or being seated "in a lotus." Those who bring to mind the name (*nāmadheyamanusmaranti*) of Avalokiteśvara are, at one point, said to go to Amitābha's pure land.[97] There, they are said not to remember the suffering of dwelling in the womb (*garbhāvāsaduḥkham*), for they are born "in that lotus" (*tasminneva padme jāyante*).[98] Next, Bali is told by Avalokiteśvara that he will go to Sukhāvatī, where, a "lotus throne made of the seven jewels" (*saptaratnamayaṃ padmāsanaṃ*) will be produced for him. Then, seating himself "in the jewel-lotus" (*ratnapadme*) in the presence of Amitābha, he will listen to the *Kāraṇḍavyūha Sūtra*.[99]

The cumulative effect of all these examples is to show that the significance of the four middle syllables of the six-syllable *mahāvidyā* would have been quite obvious to anyone remotely familiar with the idiom of the Mahāyāna. The use of *maṇipadme* connects the *paramahṛdaya* of Avalokiteśvara with one of the central symbols of the Mahāyāna vision, the "jewel-lotus," or "lotus made of jewels." The expression should be parsed as a *tatpuruṣa*, or "determinative," compound in the (masculine or neuter) locative case, meaning "in the jewel-lotus," referring to the manner in which buddhas and bodhisattvas are said to be seated in these marvelous blooms and, in particular, to the manner in which more mundane beings are believed to appear in the pure land of the buddhas. Given the predominance, in the *Kāraṇḍavyūha* and in the Mahāyāna in general, of the religious goal of the pure land of Amitābha, it may be safely assumed that *maṇipadme* would have been quite naturally associated with the mode of the rebirth of human beings there. The recitation of *Oṃ Maṇipadme Hūṃ*, then, the bringing to mind of the name of the Buddhist *īśvara*, includes a declaration of the manner in which a person is reborn in Sukhāvatī: "in the jewel lotus." The doctrinal syncretism that is set out, in large, in the *Kāraṇḍavyūha* as a whole, is also apparent, in minutia, in the sūtra's six-syllable formula.

There is, as we have seen, considerable precedent in the Mahāyāna sūtras for the use of *padma* and the locative *-e* ending to convey this particular sense (not to mention the plural locative ending *-eṣu*). The use of the simple prefix *maṇi-*, however, is comparitively rare. Indeed, the alternative word for "jewel," *ratna-*, is much more frequently found in this context. Nonetheless, *maṇiratna-* is common. The conjunction of *maṇi-* and *-padma* is also found occasionally. The *Gaṇḍavyūha Sūtra*, for instance, describes one "lion throne in the calyx of a lotus of radiant jewels" as *vairocanamaṇipadmagarbhasiṃhāsanaṃ*.[100] In the end, though, when the formula was originally "fashioned," the syllables *maṇipadme*, rather than, say, *ratnapadme*, were probably preferred due to the quality of their sound. *Oṃ-* flows more easily into the syllable *-Ma-* than it would do into the syllable *-Ra-*. The enunciation of "*maṇi*" is more discreet and compact than the mouthy "*ratna*."

For the sake of completeness, a few remarks should be made about the two surrounding syllables of the formula, *Oṃ-* and *-Hūṃ*. Neither, of course, has any intrinsic semantic meaning. Both are laden, however, with symbolic import. The Dalai Lama, for instance, presents *Oṃ* as made up of the three letters *A, U* and *M,* signifying both the impure body, speech, and mind of the practitioner and the pure, exalted body, speech, and mind of buddhahood. *Hūṃ*, the seed syllable of the Buddha Akṣobhya, "the immovable one," is said to indicate indivisibility. *Maṇi* and *Padme*, meanwhile, are said to symbolise the factors of method and wisdom. "Thus," the Dalai Lama explains, "the six syllables *oṃ maṇi padme hūṃ* mean that in dependence on the practice of a path which is an indivisible union of method and wisdom, you can transform your impure body, speech, and mind into the pure exalted body, speech, and mind of a buddha."[101]

It seems worth suggesting, however, that *Oṃ* and *Hūṃ* may also have a more direct significance. For it cannot be wholly unlikely that the frequent use of these two syllables to begin and end different mantras was originally derived from the same use that is made of the two similar syllables *A-* and *-Haṃ*. *A* is the first letter of the Sanskrit alphabet and *Ha* the last, encompassing all the other letters in between. *A-* and *-Haṃ* together also make up the word *ahaṃ*, meaning "I." The use of those two syllables at either end of a mantra, then, conveys a sense of both the identity and the all-inclusive nature of the mind engaged in mantric utterance. According, for instance, to the eleventh-century Kashmiri Śaivite master Kṣemarāja, *Ahaṃ*, "is the supreme level of speech, the great unspoken Mantra which, eternally manifest, is the life of all beings . . . it is called the vibration of the Lord because it unfolds pulsating within one's own being as does the movement of this divine universe."[102] "Mantras that did not begin with *a* and end with *m*," he writes, "would be (as useless) as autumn clouds."[103] *Oṃ* and *Hūṃ* are only slightly modified versions of *A* and *Haṃ* (the same Sanskrit characters are used with different marks above and below the letters) and may, once again, be preferred for their sound. *Oṃ Maṇipadme Hūṃ*, on this account, might be read as a declaration of, or aspiration for, the manifestation of the "I (*Oṃ . . . Hūṃ*) in the jewel-lotus (*Maṇipadme*)."

In conclusion, it would be churlish to insist that such presentations of *maṇipadme* as the "jewel in the lotus," or as a vocative to "the one with the jewel and the lotus" are nonsensical, even though, strictly speaking, they are semantically incorrect. Like the various correspondence schemes, the "meaning" of *Oṃ Maṇipadme Hūṃ* is merely an explication of the function of the formula. In so far as these other "meanings" are appropriate to a proper appreciation of this function and assist in "the turning of the twelvefold wheel of *Dharma*," they make sense. Nevertheless, the discovery of what would seem to be the original "meaning" of the formula does beg the question of why it has been interpreted so differently throughout the ages. Already, for instance, in a ninth-century Tibetan grammatical treatise, *Oṃ Maṇipadme Hūṃ* is treated as an example of the Sanskrit vocative.[104]

Two reasons present themselves. The first is that the conception of the formula as a name of Avalokiteśvara and the personification of the formula in female form would both tend to relate *Oṃ Maṇipadme Hūṃ* to the idea of calling upon a person, making the vocative interpretation an immediately attractive option from a very early stage. The second is that the Tibetans, the custodians of the formula for the last millennium, would be unlikely to be aware of the connection of *Oṃ Maṇipadme Hūṃ* with the idiom of the Mahāyāna sūtras, due to the fact that these works would generally be read in Tibetan translation. *Padme* becomes *pad ma'i nang du* in Tibetan, which provokes no immediate association with *Oṃ Maṇipadme Hūṃ*.[105]

Notwithstanding all these difficulties, the original "meaning" of *Oṃ Maṇipadme Hūṃ* does seem to have been kept alive in Tibetan minds despite, though not because of, any analysis of the "meaning" of the formula. Instead, recitation of the six syllables has remained linked, in the collective consciousness, to the idea of rebirth in Sukhāvatī due to an appreciation of the close relationship between Avalokiteśvara and Amitābha. The indignation with which the French explorer and early Tibetologist Alexandra David-Neel berates the Tibetan people on this point is, in retrospect, ironic. She writes:

> Passing to the following words of the formula, *mani padme* means "the jewel in the lotus." Here we seem to find a meaning that is immediately intelligible, and yet the usual Tibetan interpretation takes no account whatsoever of this literal meaning, the majority of devotees being completely ignorant of it. The latter believes that the mechanical repetition of *Aum mani padme hum*! secures for them a happy birth in *Nub dewa chen*: the Occidental paradise of bliss.[106]

CONCLUSION

The Original Six-Syllable Formula?

In historical terms, the six-syllable formula *Oṃ Maṇipadme Hūṃ*, we have argued, represents a Buddhist adaptation of the five-syllable Śaivite formula *Namaḥ Śivāya*. The practice of worshipping Avalokiteśvara, the Buddhist *īśvara*, by means of a concise *hṛdaya* mantra was, it seems likely, first developed in lay Buddhist circles, centred around the archetype of the *vidyādhara* or *mahāsiddha*, the persona of the *dharmabhāṇaka* who grants initiation into the use of *Oṃ Maṇipadme Hūṃ* in the *Kāraṇḍavyūha Sūtra*. In its concluding chapter on monastic discipline, the sūtra reflects the uneasy meeting of these lay practitioners with the monks of the Mahāyāna establishment. The sūtra, more generally, describes the absorption of the doctrine of the *īśvara* and his formula into the conceptual framework of the Mahāyāna sūtras. The actual form and "meaning" of the formula, it has been shown, actually reflects this process of religious syncretism.

There are two stages of doctrinal development going on here. The first, that took place prior to the writing of the *Kāraṇḍavyūha*, involves the original development of the idea of the Buddhist *īśvara* and the formula. The second, encapsulated by the sūtra, involves the merging of this idea with the categories of orthodox Mahāyāna doctrine and, in particular, with the goal of rebirth in Sukhāvatī. However, if the form and "meaning" of *Oṃ Maṇipadme Hūṃ* are informed by the processes of this secondary stage of doctrinal development, it seems quite possible, indeed highly likely, that the six-syllable formula of Avalokiteśvara took a completely different form during the first stage. The earlier form, then, would probably have been "well-fashioned" without any consideration of the goal of rebirth in Sukhāvatī. What, then, might this formula have been?

I can only give a provisional answer to this question. A satisfactory response would require the further study of material connected to Avalokiteśvara, especially, it would seem, material found in the tantras. However, one possibility does present itself. The thousand-armed bodhisattva, the form that displays the characteristics of the purāṇic *īśvara*, is also described in the *Taizokai* maṇḍala of the Japanese Shingon Buddhist tradition, based on another Mahāyāna work, the *Vairocana Sūtra*, a text itself first translated into Chinese by Subhakarasiṃha in 724 C.E. This maṇḍala has been commented on at length by Beatrice Lane Suzuki.[1] There, the formula of the thousand-armed Avalokiteśvara is listed as *Oṃ Vajradharma Hrīḥ*.[2]

APPENDIX

Annotated Précis of the *Kāraṇḍavyūha Sūtra*

The edition of the *Kāraṇḍavyūha Sūtra*, in the collection of Mahāyāna sūtras edited by P. L. Vaidya and published in 1961 by the Mithila Institute of Darbhanga, India, begins with the entry of its fuller title, *Avalokiteśvara-guṇakāraṇḍavyūhaḥ*, and then by praise to the Three Jewels and to Avalokiteśvara, "the great compassionate one" (*āryāvalokiteśvarāya bodhisattvāya mahāsattvāya mahākāruṇikāya*). There then follows the heading of the first chapter:[1]

PART ONE (*PRATHAMO NIRVYŪHAH*)

Chapter One (*prathamaṃ prakaraṇam*): The Description of the Assembly in the *Vihāra* at the Jetavana Grove

The sūtra begins, in typical fashion, with the words usually translated as "thus I have heard" (*evaṃ mayā śrūtam*), launching straight into a description of the assembly in the Jetavana grove. Śākyamuni is said to be dwelling at Śrāvasti, in the *vihāra* at the Jetavana grove of the merchant Anathapiṇḍada, surrounded by an assembly of one thousand three hundred monks and many bodhisattvas.[2]

The names of the first of these bodhisattvas are listed, in order, as: Vajrapāṇi, Jñānadarśana, Vajrasena, Guhagupta, Ākāśagarbha, Sūryagarbha, Anikṣiptadhura, Ratnapāṇi, Samantabhadra, Mahāsthāmaprāpta, Sarvanīvaraṇaviṣkambhin, Sarvaśūra, Bhauṣajyasena, Avalokiteśvara, Vajramati, Sāgaramati, Dharmadhara, Pṛthivīvaralocana, Āśvāsahasta, and Maitreya.[3]

There is also said to be a group of thirty-two gods, led by Maheśvara and Nārāyaṇa, then by Śakra, the chief of the gods (*devānāmindro*), Brahmā Sahāmpati, and then by Candra, Āditya, Vāyu, Varuṇa, and others. There are also gathered many hundreds of thousands of semidivine beings: *nāga* kings, *gandharva* kings, *kinnara* kings, *nāga* daughters, *gandharva* daughters, and *kinnara* daughters, some of whom are named. There are also many hundreds of thousands of unnamed male and female lay followers, together with wandering mendicants and hermits.[4]

Then, light rays come out of the Avīci hell and arrive in the Jetavana grove. All the beautiful features of the *vihāra* are seen (*dṛśyante*). There are pillars adorned with precious jewels, upper apartments covered in gold, doors and staircases of silver and gold, silver terraces with gold pillars studded with jewels and gold terraces with silver pillars studded with jewels. In the garden, there are various sorts of wish-fulfilling trees whose gold branches bear silver leaves, religious and nonreligious garments, food and many different kinds of jewelery. In this beautiful light, hundreds of thousands of wish-fulfilling trees manifest. There are staircases made of *vajra* and inner doors adorned with pearls. Many hundreds of thousands of lotus ponds (*puṣkariṇīśatasahasrāṇi*) manifest, some of which are full of the water endowed with the eight qualities,[5] and some with a variety of different sorts of lotuses (*utpalapadma-*) and other flowers.[6]

Chapter Two: The Destruction of Hell

The bodhisattva Sarvanīvaraṇaviṣkambhin asks where these rays of light are coming from and which *tathāgata* is responsible for them. The Lord replies that it is not a *tathāgata,* but the bodhisattva Avalokiteśvara who, saving beings in hell and proceeding to the *preta* realm, produces these rays.[7]

Sarvanīvaraṇaviṣkambhin then asks how it is possible for Avalokiteśvara to enter Avīci, describing many of the horrible aspects of the hell.[8] The Lord replies that Avalokiteśvara enters hell in the same way that a *cakravartin* king enters a garden made of different kinds of jewels (*divyaratnamayodyāne*). The bodhisattva's body is not harmed in any way. The fires of hell are extinguished as he approaches. The henchmen of Yama, the Lord of Death, become agitated and extremely frightened, asking who it is that has produced such inauspicious signs in Avīci. When Avalokiteśvara enters hell, lotuses (*padmāni*) the size of chariot wheels appear, the infernal cooking vessel is burst open and a lotus pool (*puṣkariṇī*) appears in the middle of the infernal stove.[9]

These events are relayed to Yama by his henchmen, whose report begins with the explanation that these signs took place when a being, assuming the appearance (*kāmarūpī*)[10] of a man (*puruṣaḥ*), with a head of twisted locks of hair (*jaṭāmukuṭadharo*), with a body adorned with divine ornaments (*divyālaṃkārabhūṣitaśarīraḥ*), with a mind of the utmost friendliness (*paramamaitramānasaḥ*) and like a golden orb (*suvarṇabimbamiva*) was seen (*dṛśyate*).[11]

Yama asks himself which god this could be a manifestation of: Maheśvara, Nārāyaṇa,[12] one of the other gods, or the great *rākṣasa* Rāvaṇa?[13] Looking with his divine eye, he sees a host of gods, but asks himself which of these it could be. Then, looking again around hell, he sees the great bodhisattva Avalokiteśvara.[14]

Yama then prostrates himself before Avalokiteśvara and delivers a long hymn of praise, consisting of greetings (*namo*) to fifty-nine different titles of the bodhisattva, beginning with Avalokiteśvara, Maheśvara and "to the one who has the auspiciousness of the lotus" (*padmaśriye*).[15]

Completing these praises, Yama makes three circumambulations and is gone.[16]

Chapter Three: The Liberation of the Ghost Realm

Sarvanīvaraṇaviṣkambhin then asks when Avalokiteśvara will arrive. The Lord replies that, after leaving Avīci, the great bodhisattva enters the city of the *pretas*, where the hideously deformed and suffering *pretas* call upon him. When Avalokiteśvara appears, the realm begins to cool down, Indra's thunderbolts cease to rain down and the doorkeeper, much to his own surprise, adopts a mind of incessant friendliness.[17]

Seeing this hoard of beings, Avalokiteśvara generates a mind of great compassion (*mahākaruṇācittamutpādya*). Rivers of water flow out from his ten fingers, his ten toes, and from the pores of his skin. When the *pretas* drink this water, their throats are widened, their bodies are completely restored, and their hunger is satiated. They then turn their thoughts to human beings, commenting, at some length, on how happy are they who live in Jambudvīpa. Sixteen examples are given, beginning with the happiness of those who enjoy cool shade, of those who always honor their mother and father and of those who always maintain links with a spiritual friend (*kalyāṇamitraṃ*).[18]

From among the *pretas* there then comes forth the sound of the precious king of Mahāyāna Sūtras, the *Kāraṇḍavyūha Sūtra*, whereupon all the *pretas* are established in the realm of Sukhāvatī as bodhisattvas. Thereupon, Avalokiteśvara leaves the city of the *pretas*.[19]

Chapter Four: The Birth of the Moon and so forth

Sarvanīvaraṇaviṣkambhin then asks whether Avalokiteśvara will be arriving today. The Lord replies that the bodhisattva has to bring trillions of creatures to maturity (*paripācayati*), that every day he brings beings to maturity and that there is not an illumination (*pratibhānaṃ*), even of the *tathāgatas*, that is comparable to that of the bodhisattva Avalokiteśvara.[20]

Śākyamuni explains that, in a previous life, he (Śākyamuni) was called "Sugandamukha", the son of a merchant, and heard of the qualities of Avalokiteśvara from the *tathāgata* Vipaśyin.[21]

The sun and moon are born from his eyes, Maheśvara from his brow, Brahmā from his shoulders, Nārāyaṇa from his heart, Sarasvatī from his teeth, the winds from his mouth, the earth from his feet and Varuṇa from his stomach.

Once these gods (*devā*) have been born from the body of Avalokiteśvara, the bodhisattva tells Maheśvara that, during the *kaliyuga*, he (Maheśvara) will appear in a degenerate realm (*kaṣṭasattvadhātusam*) and will be called the primordial god (*ādideva*), the creator and author (*sraṣṭāraṃ kartāram*) of the world. The beings in this realm at that time will be deprived of the path to awakening (*bodhimārgeṇa*) and the talk among those common people (*īdṛśapṛthagjaneṣu sattveṣu sāṃkathyaṃ*) will be: "It is said that space is his *liṅga* and the earth his pedestal. He is the ground of all (*ālayaḥ sarvabhūtānāṃ*) and is called *liṅga* because all beings dissolve into him."[22]

Subsequently, Śākyamuni reveals that, in a previous life as the bodhisattva Dānaśūra, he heard of the qualities of Avalokiteśvara from the *tathāgata* Śikhin.[23]

Chapter Five: The Emergence of Various Light Rays

Sarvanīvaraṇaviṣkambhin then asks about this teaching given by Śikhin. Śākyamuni explains that the *tathāgata* gave the teaching in the middle of an assembly of *nāgas, yakṣas, gandharvas, rākṣasas, asuras, marutas, garuḍas, kinnaras, mahoragas,* and men. From the mouth of the *tathāgata* emerged various light rays of different colors: blue, yellow, red, white, dark red, crystal, silver, and gold. Then, having gone to all the worlds contained within the ten cardinal and intermediate points of space, and having made three circumambulations of the *tathāgata*, these light rays re-entered the mouth of the *tathāgata* Śikhin.[24]

This concludes the first section (*kāṇḍaḥ*) known as the conversation with Sarvanīvaraṇaviṣkambhin.[25]

Chapter Six: The Conversation with the *Tathāgata*

Next, from among this assembly, the bodhisattva Ratnapāṇi asks Śikhin the reason for this. The *tathāgata* replies that he displayed this phenomenon because Avalokiteśvara was coming from the realm of Sukhāvatī.[26]

He continues to explain that when Avalokiteśvara arrives, various wish-fulfilling trees, mango trees, fragrant oleander flowers, and *campaka* trees appear, together with lotus pools (*puṣkariṇyaḥ*) abundant with flowers and hundreds of wondrous jewel trees. Flowers, jewels, various marvelous mango trees, and divine garments fall like rain. Near the *vihāra*, the seven jewels appear (*hastiratnaṃ, maṇiratnaṃ, aśvaratnaṃ, strīratnaṃ, gṛhapatiratnaṃ, pariṇāyakaratnaṃ*). The ground is seen (*saṃdṛśyate*) to be bright gold. When Avalokiteśvara leaves Sukhāvatī, the whole of creation trembles in six ways.[27]

Questioned again by Ratnapāṇi, Śikhin says that this heralds the arrival of Avalokiteśvara. When the great bodhisattva walks, a beautiful rain of lotuses (*padmavarṣaḥ*) falls. Holding brilliant, shining lotuses (*padmāni . . . gṛhītvā*), with golden stems and a thousand petals, he approaches the Lord, prostrates, offers him the flowers and says that they are sent by the *tathāgata* Amitābha, who wishes him freedom from disease, bodily ease, and happiness. Śikhin, having taken the flowers and placing them on his left, puts to the test the qualities of Avalokiteśvara. He asks what he has achieved in the hell and *preta* realms, reeling off a number of hells by their respective names. Avalokiteśvara replies that he has brought the beings in these realms to maturity and that they will all be established in complete and perfect enlightenment. But, as long as Śikhin had not come to full enlightenment, then the beings from the ten directions and all times could not be established in that exceptional *nirvāṇa*.[28]

Thereupon, having given the assembly food for thought, Avalokiteśvara prostrates himself before the Lord and vanishes into space in a ball of blazing fire.[29]

Chapter Seven: Concerning the Heaps of Merit of Avalokiteśvara

The bodhisattva Ratnapāṇi then asks about the mass of merit (*puṇya*) of Avalokiteśvara. The Lord begins by saying that the amount of merit accrued by making the customary offerings (medicine, incense, perfumes, ointments, robes, parasols, flags, bells, beds, seats, and so on) to as many *tathāgatas* as there are grains of sand in the Ganges is only equal to the merit contained in a hair's breadth (*avālāgre*) of Avalokiteśvara.[30] For instance, even though it would be possible to count each drop of rain in a downpour over the four great islands which lasted, day and night, for all twelve months of a year, and even though it would be possible to count each drop of water in the oceans, and even though it would be possible to count each hair on all the quadruped animals on the four islands, nonetheless, it would be impossible for the *tathāgata* to calculate the amount of merit accrued by Avalokiteśvara.[31] Similarly, even though the merit could be calculated if a son or daughter of good family made, and worshipped daily, enormous *stūpas* for as many buddhas as there are atoms, and even though the number of leaves in a forest could be counted, it would be impossible for the *tathāgata* to calculate the amount of merit accrued by Avalokiteśvara. The amount of merit accrued by all the men and women and sons and daughters in the four great islands, whether they be "stream-enterers," "once-returners," "non-returners," *arhats* or *pratyekabuddhas*, is less than the merit contained in the tip of a hair of Avalokiteśvara.[32]

Chapter Eight: The *Dharma*-Teaching on Conversion to the True Way

The bodhisattva Ratnapāṇi then says that all this is inconceivable and that he has never seen or heard of such a heap of merit belonging to the *tathāgatas*, let alone to a bodhisattva, as the heap of merit belonging to the bodhisattva Avalokiteśvara. Śikhin replies that were there as many buddhas like himself as there are grains of sand in the Ganges, all honored with the customary offerings, all of them would not be able to calculate the amount of merit of Avalokiteśvara. Formerly, he continues, he had coursed in this realm and had asked how it was possible to speak of such an amount of merit. In answer to this question, all the *tathāgatas* in the ten directions of space had replied in the following way.[33]

Happy are those beings in this world (*loke*), they said, who hold in their minds the name of Avalokiteśvara (*nāmadheyamanusmaranti*). They are liberated from the anguish and suffering of old age, death, disease, grief, and lamentation, they do not experience the sufferings of *saṃsāra* and, dressed in brilliant white, like swans flying as fast as the wind, go to the realm of Sukhāvatī in order, happily, to hear the *Dharma* from the *tathāgata* Amitābha. Hearing the *Dharma*, they are not troubled by the physical sufferings of *saṃsāra*, nor by greed, hatred and delusion, nor by old age and death, nor by hunger and thirst. Nor do they remember the suffering of dwelling in the womb, for they are born in "that particular lotus" (*tasminneva padme jāyante*).[34] They remain settled in this realm, their minds permeated by the essence of *Dharma*, until Avalokiteśvara's promise is fulfilled: that all beings should be liberated from all suffering and reach complete awakening.[35]

Ratnapāṇi then asks when this promise will be fulfilled. The *tathāgata* answers that, for many reasons, beings transmigrate in *saṃsāra*, but that the god (Avalokiteśvara?) brings beings to maturity (*devatā sattvān paripācayati*) and establishes them on the path to awakening. Taking whatever form is suitable to accomplish the conversion of beings (*vaineyāḥ sattvāḥ*), he teaches the *Dharma* (*dharmaṃ deśayati*). So, for instance, for those for whom the form of a *tathāgata* is suitable, he teaches the *Dharma* as a *tathāgata* (*tathāgatarūpeṇa*). On the same principle, he also takes the form of a *pratyekabuddha*, of an *arhat*, of a bodhisattva, of Maheśvara, of Nārāyaṇa, of Brahmā, of Indra, of Āditya, of Candra, of Agni, of Varuṇa, of Vāyu, of a *nāga*, of Vighnapati, of a *yakṣa*, of Vaiṣravaṇa,[36] of a king, of a king's soldier (*rājabhaṭa*), and of a mother or of a father. In whatever form is suitable, he teaches the *Dharma*. Thus, Avalokiteśvara teaches the *Dharma* to beings, matures them and establishes them in *nirvāṇa* (*nirvāṇabhūmi*).[37]

Chapter Nine: The Reviving of the *Asuras*

Ratnapāṇi then expresses his astonishment, saying that such power as Avalokiteśvara's has never been seen or heard of before. Nor, he says, is it found among the *tathāgatas*.[38]

The *tathāgata* replies. In Jambudvīpa, there is a cave called "Vajrakukṣi," the domain of countless *asuras*, where Avalokiteśvara teaches the *Dharma* in the form of an *asura*. He teaches the *Kāraṇḍavyūha Sūtra*, with the effect that the *asuras* develop minds of friendliness, peace, pity and happiness in the presence of beings (*maitracittāḥ śāntacittāḥ dayācittāḥ sattvānāmantike hitasukhacittā*).[39]

The *asuras*, then, turn with happiness towards the *Kāraṇḍavyūha Sūtra*, which is like a wish-fulfilling jewel. They listen to it, develop faith towards it, understand it, write it, have it written, memorize it, recite it, worship it, reflect on it, explain it in full to others, meditate on it and bow to it with great joy, respect and devotion. They destroy the five acts of immediate retribution (*pañcānantaryāṇi karmāṇi*),[40] honor it with purified bodies and recall their previous lives (*jātismarā*). At the time of death, Ratnapāṇi is told, the dying person is taken to the other side (*upasaṃkramiṣyanti*) by twelve *tathāgatas* and is revived by all the *tathāgatas*. He is told not to be afraid, for those who have heard the *Kāraṇḍavyūha Sūtra* will go to Sukhāvatī, where a highly decorated canopy and throne awaits them (*vivitraṃ ca te chatraṃ simhāsanaṃ sajjīkṛtam*).[41] This is how Avalokiteśvara shows the *asuras* the path to *nirvāṇa*, for the sake of quelling their evil minds and establishing them on the path to supreme *nirvāṇa*. Ratnapāṇi prostrates.[42]

Chapter Ten: The Approach to the Level "Made of Gold" and so forth

Sarvanīvaraṇaviṣkambhin says that it is extremely difficult (*atidurlabhaṃ*) to hear of the qualities and actions of Avalokiteśvara. The Lord then tells him how, in one of his previous lives, as a *ṛṣi* by the name of Kṣāntivādin, living in a mountain cave away from the world of men, he heard of the qualities and activites of Avalokiteśvara from the *tathāgata* Viśvabhū. There is a level called "Kāñcanamayī," where Avalokiteśvara teaches the *Dharma* to downcast beings. He teaches the noble eightfold path to *nirvāṇa*. Then, leaving that place, he enters the level made of silver (*rūpyamayyāṃ*), where he sees four-legged beings with the personalities of men (*catuṣpādikāni sattvāni puruṣapudgalāni*) and teaches the *Dharma* to them.[43]

Then, all these men stand before Avalokiteśvara and say: "Recover your breath and be a guide to the blind, a protector to those without protection, a shelter to those without shelter, a last resort, a mother and a father, a lamp to those whose path is lost and to those in darkness. Be benevolent and, out of compassion, show the path to liberation. Happy are they who constantly bring to mind and extol your name (*nāmamanusmaranti, udīrayanti ca*). And just as they may be spared the most violent suffering, so also may we."[44]

Avalokiteśvara puts into their ears the *Kāraṇḍavyūha Sūtra*, which they subsequently put into the ears of one another. They are then established at the irreversible level, utterly happy and perfected.

Then, his heart full of great compassion (*mahākaruṇāsampīḍitahṛdayo*), Avalokiteśvara leaves the level made of silver and enters the level made of iron, where Bali, the chief (*indra*) of the *asuras*, is bound. In the vicinity of Bali he changes form, so that, resplendent, like a golden orb (*suvarṇabimbamiva*)[46] and sending out multicolored light rays, he is seen by the chief of the *asuras* from some distance away.[47]

Chapter Eleven: The Consolation of Bali

Seeing Avalokiteśvara from afar, Bali (with his retinue of *asuras*, and hunchbacks, dwarves, and so on) throws himself at the feet of the bodhisattva and sings of his joy in four stanzas of verse.[48] Then, having offered Avalokiteśvara a bejeweled throne (*ratnapīṭhakaṃ*)[49] and having prostrated himself once again, he beseeches the bodhisattva's protection and help, both for himself and all other beings, using a variety of standard expressions.[50]

Avalokiteśvara replies that those who give rise to nonviolent thoughts towards beings, who regularly fill the alms bowls of those belonging to the order of the *tathāgatas* (*tathāgataśāsane piṇḍapātramanuprayacchanti*) and who are never overwhelmed by sloth; who write and have written the *Kāraṇḍavyūha Sūtra*, remember its name and listen to *Dharma*-teachings from it; who offer alms to a bodhisattva just once, or to the reciters of this discourse on *Dharma*, its guardians, chanters, scribes, and listeners; who offer a meal on just one day to a *tathāgata* for the sake of this discourse on *Dharma*, will all attain the realm of *cakravartin* kings. They will never experience the suffering of hunger and thirst, of the bondage of hell, and of being separated from loved ones. They will be released from all suffering and will go to Sukhāvatī, where, before Amitābha, they will listen to the *Dharma* and obtain a prediction of their future enlightenment (*vyākaraṇamanuprāpsyanti*).[51]

Avalokiteśvara tells Bali to hear him speak about the fruit of giving (*śrūyatāṃ dānapalam*) and says he will describe the amount of merit derived from filling the alms bowl of a *tathāgata*. It is, in fact, incalculable, a fact which is emphasized, at some length, by a number of impressive comparisons and examples.[52]

Expressing his delight in this teaching, a tearful and sobbing Bali speaks. What deed has he done, what offering has he given (*karma kṛtaṃ dānaṃ dattam*), he asks rhetorically, to become a prisoner in this life? He has, he concludes, put his offering in the wrong place (*kukṣetre mayā dānaṃ dattam*) and is now experiencing the fruit of this action (*karmaṇaḥ phalamanubhavāmi*). If he had thrown a handful of ashes into the place of omniscience (*sarvajñakṣetre*), it would have yielded immortality.[53]

Instead, he made his offering out of ignorance, acting in the manner of a *tīrthika*, with a mind still gripped by false notions (*tairthikadṛṣṭiparyāpannena mānagrastamānasena*).[54] Just as he was beginning to make a huge offering, a malicious beggar (*yācanako hiṃsraḥ*), in the form of a dwarf (*vāmanakarūpeṇa*), appeared. Bali then lists all the many different and extraordinarily valuable things in his possession he was prepared to give to this character. Thus, he concludes, I was about to give this offering to unworthy receptacles (*tatra mayā pātrabhūteṣvidaṃ dānaṃ dātumārabdham*).[55]

He then makes a confession of an old sin. He has, it seems, broken the hearts of the pregnant *kṣatriya* women, by depriving their sons and daughters of life, incarcerating hundred of thousands of *kṣatriyas* in an elaborate prison. He is visited by the son of Daśaratha, but, as this personage appears from one day to the next in the different forms of a fly, a bee, a wild boar, and a man, Bali does not recognize him. Thus, he prepares to make his offering.[56] The son of Daśaratha (also referred to as Nārāyaṇa) now appears, destroys Bali's fortifications and liberates the imprisoned *kṣatriyas*, who begin to prepare themselves for battle.[57]

The son of Daśaratha next manifests in the form of a brahmin dwarf, dressed in a deerskin and carrying a bamboo staff and a seat. After an exchange with Bali's gatekeepers, he is offered a jeweled throne (*ratnapītham*) by the king of the *asuras*. Bali's preceptor (*upādhyāya*) Śukra advises him that his visitor means to do him harm. But Bali, reasoning that Nārāyaṇa will surely recognize the repentance that his offering represents (*vivintya avaśyaṃ dānasya vipratisāraṃ*)[58] asks the god what his wish is.[59]

Nārāyaṇa asks for two paces of earth, to which Bali responds by offering three, a proposal which is accepted, along with some water, some sesame seeds, and some gold. Śukra continues to tell Bali that he has acted unwisely, whereupon Nārāyaṇa, having briefly left the scene of the action, reappears. He is vast in size, carrying the sun and moon on his shoulders and is armed with noose, wheel, bow, javelin, and lance.[60]

Bali falls trembling to the ground and laments that he has given the god poison to eat, that the two paces are completely filled (*dvipadāni paripūritāni*) and the third pace is not to be found (*tṛtīyaṃ padaṃ na saṃvidyate*). What evil, he asks himself, has he done?[61] The god replies that where he places him, there he will stay (*yatrāhaṃ sthāpayāmi tatra tvayā sthātavyam*). Bali then says that he will do what the god ordains and promises to be true to his word (*satyaṃ satyaṃ karomyaham*). Thus, he is bound by the fetters of his oath (*tena satyapāśairbaddhaḥ*).[62]

The place of sacrifice and all the precious offerings are then destroyed before Bali departs, supplicating the god and once more repeating the lament that he put his gift in the wrong place (*bhūtapūrvaṃ kurukṣetre mayā dānaṃ dattaṃ*) and hence must experience the fruit of this action.[63]

He then breaks into a supplicatory speech to Avalokiteśvara. He asks him to be his protector and addresses him in various ways, including: "you who holds the beautiful lotus" (*śubhapadmahasta*); "you whose body is adorned with the auspiciousness of the lotus" (*padmaśriyālaṃkṛtaśuddhakāya*) (these first two are repeated again later in the same speech); "I bow my head to the one who has the image of Amitābha" (*amitābhamūrte śirasā namāmi*);[64] "you who wear a crown of a wish-fulfilling jewel in the middle of your matted locks" (*jaṭārdhamadhye cintāmaṇimukuṭadharāya*); "you who are adorned with the auspiciousness of a lotus" (*padmaśriyā samalaṃkṛtāya*); "you who wear a crown of matted locks" (*jaṭāmukuṭadharāya*); and "you who teach the six perfections (*ṣaṭpāramitānirdeśanakarāya*).[65] Next he extemporises on the theme of how happy are they who remember the great bodhisattva's name (*nāmadheyamanusmaranti*). They are liberated from various hells, the city of the *pretas* and from suffering in general, and go to Sukhāvatī, where they remember and listen to the *Dharma* (*dharmamanusmaranti śṛṇvanti*) of the *tathāgata* Amitābha.[66]

Avalokiteśvara then predicts that Bali will become the *tathāgata* Śrī, that all the *asuras* will become converted to the true way, that there will be neither greed, nor hatred, nor delusion in his buddhafield, and that the six-syllable formula will be obtained (*ṣaḍakṣarī mahāvidyā labdhalābhā bhaviṣyati*). Bali offers him, as a fee for the *Dharma*-teaching (*dharmadakṣiṇā*) a very valuable string of pearls, a crown, earrings, and many different kind of jewels.[67]

The bodhisattva then delivers the following sermon. He says that those who think only of worldly wealth and their own families are ignorant, because the things to which they cling are dreamlike. At the time of death, none of these things will be any protection. As they see Jambudvīpa being turned inside out, they will be led away into hell (with all its various tortures), asking what evil they have done.[68]

Yama's henchmen will tell them that they did not make offerings to the alms bowl of a *tathāgata*, did not listen to *Dharma*-teachings, did not hold fast to the name of the Buddha (*na buddhanāma gṛhītam*), did not take delight in seeing pleasant offerings, and did not keep to the left of *stūpas*.[69]

These people then say that they had no faith (*aśraddho*), that they clung to evil and abandoned Buddha, *Dharma,* and *Saṃgha,* were surrounded by evil friends and abandoned spiritual friends. The henchmen reply that they will experience the fruit of their actions. They are then led away to hell (whose tortures are described at some length). Thus, Avalokiteśvara tells Bali, there will be no protection at death (*paraloke*) and that he should, therefore, exert himself in making merit (*puṇyaṃ*).[70]

He should, henceforth, be careful in his behavior and be fearful of doing evil. But, having heard this *Dharma*-teaching, his collection of evil is completely purified. He is to go to Sukhāvatī, where a lotus throne made of the seven jewels (*saptaratnamayaṃ padmāsanaṃ*) will be produced for him and, having seated himself on the bejeweled lotus (*ratnapadme*), in the presence of the *tathāgata* Amitābha, he should listen to the *Kāraṇḍavyūha Sūtra,* which extinguishes all suffering and evil, accomplishes the end of all bad rebirths, and is the instruction on endless, precious, great merit (*-puṇya-*). Thereafter, he will fulfill the prediction (*vyākaraṇamanuprāpsyase*), first taking birth as a bodhisattva called "Supariśuddhabodhicittālaṃkāra," before becoming a completely awakened buddha.[71]

Avalokiteśvara then takes his leave, saying that there is a great gathering in the Jetavana *vihāra.*[72]

Chapter Twelve: The Consolation of Yakṣas and so forth

Avalokiteśvara emanates rays of multicolored light which appear in front of the *tathāgata* Viśvabhū, whereupon the beings in the *vihāra* fall to the ground. The bodhisattva Gaganagañja asks where these rays come from and is told that they come from Avalokiteśvara in the realm of Bali. Gaganagañja then asks how he might see Avalokiteśvara and is told that, when the great bodhisattva leaves the realm of Bali, showers of flowers will fall in the *vihāra* and hundreds of very beautiful and heavily ornamented wish-fulfilling trees, countless blossoming trees with red branches and gold leaves, and countless lotus pools (*puṣkariṇīśatāni*) full of very beautiful flowers will appear.[73]

Gaganagañja asks if Avalokiteśvara is not coming. He is told that, having left the dwelling place of Bali, the great bodhisattva goes to a terrible place called "Tamondhakāra," home of hundreds and thousands of *yakṣas* and *rākṣasas,* which is lit only by the light of a wish-fulfilling jewel called "Varada," instead of by the sun and the moon. Seeing Avalokiteśvara, the *yakṣas* and *rākṣasas* prostrate themselves and say that it has been a long time since he visited their world. The bodhisattva replies that he has many things to do, that he does not manifest merely for one being, but that he generates a mind of great compassion for all beings.[74]

The *yakṣas* and *rākṣasas* then produce a bejeweled, golden lion throne (*divyasuvarṇaratname siṃhāsane*), with a canopy made of many different flowers (*puṣpamayaiḥ*), upon which Avalokiteśvara is seated and from which he begins to teach *Dharma*. He says that those who even listen to a four-*pāda* stanza (*catuṣpādikāmapi*) of the *Kāraṇḍavyūha Sūtra* and then remember it, study it, promulgate and pay proper attention to it, will create a huge amount of merit. There then follows a number of similes illustrating the incalculable merit of a four-*pāda* stanza of the sūtra.[75]

Avalokiteśvara continues to explain that he who writes or has written the *Kāraṇḍavyūha Sūtra* is doing the equivalent of writing eighty-four thousand teachings and will become a king, a *cakravartin* and a lord of the four continents (*caturdvīpeśvara*), who will bear a thousand brave, heroic sons, who, in turn, will destroy their enemies. He also describes the great benefits experienced by those who constantly bear in mind the name (*nāmamanusmaranti*) of the sūtra, by those who remember (*nāmadheyam*) a single syllable of the sūtra, and by those who have written a four-*pāda* stanza of the sūtra.[76]

Hearing this, some of the *yakṣas* and *rākṣasas* attain the fruit of the "stream-enterer," some the fruit of the "once-returner," some the fruit of the "non-returner," some the fruit of the *arhat* and some supreme enlightenment.[77] The *yakṣas* and *rākṣasas* then implore Avalokiteśvara to stay, even after the bodhisattva explains that there are many beings who need his help in putting them on the path to awakening. Finally, Avalokiteśvara tells them to go away. Eventually, having prostrated and circumambulated, they depart.[78]

Chapter Thirteen: Wandering in the Realm of the Gods

Avalokiteśvara vanishes into space in a ball of blazing fire and reappears in the realm of the gods, in the form of a brahmin, a sad beggar called "Sukuṇḍala," saying that he is hungry and thirsty.[79] When a god replies that he has nothing, the brahmin says that he must be given something. The god then enters his palace and discovers that his vessels are, in fact, full of precious jewels, delicious food, and sweet smelling garments.[80]

Concluding that the person at the door must be a worthy person (*satpātro*), having attained such riches by seeing him for a moment (*darśanamātreṇa*), the god invites the brahmin inside. The brahmin then accepts some jewels, eats some of the delicious food, puts on some of the excellent garments and, having eaten, wishes the god good luck. When the god asks him where he comes from, the brahmin says he comes from the great *vihāra* at Jetavana. When asked what kind of place it is, he replies that it is a delightful and very beautiful place, strewn with jewels, lived in by a *tathāgata*, where wish-fulfilling trees and lovely flowers appear, where many lotus pools are seen (*vividhāḥ puṣkariṇyo dṛśyante*), pervaded by those with good qualities and morality, and where many miracles of the *tathāgata* are to be seen (*dṛśyate*).[81]

Not doubting the brahmin, the god then asks him if he is a god or a man, because he has never seen a man like him. The brahmin replies that he is not a god but a man, who has become a bodhisattva, feeling sympathy for the wretched and miserable (*hīnadīnānukampako*) and pointing out the path to awakening. Finally, the god, presenting the brahmin with a crown and earrings, sings a song of praise: in a meritorious field free of all faults, today a seed has been sown and today an abundance of fruit has been harvested.[82]

Chapter Fourteen: Wandering in Siṃhala

The brahmin then leaves the realms of the gods and goes to the island of Siṃhala, where he appears before the *rākṣasīs*. When they try to seduce him, he says that, provided they obey one command, he will do whatever they want. Thereupon, he teaches them the eightfold noble path, the workings of karma (*karmapathāni*) and the four *āgamas*.[83]

The *rākṣasīs* then attain one or other of the various Buddhist "fruits," from stream-enterer to *pratyekabuddha*. They are no longer bound by greed, hatred, or delusion, no longer have murderous intent, and take up the moral life (*śikṣāsaṃvaram*). They promise not to take life, but to live, no longer like *rākṣasīs*, but (like the people of Jambudvīpa) on "rice and water" (*annena pānena*), and to uphold the discipline of a lay donor (*upāsakasaṃvaraṃ*). Then, with an unwavering gaze on that person (*tasyaiva puruṣasya purato 'nimiṣairnayanaiḥ*), they depart.[84]

Chapter Fifteen: Wandering in Vārāṇasī

Avalokiteśvara leaves Siṃhala and enters Vārāṇasī,[85] where vast numbers of worms and insects (*kṛmikula*) infest the sewer of the great city (*mahānagaryāmuccāraprasrāvasthāne*). The bodhisattva then adopts the form of a bee, whose buzzing (*ghuṇaghuṇāyamāṇam*) produces the sound: *namo buddhāya namo dharmāya namo saṃghāya*. These creatures bring this formula to mind (*nāmamanusmārayanti*). By so doing (*buddhanāmasmaraṇamātreṇa*), they destroy the "twenty-peaked false view of individuation" (*viṃśatiśikharasamudgataṃ satkāyadṛṣṭiśailaṃ*) and go to Sukhāvatī, where they are born as bodhisattvas called "Sugandhamukha," listen to the *Kāraṇḍavyūha Sūtra* in the presence of Amitābha and receive predictions about their future enlightenment (*vyākaraṇāni*).[86]

Chapter Sixteen: Wandering in Magadha

Avalokiteśvara leaves Vārāṇāsī and goes to Magadha, whose inhabitants have begun to eat each other, having suffered from famine and drought for twenty years. The bodhisattva produces showers of rain, then cakes (*piṣṭakāni*), a variety of grains and pulses, clothes, and so on, until, eventually, everyone's desires are satisfied. The people ask which god could be responsible for this, at which point an old man, many hundreds of thousands of years old (*anekavarṣaśatasahasrāyuṣikaḥ*) appears. He tells them that this could be produced by no god, but only by Avalokiteśvara. Asked about the characteristics of Avalokiteśvara, the old man begins to expound on the qualities of the bodhisattva.[87]

Happy are they, he says, who bring to mind the name (*nāmamanusmaranti*) of the bodhisattva. He also says that those who offer Avalokiteśvara the four-cornered diagram (*caturasraṃ maṇḍalakaṃ*) become *cakravartin* kings, attended by the seven great jewels. At the end of his talk, everyone, including the old man, returns to his own home. Avalokiteśvara disappears into space (*ākāś 'ntarhitaḥ*)[88] and conceives an intention to go back to the Jetavana *vihāra*. He returns there, circumambulates the *tathāgata* Viśvabhū three times and takes a seat on his left.[89]

Avalokiteśvara tells the assembled company what he has been doing. The bodhisattva Gaganagañja says that he has never seen or heard of such power (*viṣayaṃ*) belonging to a bodhisattva and that it is not found even among the *tathāgatas*. He asks Avalokiteśvara if he is tired or worn out. The great bodhisattva replies that he is not tired or worn out. The two bodhisattvas then sit down in silence.[90]

Then the Lord teaches the six perfections, after which each member of the assembly proceeds to their respective domains and all the bodhisattvas go to their respective buddhafields. This is said to conclude the first part (*prathamo nirvyuhaḥ*) of the *Kāraṇḍavyūha Sūtra*.[91]

Part Two (*dvitīyo nirvyūhaḥ*).

Chapter One: The Story of the King of Horses

Sarvanīvaraṇaviṣkambhin asks to be told about the many different *samādhis* achieved by Avalokiteśvara. The Lord replies that these are immeasurable and that they cannot be counted by the *tathāgatas*. He then gives a list of sixty-two of these different *samādhis*. Avalokiteśvara, he concludes is, furnished with (*samanvāgataḥ*) *samādhis*. There are hundreds of thousands of *samādhis* in each of his hair pores. This is the greatest collection of merit (*paramapuṇyasaṃbhāraḥ*) of the great bodhisattva. Such a collection of merit is not be found among the *tathāgatas*, let alone among the bodhisattvas.[92]

Śākyamuni then tells the story of how, in a past life, he was born as the bodhisattva king Siṃhala, who set out to visit the island of Siṃhala with a band of five hundred merchants. The *rākṣasīs* that live on the island send a storm that shipwrecks the boat. They then appear in the form of beautiful women, meeting the castaways on the shore and seducing them all into becoming their lovers. Siṃhala himself goes to live with the oldest of these *rākṣasīs*.[93]

One night, he is warned by his bedside lamp (*ratikara*)[94] that his lover is really a *rākṣasī* and that she will eventually kill him. In order to convince him of this, the lamp tells him to take the road to the south where there is a place, fortified by a very high iron wall, where other merchants are imprisoned among the bones and corpses of their former comrades. Siṃhala sets out in the moonlight to find this place and climbs a tree besides the fortress walls. The incarcerated merchants tell him that, every day, one of their number is taken away by the *rākṣasīs* to be eaten and that the bones are then thrown back into the iron fortress.[95]

Siṃhala hurries back and asks the lamp if there is a means of escape. There is, he is told, a king of horses named Bālāha, who feels sympathy for the wretched and miserable (*hīnadīnānukampakaḥ*). This horse, having eaten the herbs called "All White" (*sarvaśvetānāmauṣadhīṃ buktvā*), having turned round and round and round on the place of golden sand (*suvarṇavālukāsthale āvartanaparivartanasaṃparivartanaṃ kṛtvā*), will stretch out his body (*śarīraṃ pracchoḍayati*)[96] and make this address (*pratyāhāraṃ kurute*): "Who is going to the other side? Who is going to the other side? Who is going to the other side? (*kaḥ pāragāmī*)?" Siṃhala, he is told, should say: "I, master, am coming to the other side (*ahaṃ deva pāragāmī*)." Returning to bed, he explains to his suspicious lover that his body is cold because he has been outside to relieve himself.[97]

The next day, Siṃhala gathers his band of merchants together outside the town and tells them that their wives (whose great love and generosity they have been discussing among each other) are, in fact, *rākṣasīs*. The frightened merchants are persuaded, reflecting on the fact that *rākṣasīs* are, traditionally, the inhabitants of the island of Siṃhala. "Truly, truly," they say, "by the Buddha, *Dharma* and *Saṃgha*, she is not a woman but a *rākṣasī*." Siṃhala asks them if they have a source of refuge (*gatiḥ śaraṇaṃ parāyaṇaṃ*) and describes Bālāha in almost exactly the same terms as given above. He tells them that they will leave in three days time and that each man should bring his own provisions (*saṃbalaṃ*).[98]

Upon returning to their homes, the merchants are told by the *rākṣasīs* that they look tired and are asked whether they have seen the pleasant gardens and hundreds of pleasant lotus pools (*puṣkariṇīśatāni*). No, they reply, they have not seen them at all. The *rākṣasīs* then explain that there are many different gardens on the island of Siṃhala, containing hundreds of lotus pools full of different colored lotuses. The merchants reply that, on the third day, they will go to the other side in order to see the place of the gardens and the lotus pools. Then, having picked various lotuses (*puṣpāṇi gṛhītvā*), they will return.[99]

The merchant alternates between thinking about the body of the *rākṣasī* and wondering if the *rākṣasīs* know his plan and are going to kill him. He is quiet. The *rākṣasī* then brings him many offerings. When he has eaten them, he lets out a sigh, explaining that the men of Jambudvīpa delight in their own country. The *rākṣasī* asks him why, when the island of Siṃhala is so well provided with food, water, clothes, gardens, and lotus pools. He remains quiet. This is how the first day passes.[100] The second day passes in a rapid succession of making offerings and finalizing preparations.[101]

On the third day, the merchants leave at sunrise and convene outside the town. Siṃhala says that none of them must ever look back at the island of Siṃhala and they hurry on to find Bālāha. The horse is, once again, described in the same terms. He eats the herb, turns around on the place of golden sand, stretches out his body and shakes (*calati*) the island of Siṃhala. He asks, three times: " Who is going to the other side?" and repeats the warning that, when he stretches out his body, none of them should look back at the island of Siṃhala or open their eyes. Siṃhala and the merchants then climb aboard the horse, whereupon the *rākṣasīs* begin to weep and wail. Opening their eyes and looking back, the merchants fall headlong into the sea, where they are eaten by the *rākṣasīs*.[102]

Siṃhala, therefore, returns to Jambudvīpa alone, where he makes three circumambulations of Bālāha on the shore. He then proceeds to his home. His parents embrace him and, once they can see through their tears, begin to look at him (*draṣṭumārabdhau*). After Siṃhala has told them his story, his parents say that, since he is still alive, they have no need of money (*nāsmākaṃ dravyeṇa kṛtyam*). In their old age, they say, he is their support; in the darkness he shows them the path; at the time of death he gives them the sacred cake (*maraṇakāle piṇḍadātā*); he offers protection to the dead and like a cooling wind, he is a giver of delight.[103]

This, Śākyamuni tells Sarvanīvaraṇaviṣkambhin, is how he experienced suffering as the bodhisattva caravan leader. Because Avalokiteśvara was Bālāha, the king of horses, so he, Śākyamuni, was liberated from the fear of death. As it is impossible, he says, to calculate the amount of merit of Avalokiteśvara, he offers to give a brief discourse on the individual hair pores, one by one.[104]

Chapter Two: The Description of the Hair Pores

The first pore described by Śākyamuni is called "Suvarṇa". A huge number of *gandharvas* live there, no longer bound by the sufferings of *saṃsāra* (*tena ca sāṃsārikena duḥkhena na bādhyante*),[105] enjoying supreme happiness and heavenly riches. They are not bound by greed, hatred, or delusion. They think no aggressive or violent thoughts, constantly practise the eightfold noble path and are always thirsting for *Dharma*. There is a wish-fulfilling jewel called "Avabhāsaṃ," which spontaneously grants all desires.[106]

Leaving Suvarṇa, the second pore is called "Kṛṣṇa." Huge numbers of *ṛṣis* live there, with one, two, three, four, five, or six of the supernatural faculties (*abhijñā*). The ground is made of silver, the mountains of gold, which are studded with rubies and have summits made of silver, like the seventy-seven mountains, which are each home to sixty thousand *ṛṣis*. There are wish-granting trees, with red branches and gold and silver leaves.[107]

On each side of the pore (*ekaikapārśve romavivare*) there are four lotus pools (*puṣkariṇyaḥ*), some of which are full of water endowed with the eight qualities and others which are full of flowers (*kecitpuṣpaparipūrṇāḥ*). Nearby, there are sweet-smelling trees and beautiful wish-granting trees, bearing jewelery of various kinds and gold leaves. In each of these trees reside a hundred *gandharvas*, whose music and singing instills a desire for emancipation (*saṃvegam*) in the animals and birds, who ponder the suffering of *saṃsāra* experienced by the people of Jambudvīpa. The animals and birds bring to mind the name (*nāmānusmaranti*) of the *Kāraṇḍavyūha Sūtra*, whereupon delicious food, sweet-smelling substances and divine clothes appear before them. All their wishes are granted.[108]

Sarvanīvaraṇaviṣkambhin expresses his astonishment that the bringing to mind the name (*nāmānusmaranti*) and the remembrance of the name (*nāmadheyamātreṇa*) of the sūtra should possess such power. Happy are they, he says, who listen to the sūtra, have it written, remember it, speak it, study it, and fundamentally make it their own. Even those who have written a single syllable of the sūtra do not see (*paśyanti*) the suffering of *saṃsāra*, are not born into families of the lowest or mixed social level (*caṇḍālakukkurakuleṣu*) and have bodies that are strong and free from deformity and disease of various kinds. Śākyamuni expresses his approval of such an illumination (*pratibhānaṃ*). Numerous gods, *nāgas*, *yakṣas*, *gandharvas*, *asuras*, *garuḍas*, *kinnaras*, *mahoragas*, men, women, and thousands of lay followers are gathered around. Such a *Dharma*-talk (*dharmasāṃkathyaṃ*) is equivalent to the illumination of the *vaipulya* sūtras (*vaipulyapratibhānaḥ*).[109]

Sarvanīvaraṇaviṣkambhin says that when the Lord answers in such a way, there is born an unbreakable faith in the sons of the gods (*devaputreṇa*).

Śākyamuni again expresses his approval and says that the bodhisattva must ask the *tathāgata* again and again for instruction.[110]

Leaving Kṛṣṇa, the next pore is called "Ratnakuṇḍala," where many beautiful and brilliantly adorned female *gandharvas*, or *apsaras*, live. They are not bound by the suffering of greed, hatred, or delusion. Nor do they experience the bodily suffering of human beings. They bring to mind the name (*nāmamanusmaranti*) of Avalokiteśvara, which, on the third instance, produces all good things.[111]

Sarvanīvaraṇaviṣkambhin then expresses his desire to go and see these hair pores, only to be told by the Buddha that these pores are ungraspable (*agrāhyāste*) and untouchable (*asaṃsparśāḥ*), just as the dimension of space is ungraspable and untouchable (*yathā ākāśadhāturagrāhyo 'saṃsparśaḥ*). The great bodhisattva Samantabhadra, he is told, roamed these pores for twelve years, but the pores and the hundred buddhas residing in each one were not seen (*na . . . dṛṣṭāṇi*) by him. What chance, then, do other bodhisattvas have?[112]

Śākyamuni explains that the pores were not seen (*na dṛśyate*) by himself, despite investigation and exploration. This one (*ayaṃ*), he concludes, is a master of illusion (*māyāvī*), beyond being mastered (*asādhyaḥ*) and subtle (*sūkṣma*): only in this way can he be perceived (*evamanudṛśyate*). He has a great, pure (*nirañjano*) body, with one hundred thousand arms (*śatasahasrabhujaḥ*), one hundred thousand *koṭis* of eyes (*koṭiśatasahasranetro*), an omnipresent body (*viśvarūpī*) and eleven heads (*ekādaśaśīrṣaḥ*). He is the great yogin (*mahāyogī*), established in *nirvāṇa* (*nirvāṇabhūmivyavasthitaḥ*), distinguished (*sucetano*), greatly wise (*mahāprajñaḥ*), a deliverer of beings (*bhavottārakaḥ*), well-born (*kulino*), invisible (*anādarśī*), wise (*prājño*) and in his exposition he casts no shadows on any elements (*nirdeśastathācchāyābhūtaḥ sarvadharmeṣu*). He is not heard or seen by anyone (*na śruto na kenacit dṛṣyate*). The other self-existent (*svabhāvakā*) *tathāgatas* do not see (*na paśyanti*) him, and nor, therefore, do Samantabhadra and the other bodhisattvas. This inconceivable one (*acintyo*) manifests miracles (*prātihāryāṇi samupadarśayati*) and brings to maturity (*paripācayati*) countless numbers of bodhisattvas, whom he stands on the path of *Dharma* (*bodhimārge pratiṣṭhāpayati*). He leads them to the realm of Sukhāvatī, where, in the presence of Amitābha, he teaches them *Dharma* (*dharmamanuśṛṇoti*).[113]

Sarvanīvaraṇaviṣkambhin asks the Buddha how he might see (*paśyāmi*) the great bodhisattva. Śākyamuni replies that Avalokiteśvara comes to this realm in order to see, praise and give worship to him (the Buddha) (*mama darśanāya vandanāya paryupāsanāya*). Sarvanīvaraṇaviṣkambhin asks when the great bodhisattva is coming. Śākyamuni replies that when he is mature in spirit (*yadā . . . sattvaparipāko bhavati*), then Avalokiteśvara will come. Sarvanīvaraṇaviṣkambhin reflects on the chronic attachment to evil (*pāparatena*) that has deprived him from seeing (*-darśana-*) Avalokiteśvara. He then, again, asks when the great bodhisattva will come. Śākyamuni laughs and laughs (*hasati vyavahasati*). The appointed time of Avalokiteśvara's coming, he says, is unpredictable (*akālaste*).[114]

Leaving Ratnakuṇḍala, the next pore is called "Amṛtabindu," where numerous sons of the gods (*devaputra*) live. Great bodhisattvas live there, established on any one of the ten levels (*bhumikāḥ*). There are sixty mountains made of gold and silver, sixty thousand *yojanas* high, with ninety-nine thousand summits, covered in gold and jewels. On its slopes, bodhisattvas live in one-pointed concentration (*ekacittotpādikā*). On the king of mountains, numerous *gandharvas* live, who sustain a constant chant. There are numerous, brilliantly decorated palaces, where bodhisattvas prepare *Dharma*-talks (*dharmasāṃkathyaṃ*) before proceeding to their respective promenades (*caṃkramaṇāni*). In each of these promenades, there are numerous lotus pools (*puṣkarinyaḥ*), some of which contain water endowed with the eight qualities and others which are full of many different kinds of lotuses (*utpalapadma-*). There are also many marvelous wish-granting trees. During the night, the bodhisattvas promenade (*caṃkramanti*), bringing to mind the diversity of the Mahāyāna (*vividhaṃ ca mahāyānamanusmaranti*), meditating upon (*anuvicintayati*) the state of *nirvāṇa* and the sufferings of *saṃsāra* and thinking about (*cintayanti*) the state of hell, causing them to develop loving-kindness (*maitrīṃ bhāvayanti*).[115]

Leaving Amṛtabiṇḍu, the next pore is called "Vajramukha." Numerous *kinnaras* live there, constantly thinking positively (*abhiprasannāḥ*) towards Buddha, *Dharma* and *Saṃgha*, one-pointedly delighting in loving-kindness, reflecting on patience, thinking of *nirvāṇa* and longing for the emancipation of human beings (*saṃvegamānuṣyakāḥ*). The *kinnaras* thirst for *Dharma*. There are numerous mountain chasms (*parvatavivarāṇi*), some of which are made of *vajra*, some of rubies, some of sapphires, and some of the seven jewels. There are also numerous marvelous trees, lotus pools, and palaces, where the *kinnaras* prepare *Dharma*-talks on the six perfections and walk about on their own respective promenades. These promenades are also heavily ornate, some made of gold, all enlivened by marvelous trees, which are like homes to the *kinnaras*. The *kinnaras* meditate on *saṃsāra* and cry out aloud about the sufferings of birth, old age, death, and poverty, about the suffering of being separated from what one loves and wants, and about the suffering of being joined to what one does not love. They also meditate on the sufferings of a variety of hells, of the city of the *pretas* and, finally, of all beings. They meditate on the state of *nirvāṇa* and, thirsting for *Dharma*, constantly bring to mind the name (*nāmānusmaranti*) of Avalokiteśvara. Thereby, they become endowed with all benefits (*sarvopakaraṇairupasthitā*).[116]

How difficult to meet (*durlabhaḥ*), Śākyamuni concludes, is Avalokiteśvara, who is, to all beings, both mother and father, giver of fearlessness, revealer of the path and spiritual friend. How difficult (*durlabhaṃ*) it is to grasp his name (*nāmagrahaṇam*). Those who bring to mind (*nāmānusmaranti*) his (*tasya*) six-syllable formula will be born in these pores (*teṣu romavivareṣu jāyante*), never again to wander in *saṃsāra*, traveling from one pore to another until they achieve the state of *nirvāṇa*.[117]

Chapter Three: The Description of the Glory of the Six-Syllable Formula

Sarvanīvaraṇaviṣkambhin asks how the six-syllable formula may be obtained. Śākyamuni replies that the formula is difficult to obtain (*durlabhā*) and that it is not known by the *tathāgatas*, let alone by the bodhisattvas. When asked why, the Lord explains that the formula is the innermost heart (*paramahṛdayam*) of Avalokiteśvara. Whoever knows this innermost heart knows liberation (*mokṣaṃ jānāti*). Sarvanīvaraṇaviṣkambhin asks if anyone knows the formula and is told that no one knows it. The yogins and *tathāgatas* (*yoginastathāgatā*) know it to be difficult to be met with (*durāsadā*) and immeasurable (*aprameyā*): so much more so do the bodhisattvas. All the *tathāgatas* have wandered for sixteen *kalpas* in this cause and the bodhisattvas will do so for even longer.[118]

This is the innermost heart (*paramahṛdayaḥ*) of Avalokiteśvara. But he who wanders in this world does not know the formula.[119] Meritorious are they (*puṇyavantaste*) who are always and utterly engrossed in reciting (*japābhiyuktā*) the formula. At the time of reciting it (*tasyā japakāle*), as many *tathāgatas* as there are sands in the waters of the ninety-nine Ganges and as many bodhisattvas as there are atoms assemble. They stand at the door of the six perfections (*ṣaṭpāramitā dvārasthā*). Another three thousand two hundred groups of sons of gods assemble. The four kings rule the four directions. The *nāga* kings rule the earth (*dharaṇīṃ parirakṣanti*). The *yakṣas* rule space. In each hair pore, *koṭis* of *tathāgatas* sit and express their approval.[120]

Well done (*sādhu*), the *tathāgatas* say, to those who have attained this wish-fulfilling jewel. Seven generations of their family will be saved. Those who have taken bad rebirth will become irreversible bodhisattvas. Those who keep it (*dhārayet*) on their body (*kāyagatāṃ*) or around their neck (*kaṇṭhagatāṃ*) are to be known (*veditavyaḥ*) as having a body made of *vajra* (*vajrakāyaśarīra*), like a *stūpa* full of relics (*dhātustūpa iti*) and as the ultimate in the wisdom of the *tathāgatas* (*tathāgatajñānakoṭiriti*). He or she (*kulaputro vā kuladuhitā vā*) who recites (*japanti*) the formula will become one of indestructible brilliance (*akṣayapratibhāno*), purified by esoteric wisdom (*jñānarāśiviśuddho*), furnished with a great compassion (*mahākaruṇayā samanvāgato*) and will, every day, fully accomplish the six perfections. He will receive the initiation of a *vidyādhara-cakravartin* (*vidyādharaca-*

kravartyabhiṣekaṃ pratilabhate). Whoever is given solace (*praśvāsaṃ*) by it, whether by a friend or an enemy (*maitryā vā dveṣena vā*), will become an irreversible bodhisattva and, soon, a fully enlightened buddha. Even those who merely touch the garments (*vastrasparśanenāpi*) of those who bestow the formula will become "last-existence" bodhisattvas (*caramabhavikā*). Even by merely seeing (*darśanamātreṇa*) one such person,[121] men, women, children, and animals, will become "last-existence" bodhisattvas, free of the suffering of birth, old age, sickness, and death, inconceivable (*acintyā*) and accomplished (*yoginaśca*). These are the consequences of reciting (*japamānasya*) the six-syllable formula.[122]

Sarvanīvaraṇaviṣkambhin asks how he might obtain the formula, this inconceivable method (*acintyo yogānām*) and inconceivable, immeasurable meditation (*aprameyadhyānānāṃ*), the incomparable teaching on supreme enlightenment and *nirvāṇa* (*aparisthitaścānuttarāyāṃ samyaksaṃbodhau nirvāṇasyopadarśakaḥ*). He wishes, he says, to hear this entrance to liberation (*mokṣasya praveśanam*), this cessation of greed and hatred (*rāgadveṣasya vyupaśamanam*), this supreme *Dharma*-king (*dharmarājasya paripūrṇam*), destruction of rebirth in the five realms of *saṃsāra* (*unmūlanaṃ saṃsārasya pañcagatikasya*), drying up of the hellish *kleśas* (*saṃśoṣaṇaṃ nārakāṇāṃ kleśānām*), destruction of the animal realms (*samuddhātanamuttāraṇaṃ tiryagyonigatanām*), definitive taste of *dharmas* (*āsvādo dharmāṇāṃ paripuraṇam*) and indestructible instruction on all wisdom (*sarvajñānasya akṣayaṃ nirdeśaṃ*). He will give the four continents full of the seven jewels to whoever bestows (*anuprayacchati*) the formula on him. If no bark, ink, or reed can be found with which to write the formula, his own skin, blood, and bones may be used. He (who bestows on him the formula) will become his mother and father and the guru of gurus (*gurūṇāmapi guruśca*).[123]

Śākyamuni then says that he remembers (*smarāmyahaṃ*) how, for the sake of the formula, he traversed countless realms and served numerous *tathāgatas*, but was still not able to obtain or hear the formula. However, there was one *tathāgata* called "Ratnottama," before whom Śākyamuni (in a previous life as a bodhisattva) prostrated himself in tears. He is advised to go to the realm called "Padmottama," home of a *tathāgata* called "Padmottama," who will teach him the formula. So, taking leave of Ratnottama and finding Padmottama, before whom he once again prostrates, Śākyamuni asks to be given the six-syllable formula by which, merely through bringing to mind its name (*namānusmaraṇamātreṇa*), all evil is destroyed, and enlightenment (*bodhiṃ*) is attained. He asks that his wearisome search may not be in vain.[124]

Padmottama then brings to mind the qualities of the formula (*mahāvidyāguṇāṃ saṃsmārayati*), a long speech consisting of elaborate similes and examples of vast numbers and huge quantities which are, nonetheless, deemed calculable. In contrast, however, the amount of merit accrued by even one recitation (*ekajāpasya*) of the formula is said, repeatedly, to be incalculable. For example, he says, although it would be possible to count the number of all the atoms of dust, it is not possible to calculate the amount of merit accrued in one recitation of the six-syllable formula. For example, although it would be possible to calculate the number of grains of sand in the four oceans, it is not possible to calculate the amount of merit accrued in one recitation of the six-syllable formula.

For example, although, if a man built a house a thousand *yojanas* wide and five hundred *yojanas* high and filled it to the brim with sesame seeds, it would be possible to calculate the amount of time it would take for the house to become empty if a man (free from old age and death) were to stand at the door and, after every hundred *kalpas*, throw out one seed, it is not possible to calculate the amount of merit accrued in one recitation of the six-syllable formula. For example, although, if all the four islands were sown with barley, wheat, rice, beans, sesame seed, pulses, and other seeds, and if these crops grew and were harvested, if Jambudvīpa was made into a threshing floor and was filled with all these crops, it would be possible to count each grain, it is not possible to calculate the amount of merit accrued in one recitation of the six-syllable formula. For example, although it would be possible to count each drop of water in all the great rivers (whose names are given) of Jambudvīpa which, together with each one's five thousand tributaries, run night and day to the sea, it is not possible to calculate the amount of merit accrued in one recitation of the six-syllable formula.

For example, although it would be possible to count each hair on all the four-legged animals (examples of which are given) in the four islands, it is not possible to calculate the amount of merit accrued in one recitation of the six-syllable formula. For example, there is a great mountain called "Vajrāṅkaśa" ninety-nine thousand *yojanas* high and eighty-four thousand *yojanas* deep, on one face of which, eighty-four thousand *yojanas* high, there is a man (free from old age and death) who wipes the mountain with a silk cloth once every *kalpa*; although it would be possible to calculate the number of years, months, days, hours, minutes, and seconds it would take before the mountain was completely destroyed by this process, it is not possible to calculate the amount of merit accrued in one recitation of the six-syllable formula.[125] For example, although it would be possible to count each drop of water in the great ocean, eighty-four thousand *yojanas* deep and extending as far as the mare's mouth (*vaḍavāmukhaparyantaṃ*), it is not possible to calculate the amount of merit accrued in one recitation of the six-syllable formula.[126]

For example, although it would be possible to count the number of leaves in a forest of acacia trees, it is not possible to calculate the amount of merit accrued in one recitation of the six-syllable formula. For example, the amount of merit that would be accrued if all the men, women, boys, and girls of the four islands became tenth-level bodhisattvas is equivalent to the amount of merit accrued in one recitation of the six-syllable formula. For example, although it would be possible to count each drop of water if the gods made it rain night and day for a *kalpa* of years made up, not of twelve, but of thirteen months, it is not possible to count the amount of merit accrued in one recitation of the six-syllable formula. Indeed, if several *koṭis* of *tathāgatas* were gathered together in one place and, over the course of a divine *kalpa*, were made offerings of such things as clothes, alms bowls, beds, seats, and medicines, these *tathāgatas* would not be able to calculate the amount of merit of the six-syllable formula.[127]

Padmottama now says that he wandered alone in this world. He developed a state of accomplishment, through inconceivable meditation and effort, which was the achievement of the innermost heart essence, that is the subtle *Dharma*, the imperceptible *Dharma* and the future *Dharma* (*sa ca sūkṣmo dharmaḥ avyakto dharmaḥ anāgato dharmaḥ paramahṛdayaprāptaḥ*). He established himself in the skillful means (*upāyakuśalairdharmaiḥ pratiṣṭhaḥ*) of Avalokiteśvara. In this state (*evaṃ*), for the sake of achieving the skillful means of the six-syllable formula, he traversed many realms, before arriving in front of the *tathāgata* Amitābha. He prostrated himself before Amitābha, weeping with desire for the *Dharma*.[128]

Amitābha asks him if he wishes to attain the method (*bhāvanāyoga-manuyuktaḥ*) of the formula. In reply, Padmottama outlines the great lengths to which he has gone to attain the formula and asks the *tathāgata* to be his protector, refuge, and last resort (*trātā bhava, śaraṇaṃ parāyaṇam*), the eyes of one who is blind, the guide to one who is lost, and so on.[129]

Amitābha alerts Avalokiteśvara with the sound of a cuckoo (*lambikarutena svareṇa nirghoṣeṇārocayati*), points out the great pains to which Padmottama has gone for the sake of the formula, tells him to give (*dadasva*) it to the *tathāgata* and wanders off (*paribhramati*).[130]

Chapter Four: The Description of the Maṇḍala of the Six-Syllable Formula

Avalokiteśvara says that it should not be given to one who has not seen the maṇḍala (*adṛṣṭamaṇḍalasya na dātavyāṃ*). How can he take on the *mudrā* of the sign of the lotus (*kathaṃ bhagavatpadmāṅkamudrāmanugṛhṇāti*)? How can he make his own the *mudrā* of Maṇidhara (*kathaṃ maṇidharāṃ mudrāṃ saṃjānīte*)? How can he make his own Sarvarājendrā (*kathaṃ sarvarājendrāṃ saṃjānīte*)? How can he make his own the purification of the maṇḍala (*maṇḍalapariśuddhiṃ kathaṃ saṃjānīte*)?[131]

In the middle of the maṇdala, which is four-cornered and about the size of five hands (*pañcahastapramāṇaṃ sāmantakena*), should be drawn Amitābha, using the powder of sapphires, rubies, emeralds, quartz, gold, and silver. The bodhisattva Mahāmaṇidhara should be on the right. The six-syllable formula should be on the left (*vāmapārśve ṣaḍakṣarī mahāvidyā kartavyā*), with four arms, the color of autumnal yellow (*śaratkāṇḍagauravarṇā*), decorated with many ornaments (*nānālaṃkāravibhūṣitā*), holding a lotus (*padmaṃ*) in the left hand, a string of prayer beads (*akṣamālā*) in the right, with her two joined hands in the *mudrā* of Sarvarājendrā. At the feet of the six syllable formula stands a *vidyādhara*, holding a spoon of smoking incense (*dhūpakaṭacchukaṃ dhūmāyamānam*) in his right hand and a basket of various ornaments (*nānāvidhālaṃkāraparipūrṇaṃ piṭakaṃ*) in his left. At the four doors of the maṇḍala are the four great kings holding various weapons. At the four corners of the maṇḍala are four jars full of various precious stones.[132]

Whichever son or daughter of noble family wishes to enter the maṇḍala, should write the names of all the various clans (*sarvagotrasyāparaṃparasya nāmāni*) and throw them into the maṇḍala (*maṇḍale prathamataraṃ tāni nāmāni prakṣipet*). They will then all become "last-existence" bodhisattvas, free of human suffering and, before long reach full enlightenment. It is not to be given by a preceptor in an unsuitable manner (*asthāne*). It may be given to one who has exhibited faith (*śraddhādhimuktakasya*) or to one who has exhibited faith in the Mahāyāna (*mahāyānaśraddhādhimuktakasya*), but not to a *tīrthika* (*na ca tīrthikasya dātavyā*).[133]

Amitābha then tells Avalokiteśvara that if someone is poor and cannot obtain the precious stones, gold and so on, then colored dyes, flowers, and other fragrant substances (*gandhaiḥ*) may be used. If even this cannot be obtained, in the case of someone who has come from abroad (*deśāntara-gatasya*) or who has fallen on hard times (*sthānapadacyutasya*), then the maṇḍala may be conceived of mentally by the preceptor (*ācaryeṇa mānasikaṃ maṇḍalaṃ cintitavyam*), who will teach the mantras, *mudrās* and other details (*mantramudrālakṣanānyupadarśayitavyāni*).[134]

Chapter Five: The Teaching of the Formula

Padmottama then asks Avalokiteśvara to give him the six-syllable formula, by which he (Padmottama) might liberate from suffering numerous beings, who will subsequently achieve complete enlightenment. Avalokiteśvara then bestows (*anuprayacchati*) the formula: *Oṃ Maṇipadme Hūṃ*. At that moment, the four islands shake, the four oceans are churned about and *yakṣas, rākṣasas, kumbhāṇḍas,* and the female *mahākāla* deities run away. Padmottama offers a valuable string of pearls to Avalokiteśvara who, in turn, offers the string of pearls to Amitābha. Padmottama then returns to the realm called Padmottama. This, says Śākyamuni, is what he heard from Padmottama in a previous lifetime.[135]

Sarvanīvaraṇaviṣkambhin asks how he might obtain the formula. Just as those who have tasted immortality, he says, cannot be satisfied with something tasteless, so he cannot be satisfied with merely hearing about the formula. For meritorious are they who recite (*japanti*), listen (*śṛṇvanti*), meditate on (*cintayanti*) and mentally hold on to (*adhyāśayena dhārayanti*) the formula. Śākyamuni replies that anyone who has written the formula has written the eighty-four thousand parts of the *Dharma* (*caturāśītidharmaskandhasahasrāṇi*). The fruit of making as many *stūpas* for as many *tathāgatas* as there are atoms, made of gold and jewels and filled each day with relics (*ekadine dhātvāvaropaṇam kuryāt*)[136] is equivalent only to the fruit of one syllable of the formula. Whoever recites (*japet*) the formula, attains eight hundred different *samādhis*, some examples of which are given, beginning with the *samādhi* called "holding the jewel" (*maṇidhara*). The others are the *samādhis* of: the purifying of hell (*narakatiryaksaṃśodhana*); *vajra*-armour (*vajrakavaca*); going about properly established (*supratiṣṭhitacaraṇa*); entering into all skilful means (*sarvopāyakauśalyapraveśana*); changing one's state (*vikiriṇa*);[137] seeing all buddhafields (*sarvabuddhakṣetrasaṃdarśana*); entering into all *dharmas* (*sarvadharmapraveśa*); the ornament of meditation (*dhyānālaṃkara*);[138] riding the chariot of *Dharma* (*dharmarathābhirūḍha*);[139] liberation from greed, hatred, and delusion (*rāgadveṣamohaparimokṣana*); endless years (*anantavatsa*);[140] pointing out the six perfections (*ṣaṭpāramitānirdeśa*); holding the great Meru (*mahāmerudharo*); rescuing from all states of existence (*sarvabhavottāraṇa*); viewing all the *tathāgatas* (*sarvatathāgatavyavalokana*) and the well-established seat (*supratiṣthitāsana*).[141]

Chapter Six: The Description of the Maṇḍala of the Formula

Sarvanīvaraṇaviṣkambhin asks where he must go to obtain the formula and is told that there is, in the great city of Vārāṇasī, a *dharmabhāṇaka* who remembers the formula (*dhārayati*), speaks it (*vācayati*) and pays proper attention to it (*yoniśca manasi kurute*).[142] He says that he will go to the city in order to see, praise and give worship (*darśanāya vandanāya paryupāsanāya*) to this *dharmabhāṇaka*. Śākyamuni congratulates him and tells him that the *dharmabhāṇaka* is difficult to meet (*durlabhaḥ*) and is to be seen as the same as a *tathāgata* (*tathāgatasamo dṛṣṭavyaḥ*), as like a heap of merit (*puṇyakūṭa iva dṛṣṭavyaḥ*), as like the Ganges with all its sacred bathing places (*sarvatīrthī gaṇgeva dṛṣṭavyaḥ*),[143] as like one who does not speak lies (*avitathavādīva dṛṣṭavyaḥ*), as like one who speaks the truth (*bhūtavādīva dṛṣṭavyaḥ*), as like a heap of jewels (*ratnarāśiriva dṛṣṭavyaḥ*), as like a boon-giver and a wish-fulfilling jewel (*varadaścintāmaṇiriva dṛṣṭavyaḥ*), as like a *Dharma*-king (*dharmarāja iva dṛṣṭavyaḥ*) and as like a rescuer of the world (*jagaduttāraṇa iva dṛṣṭavyaḥ*). Having seen (*dṛṣṭvā*) the *dharmabhāṇaka*, he should not develop a mind of doubt (*vicikitsācittamutpādayitavyam*). Having attained the level of a bodhisattva (*bodhisattvabhumeścyutvā*), he should not fall back into a lower state (*mā . . . adāye prapatsyase*). The *dharmabhāṇaka* neglects moral precepts and proper behavior (*śīlavipannaḥ ācaravipanno*),[144] is surrounded by wives and children (*bhāryāputraduhitṛbhiḥ parivṛtaḥ*), has a robe covered in urine and excrement (*kāṣāyoccāraprasrāvaparipūrṇaḥ*) and is not a celibate (*asaṃvṛtteryāpathaḥ*).[145]

Sarvanīvaraṇaviṣkambhin says he will do as Śākyamuni says. Gathering a retinue of bodhisattvas, householders, renunciants, boys and girls, as well as a huge number of choice offerings with which to worship the *dharmabhāṇaka*, he sets out for Vārāṇasī. He finds the *dharmabhāṇaka*, prostrates before him and sees him to be without moral code and moral behavior and to be a non-celibate (*sa tena dṛṣṭaḥ śīlavipanna ācāravipanno 'saṃvṛteryāpathaḥ*). Having made his offerings (*pūjāṃ kṛtvā*), he praises the *dharmabhāṇaka*. He is, he says, a great storehouse of *Dharma*. When he preaches the *Dharma*, he is surrounded by gods, *nāga*s, *yakṣas,* and so on. Many beings are bound in *saṃsāra*, but meritorious are they who live in Vārāṇasī, who can see (*paśyanti*) and pay homage (*parigrahaṃ kurvanti*) to him. Merely by seeing him (*darśanamātreṇa*), all evil is destroyed, just as a forest is destroyed by fire. The *tathāgatas* are taught by him (*jānante tava tathāgatā*) and numerous bodhisattvas worship him (*tava pūjākarmaṇa upasaṃkrāmanti*). He is also worshipped by Brahmā, Viṣṇu, Maheśvara, Candra, Āditya, Vāyu, Varuṇa, Agni, and Yama, the other *Dharma* kings and the four great kings.[146]

The *dharmabhāṇaka* tells Sarvanīvaraṇaviṣkambhin not to beget wickedness (*mā tvaṃ kulaputra kaukṛtyamutpādayasi*).[147] How many fools, obscurations, and enjoyments are there, he says, that are produced in *saṃsāra* which give rise to birth in the wheel of life.[148] But, he says, those who know (*jānante*) the six-syllable formula are not tainted by greed, hatred, and delusion; they are not attached to gold. Those who wear the formula on their body (*ṣaḍakṣarī mahāvidyā kāyagatā*) will not be tainted by bodily greed, hatred, and delusion.[149]

Embracing the feet of the *dharmabhāṇaka,* Sarvanīvaraṇaviṣkambhin beseeches him to act as the eyes of one who is blind, to teach the noble eightfold path, and to refresh with the taste of *Dharma* one who anxiously longs for the *Dharma*. He asks to be given (*dadasva*) the formula, which is described as the seed of enlightenment (*bodhibījaṃ*) for one deprived of complete and perfect enlightenment, as a space of *dharma*s (*dharmāṇāmavakāśaṃ*), as the complete remedy to obtain perfect bodily health (*supratiṣṭhitarūpāṇāṃ kāyapariśuddhiṃ*). Everyone, he says, speaks of this melodious phrase (*vākyaṃ madhuropacayam*) as the accomplishment of indestructible blessings (*abhedyānāṃ kuśalānāṃ pratilambha iti*). Give me, he says, the six-syllable formula by which I may soon be deeply versed in complete and perfect enlightenment, turn the twelvefold wheel of *Dharma* (*dvādaśākāraṃ dharmarandhra-cakramāvartayeyam*), and liberate all beings from the suffering of *saṃsāra*. Asking twice more for the formula, he ends by beseeching the *dharmabhāṇaka* to be his protector, refuge and last resort (*trātā śaraṇaṃ parāyaṇam*), and finally an island to those without an island (*advīpānāṃ dvīpo*).[150]

The *dharmabhāṇaka* replies by saying that the six-syllable formula is a phrase (*-padam*) which is: a *vajra* without equal (*asamavajrapadam*); an indestructible *vajra* (*abhedyavajrapadam*); a showing of supreme wisdom (*anuttarajñānadarśanapadam*); undecaying wisdom (*akṣayajñānapadam*); supreme (*niruttarapadam*); the entrance to liberation (*mokṣapraveśanapadam*); the complete purity of the wisdom of the *tathāgatas* (*tathāgatajñāna-viśuddhipadam*); an escape from the suffering of *saṃsāra* caused by greed, hatred, and delusion (*rāgadveśamohasaṃsāraduḥkhaparivarjanapadam*); all skillful means (*sarvopāyakauśalyapadam*); completely filled with meditation, liberation, and *samādhis* (*dhyānavimokṣasamādhisamāpūrtipadam*); the entering into all *dharmas* (*sarvadharmapraviśanapadam*) and constantly striving for the divine (*nityakāladevatābhikāṅkṣipadam*).[151]

Then, the *dharmabhāṇaka* points to those who have taken various robes (*nānāsthāṇeṣu dīkṣante / mokṣārtheṣu nānāpaṭeṣu dīkṣante / tadyathā indrapaṭaṃ śvetapaṭaṃ dhyuṣitapaṭam*) and ascetics who are consecrated into the Maheśvaras and other sects (*divasanirīkṣakā maheṣvareṣu dīkṣante / bailmavegarudreṣu nagnaśramaṇeṣu ca*). They who have taken these various consecrations will not achieve liberation (*eṣu sthāneṣu dīkṣante / na teṣāṃ mokṣaṃ saṃvidyate*). There will be no end to their eternal round of birth and rebirth (*anādigatikānāmapi nāpi nāśo bhavati*). All the gods, Brahmā, Viṣṇu, Maheśvara, and so on, are constantly longing for the six-syllable formula.[152]

Sarvanīvaraṇaviṣkambhin asks again how to obtain the six-syllable formula, by which we may quickly become better (*yena vayaṃ kṣipravarā bhavāmaḥ*).[153] The *dharmabhāṇaka* replies that all the *tathāgatas* are born from the Perfection of Wisdom and the Perfection of Wisdom is said to be the mother of the *tathāgatas* (*prajñāpāramitānirjātāḥ sarvatathagatāḥ / tatprajñāpāramitā sarvatathāgatānāṃ ca netrītyākhyāyate*). If she makes obeisance, with hands clasped, to the six-syllable formula, then so much more so will the *tathāgatas* and the bodhisattvas (*sāpi ca ṣaḍakṣarīṃ mahāvidyārājñīṃ praṇamate kṛtāñjalipuṭā bhavantī, prāgeva tathāgatā arhantaḥ samyaksaṃbuddhā bodhisattvagaṇāḥ*).[154]

The formula, the *dharmabhāṇaka* says, is the grain of rice (*taṇḍulavatsāraṃ*) of the Mahāyāna, equivalent to the many Mahāyāna sūtras being sung (*geyaṃ*) and the teaching of a great variety of Buddhist texts (*vyākaraṇagāthānidānetivṛttajātakavaipulyādbhutadharmopadeśakaḥ*). Merely reciting it (*japitamātreṇa*) brings sublime liberation (*śivaṃ mokṣaṃ*) and happiness (*kuśalam*). To obtain it is to possess the pith (*sāram*), just as one obtains the pith of rice grains, by taking them home, filling jars with them, drying them in the sun, threshing them, and leaving them for four years. What is the pith? The rice grain.[155]

Just so, all other yogas are like chaff, while the six-syllable formula is to be seen as like the rice grain of all yogas. For its sake, bodhisattvas practice the six perfections. By one recitation (*ekajāpena*), the six perfections are accomplished. Merely by touching the garment (of one who grants the formula) one attains the irreversible level. Thus, it is difficult (*durlabham*) to grasp its name (*nāmagrahaṇam*). Merely grasping its name once (*ekavāranāmagrahaṇena*) is equivalent to all the *tathāgatas* being offered robes, alms bowls, beds, seats, and medicine.[156]

Sarvanīvaraṇaviṣkambhin then asks to be given the formula. The *dharmabhāṇaka* pauses for reflection (*saṃcintya saṃcintya vyavasthitaḥ*) and a voice sounds from space (*ākāśe śabdo niścarati sma*), telling him to give (*dadasva*) the formula and saying that the bodhisattva has undergone various hardships. Again, the *dharmabhāṇaka* reflects (*saṃcintayati*) on the question of where the voice is coming from (*kutaḥ śabdo niścarati*)[157] and, once again, almost exactly the same instructions are heard.[158]

The *dharmabhāṇaka* gazes into space (*ākāśaṃ vyavalokayati sma*) where he sees (*paśyati*) a figure (*śarīram*) the yellowish color of arrow shafts (*śaratkāṇḍagauravarṇaṃ*), wearing twisted locks (*jaṭāmukuṭadharaṃ*), with the omniscient one on his head (*sarvajñaśirasikṛtaṃ*), holding a beautiful lotus (*śubhapadmahastaṃ*) and adorned with the auspiciousness of the lotus (*padmaśriyālaṃkṛtaṃ*). Seeing such a figure (*tādṛśaṃ rūpaṃ dṛṣṭvā*), the *dharmabhāṇaka* tells Sarvanīvaraṇaviṣkambhin that the formula is granted to him (*anujñātaste*) by Avalokiteśvara. Sarvaṇīvaraṇaviṣkambhin eagerly joins both hands together and begins to recite (*udgṛhītumārabdhaḥ*): "*Oṃ Maṇipadme Hūṃ*."[159]

Immediately, the earth trembles in six uncommon ways (*ṣaḍvikāraṃ pṛthivī prakampitā*). Sarvanīvaraṇaviṣkambhin obtains seven different *samādhis* called: "to give birth to the subtle state" (*sūkṣmajano*); "rejoicing in loving-kindness and compassion" (*maitrīkaruṇāmudito*); "conduct of yoga" (*yogācāro*); "abiding at the entrance to liberation" (*mokṣapraveṣavyavasthāno*); "spreading light all around" (*sarvālokakaro*); "king of display" (*vyūharājo*), and "holding Dharma" (*dharmadharo*).[160] He then begins to offer, as payment to his teacher, the four islands full of the seven jewels. This, however, is refused by the *dharmabhāṇaka*, who says that as not even one syllable (*ekasyākarasyāpi*) can be paid for (*na bhavati dakṣinā*), how can six. He tells him that, having become a bodhisattva, he (Sarvanīvaraṇaviṣkambhin) is an *ārya* and not a non-*ārya* and that he is converted (*vaineyaśca*). Sarvanīvaraṇaviṣkambhin offers him a very valuable string of pearls, which is also refused. Instead, he is told to take it to Śākyamuni. So, prostrating himself once again, Sarvanīvaraṇaviṣkambhin leaves his preceptor for the Jetavana *vihāra*, taking with him his heart's desire (*labdhamanorathaḥ*). He prostrates himself before Śākyamuni and stands to one side.[161]

Chapter Seven[162]

Śākyamuni asks if he has achieved his aim. Sarvanīvaraṇaviṣkambhin replies that wisdom has been obtained (*jñānaṃ saṃjānīte*), whereupon seventy-seven families of buddhas assemble and begin to speak the following *dhāraṇī*: *"Namaḥ Saptānāṃ Samyaksaṃbuddhakoṭīnām Oṃ Cale Cule Cunye Svāhā,"* the *dhāraṇī* known as "Spoken by seventy-seven families of completely perfect buddhas" (*saptasaptatisamyaksaṃbuddhakoṭibhirudkkā nāma dhāraṇī*).[163]

The narrative abruptly returns to the tour of Avalokiteśvara's marvelous body, the text stating simply that after leaving one hair pore there is another pore called "Sūryaprabha." This is inhabited by numerous bodhisattvas, in a familiar landscape of fabulous mountains, trees, and lotus pools, together with a wish-fulfilling gem called "Sārada," which endows bodhisattvas with all services (*sarvopakaraṇairupasthānaṃ*). The bodhisattvas enter top floor apartments (*kūṭāgāreṣu*), bring to mind (*anusmaranti*) the six-syllable formula and see (*paśyanti*) Avalokiteśvara. Having seen him (*dṛṣṭvā*), they know his "mind-brightness" (*cittaprasādaṃ janayanti*).[164] Then, leaving the apartments, some walk about on promenades, while others go either to gardens made of precious jewels, or to lotus pools, or to mountains made of rubies. Once there, they sit down cross-legged with a straight back and focus their minds upon happiness (*praṇidhāya abhisukhāṃ smṛtimupasthāpya*).[165]

Leaving this pore, the next pore is called "Indrarājaḥ," containing numerous irreversible bodhisattvas who inhabit a landscape of eighty thousand mountains made of gold and jewels, in the middle of which there is a wish-fulfilling jewel called "Padmāvabhāsa." The bodhisattvas do not experience the suffering of *saṃsāra* and are not tainted by the *kleśas* of *saṃsāra*, their minds being all the time absorbed in *nirvāṇa* (*nirvāṇacintā*).[166]

Thence to the pore named "Mahoṣadhīḥ," inhabited by numerous bodhisattvas in whom has arisen the "first thought" (*prathamacittotpādika*). They inhabit a landscape of ninety-nine thousand mountains, each of which, individually, is made either of gold, or of silver, or of a jewel, and each of which contains eighty thousand resplendent and jewel-studded summits, upon which *gandharvas* make music. The bodhisattvas contemplate emptiness and signlessness (*śūnyatānimittaṃ cintayanti*)[167] and bewail the sufferings of birth, old age and death, of being separated from what is dear, and of being born either in the Avīci hell or in the city of the *pretas*. They are then said, in exactly the same terms used to describe the bodhisattvas in the pore of Sārada, to sit cross-legged and to focus their minds upon happiness.[168]

In the next pore, "Cittarāja," *pratyekabuddhas* perform miracles of shining, heating, lightning, and raining (*jvalanatapanavidyotanavarṣaṇaprātihāryāṇi kurvanti*). There are a hundred thousand mountains made of the seven jewels, containing wish-granting trees. The *pratyekabuddhas* give teachings to one another on the sūtras and on other texts (*sūtrageyavyākaraṇagāthodānetivṛttakajātakavaipulyāṅgāt*).[169]

Sarvanīvaraṇaviṣkambhin now enters the final pore, which is called "Dhvajāgra." It is vast and contains eighty thousand bejewelled mountains and a variety of different kinds of marvelous trees, a level made of *vajra* and ninety thousand brilliantly decorated apartments, in which groups of *tathāgatas* are teaching Dharma (*dharmaṃ deśayanti*). They teach the six perfections to the people of Jambūdvīpa, who thus see (*paśyanti*) the hair pores of Avalokiteśvara. This statement is immediately followed by the statement that there is a gathering in the *vihāra* at Jetavana of gods, *nāgas*, *yakṣas* and so on, Maheśvara and Nārāyaṇa, sons of gods and bodhisattvas.[170]

Sarvanīvaraṇaviṣkambhin then asks if there are any more pores to be met with. Śākyamuni replies that the four oceans emerge from the right big toe of Avalokiteśvara (*dakṣinaṃ pādāṅguṣṭhaṃ yatra te catvāro mahāsamudrāḥ paribhramanti*), but his knees are not immersed (*na ca jānanyavagāhayanti*). When the waters pour out from there, they fall into the mouth of the mare (*vaḍavamukhe*),[171] whereupon they extinguish the heap of ashes (*tadā bhasmarāśimanugacchanti*). Thus, the blessing (*adhiṣṭhānaṃ*) of Avalokiteśvara is experienced. Asked if there is another pore to be met with, Śākyamuni replies that there is not.[172]

Sarvanīvaraṇaviṣkambhin then asks if Avalokiteśvara is coming and is told that he is indeed coming to the great *vihāra* at Jetavana, in order to see, praise, and worship Śākyamuni (*mama darśanāya vandanāya paryupāsanāya*) and also to give a prediction to Maheśvara of his future enlightenment (*vyākaraṇam-*) in the Sahā world system.[173]

Next, Avalokiteśvara produces rays of multicolored light. These arrive in the Jetevana *vihāra* and circumambulate Śākyamuni three times. Many wonderful phenomena now manifest in the *vihāra*, such as fragrant trees and lotus pools. The light rays then proceed on to the Avīci hell, which they freeze over.[174]

Avalokiteśvara is then said to leave Sukhāvatī and to appear in the *vihāra*, where he prostrates himself before Śākyamuni and takes a seat to one side. In a voice which resembles the sound of a cuckoo (*kalaviṅkarutasvarābhinirghoṣeṇa*), Śākyamuni asks Avalokiteśvara where he has come from and if he has brought beings to maturity (*kṛtaste sattvaparīpākaḥ*). "Just as the Lord has ordered," replies Avalokiteśvara, "thus have I established the levels of my activity (*evaṃ ca mayā karmabhūmirniṣpāditā*)." The Buddha congratulates him. Then, Avalokiteśvara presents Śākyamuni with some lotus flowers (*padmānyupanāmayati*). They are, the bodhisattva reports, sent by the *tathāgata* Amitābha, who asks that Śākyamuni be free from pain and disease, and have good health and enjoyment of the senses (*pṛcchatyalpābādhatāṃ ca alpātaṅkatāṃ ca laghūtthānatāṃ ca sukhasparśavihāratāṃ ca*). Śākyamuni accepts the lotuses and places them on his left.[175]

Maheśvara (*maheśvaro devaputro*) appears and prostrates himself at the feet of Śākyamuni and asks how he might receive a prediction of his future enlightenment (*vyākaraṇanirdeśasya*). He is told to go to Avalokiteśvara, before whom he prostrates and praises (*namo*) with various epithets, including: "Maheśvara" (*maheśvarāya*); "you who holds a lotus" (*padmadharāya*); "you who is seated on a lotus" (*padmāsanāya*); "you who is beloved of the lotus" (*padmapriyāya*); "you who holds a beautiful lotus" (*śubhapadmahastāya*), and "you who has the glory of the lotus" (*padmaśriye*).[176]

Maheśvara stands quietly to one side and is asked why he does so by Avalokiteśvara. He replies by asking to be given a prediction of his future enlightenment (*vyākaraṇa*). Avalokiteśvara then says that he will be a *tathāgata* called "Bhasmeśvara."[177]

Umādevī now appears, prostrating herself before Avalokiteśvara, whom she addresses (*namo*) in similar terms: "Maheśvara" (*maheśvarāya*); "you who gives life" (*prāṇamdadāya*); "you who rules the whole world" (*pṛthivīvaralocanakarāya*); "you who has the auspiciousness of a beautiful lotus" (*śubhapadmaśriye*); "you who turns the world" (*parivṛtāya*); "you who has set out for *nirvāṇa*" (*nirvāṇabhūmisaṃprasthitāya*); "you who is benevolent" (*sucetanakarāya*); "you who holds the *Dharma*" (*dharmadharāya*). She then asks to be liberated from the disgusting state of womanhood (*strībhāvājjugupsanīyāt*) and from the suffering inherent in a body full of the impurities of the *kali* age (*kalimalaparipūrṇagarbhāvāsaduḥkhāt*). Avalokiteśvara replies that she will be a *tathāgata* called "Umeśvara" and that her realm will be the right flank of the great Himālaya mountain (*himavataḥ parvatarājasya*).[178]

Śākyamuni points out to Sarvanīvaraṇaviṣkambhin that just as Avalokiteśvara has transformed Umādevī, so he brings all beings to complete enlightenment. This concludes the story (*khyāta*) called the description of Maheśvara (*maheśvaranirvyūho*).[179]

Chapter Eight

Sarvanīvaraṇaviṣkambhin rejoices in the fact that Avalokiteśvara has arrived and asks Śākyamuni to expound on the qualities of the great bodhisattva. This he does, in typical fashion, by means of similes demonstrating the incalculable enormity of Avalokiteśvara's merit.[180]

Śākyamuni then says that Avalokiteśvara is furnished with (*samanvāgataḥ*) hundreds of *samādhis* and proceeds to name thirty-seven of them.[181]

Next, Śākyamuni says that, in a previous life as a bodhisattva called Dānaśūra, during the time of a *tathāgata* named "Krakucchanda," he saw a "*samādhi*-contest" (*samādhivigraho mayā dṛṣṭaḥ*) between Avalokiteśvara and Samantabhadra, made on the basis of blessedness and so on (*bhadrādibhiḥ*). The contest takes the form of Samantabhadra obtaining (*samāpede*) one specific *samādhi* and Avalokiteśvara another: seven pairs, or duels, are mentioned. Then, Samantabhadra displays (*duddhāṭayati*) his hair pores and Avalokiteśvara reveals his (*apāvṛṇoti*), at which point Samantabhadra congratulates (*sādhu sādhu*) Avalokiteśvara on possessing such brilliancy (*pratibhānavān*). Finally, Krakucchanda tells Dānaśūra that this is just a small part (*alpaṃ*) of the brilliancy of Avalokiteśvara and that such brilliancy is not met with among the *tathāgatas*.[182]

Sarvanīvaraṇaviṣkambhin now asks Śākyamuni to teach him the *Kāraṇḍavyūha Sūtra*, so that he might be refreshed by the taste of the *Dharma*. Śākyamuni replies that those who hear the sūtra will no longer experience the obscurations produced by their previous actions. The sūtra liberates from all evil all those attached to evil, such as adulterers, butchers, those who have killed their mother and their father, those who have broken into *stūpas* (*arhaddhātastūpabhedakā*) and those who have developed evil thoughts in front of a *tathāgata* (*tathāgatasyāntike duṣṭacittarudhirotpādakāḥ*).[183]

Sarvanīvaraṇaviṣkambhin asks how he should view (*kathaṃ jānāmy-ahaṃ*) the sūtra. Śākyamuni replies that on the right flank of Mount Sumeru there are two pools (*tīrthau*), one pure and one impure (*malanirmalau*), created (*parikalpitau*) by seven *tathāgatas* and arranged (*vikalpitau*) by Śākyamuni himself. The accumulation of evil should be seen in the same way that a white garment becomes dark. The sūtra destroys all evil and makes everything spotlessly white, just as the rainy season gives a darker color to all the grass, bushes, herbs, and trees, and just as the *nāga* king Śatamukha, emerging from his realm, destroys all this plant life. Happy are they who hear the sūtra. They should not be spoken of as ordinary men (*pṛthagjanā*), but should be seen as like irreversible bodhisattvas (*avaivartikā bodhisattvā iva draṣṭavyāḥ*). When they die, twelve *tathāgatas* will console them, telling them to have no fear, on account of having heard the *Kāraṇḍavyūha Sūtra*. They will be told that they will no longer wander in *saṃsāra*, experience birth, old age and death, or separation from what is dear. They will go, the *tathāgatas* will say, to Sukhāvatī, where they will listen unceasingly to the Dharma of Amitābha. They will have a happy death (*sukhamaraṇaṃ*). Then, Avalokiteśvara prostrates himself before Śākyamuni and stands to one side. Sarvanīravaṇaviṣkambhin stands up, together with a gathering of all the gods, *nāgas*, *yakṣas*, *gandharvas*, *asuras*, *garuḍas*, *kinnaras*, *mahoragas*, humans, and nonhumans.[184]

The venerable Ānanda now appears, asking to be given a teaching on monastic moral conduct (*śikṣāsaṃvaram*). Śākyamuni replies that those wishing to be ordained (*upasaṃpadābhāvam*) should first of all go and look carefully at their cell (*āvāsaṃ samyagavalokayitavyam*) and pronounce it to be clean: free of any bones or filth.[185]

Śākyamuni continues by saying that neither ordination nor " proposal" should be given by a mendicant of bad moral character (*duḥsīlena bhikṣunā nopasaṃpādayitavyam / na ca jnaptirdātavyā*).[186] Why not? A cell should not be made by mendicants of bad moral character, let alone the "fourth proposal" (*bhikṣavo duḥśīlena bhikṣuṇā nānāvāsaṃ na kartavyam, prageva jñapticaturtham*).[187] They do not obey the rules (*śāsanadūṣakāḥ*).[188] These mendicants of bad moral character should not be given a cell among the moral and the venerable (*duḥśīlānāṃ bhikṣūṇāṃ śīlavatāṃ dakṣiṇīyāṇāṃ madhye āvāso na dātavyaḥ*), but outside the *vihāra* (*teṣāṃ bahirvihāre āvāso dātavyaḥ*). No *Saṃgha* food should be given them (*saṃghālāpo na dātavyaḥ*).[189] They are neither worthy of the rank of the *Saṃgha* (*na ca teśāṃ sāṃghikī bhūmimarhati*), nor are there any genuine monks among them (*na ca teṣāṃ kiṃcidbhikṣubhāvaṃ saṃvidyate*).[190]

Śākyamuni says that such characters will only become worthy of offerings three hundred years after he has passed away as a *tathāgata* (*tṛtīye varṣaśatagate mama parinirvṛtasya tathāgatasya īdṛśādakṣiṇīyā bhaviṣyanti*).[191] They who hold the title of householder in the *vihāra* (*ye vihāre gṛhisaṃjñāṃ dhārayiṣyanti*), who are surrounded by sons and daughters (*dārakadārikāparivṛtā bhaviṣyanti*), who misuse their cells by filling them with high seats and comfortable beds (*te sāṃghikaṃ mañcapīthaṃ vaṃśikopabimbopadhānakaṃ śayanāsanaṃ asatparibogena paribhokṣyante*), who make excrement and urine on the customs of the *Saṃgha* (*ye ca sāṃghikopacāre uccāraṃ prasrāvaṃ kurvanti*),[192] will be born as creatures in the filth of Vārāṇasī (*te vārāṇasyāṃ mahānagaryāmuccāraprasrāve gūdhamṛttikodare prāṇino jāyante*).[193] Those who misuse the teeth-cleaning wood (*dantakāṣṭhamasatparibhogena paribhuñjante*) will be born among the creatures of the sea (*kūrmamakaramatsyeṣu jayante*).[194] Those who misuse the community rice and grain will be reborn in the city of the *pretas*, where they will endure various misfortunes and tortures. Those who misuse the community food and drink will be reborn hideously deformed in low-caste families (*alpaśruteṣu kuleṣu jāyante*). Those who misuse the rank of the *Saṃgha* (*sāṃghikīṃ bhūmim*), will be reborn in hell for twelve *kalpas*, where they will suffer terribly before eventually taking rebirth in Jambudvīpa as blind beggars (*daridrāḥ jātyandhāḥ*). That, Śākyamuni concludes, is why the precepts are to be kept (*tasmātte hyanindānyuttarāṇi sāṃghikāni vastūni rakṣitavyāni*).[195]

Śākyamuni continues by saying that a monk should have three robes: one for while he is with the *Saṃgha* (*saṃghasya viśvāsena saṃghaparibhogāya*), one for visiting dignitaries (*rājakuladvāragamanāya*) and one for going to the towns and villages (*grāmanagaranigamapallīpattaneṣu*). Those possessed of moral discipline, quality, and wisdom will hold and spread these moral precepts (*ye śīlavanto guṇavantaḥ prajñāvantastairbhikṣava imāni śikṣāpadāni mayā prajñaptāni dhārayitavyāni*). Misconduct should never be indulged in. That which relates to the community (*sāṃghikaṃ vastu*) is like a vase of fire (*agnighaṭopamam*), a poison (*viṣopamam*), a *vajra* (*vajropamam*), a burden (*bharopamam*). It is possible to make an antidote to poison, but it is not possible to make an antidote to misuse of that which relates to the community (*viṣasya pratīkāraṃ kartuṃ śakyate, na tu sāṃghikasya vastunaḥ pratīkāraṃ kartuṃ śakyate*).[196]

Ānanda then tells Śākyamuni that those mendicants who uphold the moral precepts (*ājñaptāni bhagavatā śikṣāpadāni*) will arrive at forbearance and liberation (*pratimokṣasaṃvarasaṃvṛtā*), be inclined towards the *vinaya* and the *kośa* (*vinayābhimukhā bhavanti / kośābhimukhā bhavanti*), and be prosperous and accomplished (*śikṣākuśalā bhavanti / tāni ca bhagavataḥ śikṣāpadāni bhavanti*). Then Ānanda prostrates himself before Śākyamuni. The great *śrāvakas* go to their respective buddhafields and all the gods, *nāga*s, *yakṣas, gandharvas, asuras, garuḍas, kinnaras*, and men disappear. All the assembly rejoices in what Śākyamuni has said. This is said to conclude the Maheśvara, the display of the *dhāraṇīs*, the jewel-king of Mahāyāna sūtras, the *Kāraṇḍavyūha Sūtra (-ratnarājasya dhāraṇivyūhaḥ maheśvaraḥ samāptaḥ)*.[197]

NOTES

Introduction

1. William W. Rockhill, *The Journey of Friar William of Rubruck to the Eastern Parts of the World, 1253–55, as Narrated by Himself* (London: Hakluyt Society, 1900), p. 145f.

For a recent survey of the various Western treatments of *Oṃ Maṇipadme Hūṃ* see the chapter entitled "The Spell," in *Prisoners of Shangri La, Tibetan Buddhism and the West*, by Donald S. Lopez (Chicago: University of Chicago Press, 1998).

2. Robert Ekvall has described the various uses of *Oṃ Maṇipadme Hūṃ* in Tibetan society in the course of a discussion of *chos 'don*, or "express verbalized religion." He writes, at one point: "When a Tibetan takes a vow of silence for a period of time, the only utterance permitted is the verbalization of religion; therefore, in theory he is bound to the utterance of prayers alone. In such a case, the mantra *Oṃ Maṇipadme Hūṃ* may serve many conversational needs. The tent wife who is bound by a vow of silence for the day may shout it in your ear to call attention to the fact that she waits to fill your tea bowl, and I have seen many a trespassing dog rise and depart with speed when told *Oṃ Maṇipadme Hūṃ*." See Robert Ekvall, *Religious Observances in Tibet: Pattern and Function* (Chicago: University of Chicago Press, 1964), pp. 98–149.

3. See Lorne Ladner, *Wheel of Great Compassion: The Practice of the Prayer Wheel in Tibetan Buddhism* (Somerville: Wisdom, 2000), for a survey of the prayer wheel tradition.

4. Lama Anagarika Govinda, *Foundations of Tibetan Mysticism* (London: Rider, 1969), p. 256f.

5. For instance, *Oṃ Maṇipadme Hūṃ* is used as a means of preliminary purification in the practice, often performed early in the morning, of making an offering of *sang*, or incense.

6. A text attributed to the late-eleventh- and early-twelfth-century Tibetan teacher Ma cig Lab kyi sgron ma says: ". . . infants learn to recite the six-syllable (mantra) at the very same time that they are beginning to speak . . ." Karma Chags med, *Thugs rje chen po*, translated in Matthew Kapstein, "Remarks on the *Maṇi bKa' 'bum* and the Cult of Avalokiteśvara in Tibet," in *Tibetan Buddhism, Reason and Revelation*, Steven D. Goodman and Ronald M. Davidson eds. (Albany: State University of New York, 1992), p. 85.

Thang stong rgyal po, the fourteenth- and fifteenth-century Tibetan yogin who was highly influential in the propagation of the use of *Oṃ Maṇipadme Hūṃ* by his countrymen, is said, as a youth, to have taught a group of traders to recite the mantra five hundred times a day as a minimum Buddhist practice. See Janet Gyatso, *The Literary Transmission of the Traditions of Thang stong rgyal po: A Study of Visionary Buddhism in Tibet* (Ph.D. diss., University of California, 1981), p. 107.

7. This point is particularly well illustrated in a story about the thirteenth-century *rNying ma* guru Chos kyi dbang phyug, who, when asked by a disciple whether he had achieved *siddhi,* or supernatural power, through his meditations, replied: "I have reached the real point of their practical application, but because I devote myself to reciting the mantra *Oṃ Maṇipadme Hūṃ* I have no leisure to practise them." The guru, though capable of performing magic, considered it more important to recite the six-syllable mantra. See Dudjom (bDud 'joms) Rinpoche, *The Nyingma School of Tibetan Buddhism* (Boston: Wisdom, 1991), p. 767.

8. In the *'Drol ba zang mo,* a play depicting the struggle to establish Buddhism within the Tibetan cultural realm that is performed at the *Maṇi Rim 'Dus* festival held at Tengboche monastery in Nepal, *Oṃ Maṇipadme Hūṃ* is treated as if it is the essence of Buddhist practice. For instance: "The basis of religion is reciting the six-syllable prayer." Regions which have not been converted to Buddhism are described as follows: "They did not know how to pronounce the magic formula of six syllables." Luther G. Jerstad, trans., *Maṇi Rimdu: Sherpa Dance Drama* (Washington: University of Washington Press, 1969), pp. 22 and 24.

See also Dilgo Khyentse, *The Heart Treasure of the Enlightened Ones* (Boston: Shambhala, 1992), for a presentation of *Oṃ Maṇipadme Huṃ* as the distilled essence of the complete Buddhist path.

9. I have counted ten of these *sādhana* texts listed in the index of the Peking *bsTan 'gyur*.

10. One of the most famous of these is the *'Gro don mkha' ma,* "For All Beings Throughout Space," composed by Thang stong rgyal po. See Janet Gyatso, "An Avalokiteśvara Sādhana," in *Religions of Tibet in Practice,* Donald S. Lopez, ed. (NJ: Princeton University Press, 1997), pp. 266–270.

11. See Nik Douglas and Meryl White, *Karmapa: The Black Hat Lama of Tibet* (London: Luzac, 1976), p. 64.

12. See the chapter entitled "The Great Festival of the Maṇi Prayer" (*maṇi rgya bzhag*), in *Journey Among the Tibetan Nomads,* by Namkhai Norbu (Dharamsala: Library of Tibetan Works and Archives, 1997), for an account of this collective practice as performed by Tibetan nomad communities.

See also Lama Thubten Zopa, *Teachings from the Mani Retreat* (Weston: Lama Yeshe Wisdom Archive, 2001), for teachings given to a group of western Buddhists engaged in this kind of practice.

13. Hereafter, referred to simply as "Vaidya," together with the page and line number of each reference.

14. Hereafter, referred to simply as "Peking," with the number of the Tibetan page and line number (rather than the number of the page of the bound photocopied edition published by the Suzuki Research Foundation, Tokyo, 1962).

15. Vaidya's edition cannot be regarded as "definitive." See the discussion of this issue in chapter 1.

Chapter 1: Background to the *Kāraṇḍavyūha Sūtra*

1. See Eugène Burnouf, *L'Introduction à l'Histoire du Bouddhisme Indien* (Paris: Imprimerie Royale, 1844), p. 196.

2. The prose version in Vaidya's edition is divided up into two sections of sixteen and eight chapters.

3. The verse version also occasionally breaks into *upajāti* and *sragdharā* meters. See P. C. Majumder, "The *Kāraṇḍavyūha:* Its Metrical Version," *Indian Historical Quarterly* 24 (1948): 294.

4. Nanjio 168 and 169, or Taisho 461 and 462, respectively.

5. Vaidya, p. 258, l. 1. Majumder "The *Kāraṇḍavyūha,*" p. 294 also gives *Āryāvalokiteśvaraguṇakāraṇḍavyūha* as the full title of the verse text.

6. See Luis Gomez, trans., *The Land of Bliss, The Paradise of the Buddha of Measureless Light* (Honolulu: University of Hawaii Press, 1996), p. 3.

7. That is, the *Sarvatathāgatādhiṣṭhānasattvāvalokanabuddhakṣetrasandarśanavyūha Sūtra* and the *Mañjuśrībuddhakṣetraguṇavyūha Sūtra*.

8. See Jan Gonda, *Viṣṇuism and Śivaism, A Comparison* (London: Athlone Press, University of London, 1970), p. 49.

9. See Monier Monier-Williams, *A Sanskrit-English Dictionary* (London: Oxford University Press, 1899), p. 254. Burnouf uses the French word "corbeille" (Burnouf, *L'Introduction*, p. 196).

10. See Monier-Williams, A Sanskrit-English Dictionary, p. 254.

11. Majumder, "The *Kāraṇḍavyūha,*" p. 294.

12. Edward Conze, *Materials for a Dictionary of the Prajñāpāramitā Literature* (Tokyo: Suzuki Research Foundation, 1967), p. 145.

13. See E. Conze, trans., *The Perfection of Wisdom in Eight Thousand Lines and its Verse Summary* (San Francisco: Four Seasons Foundation, 1973), for translations of these passages (*Aṣṭasāhasrikā,* 98 and *R.*, iv, 3).

14. See John Reynolds, *The Golden Letters* (New York: Snow Lion, 1996), p.139f.

15. I am following the translation of the text by John Reynolds. See Reynolds, *The Golden Letters,* p. 172.

The term *za ma tog* seems also to have been used by the Tibetans to refer to the large, round object often seen, in Tibetan religious painting, sitting beside *mahāsiddhas* and *vidyādharas*, such as dGa' rab rDorje. See for instance, Namkhai Norbu, *The Dzogchen Ritual Practices* (London: Kailash Editions, 1991), p. xi: "By his [dGa' rab rDorje's] left side is a spherical object known as a *za ma tok* [*sic*]. This was a yogi-practitioner's personal kit container in which he kept his ritual implements, sacred relics, medicine, and the like."

16. Vaidya, p. 269, ll. 15–19.

See, for instance, *Aṣṭasāhasrikā*, 57 ff. (Conze, *The Perfection of Wisdom*, p. 105f.) for an example of the way in which the Prajñāpāramitā (implicitly, in book form) is said to be copied and worshipped in the same way.

For a more detailed discussion of this issue, see Gregory Schopen, "The phrase '*sa pṛthivīpradeśaś caityabhūto bhavet*' in the *Vajracchedikā*: notes on the cult of the book in the Mahāyāna," in *Indo-Iranian Journal* 17 (1975): 147–181.

17. See Giuseppe Tucci, "La Redazione Poetica del Kāraṇḍavyūha," *Atti della Reale Accademia delle Scienze di Torino, Classe di Scienza di Morali, Storiche e Filologique* 58 (1922–23): 607.

18. As Tucci points out, although the verse sūtra contains four hundred and fifteen of the nine hundred and thirteen verses of the *Bodhicaryāvatāra*, it contains no trace of the tenth chapter, an omission which would support the hypothesis that this chapter was not actually written by Śāntideva and was a later addition. See Tucci, "La Redazione," p. 616.

19. See Tucci, "La Redazione," p. 608 ff.

20. Ibid., p. 609.

21. See David Gellner, *Monk, Householder and Tantric Priest* (Cambridge: Cambridge University Press, 1992), p. 366, n. 12. Gellner refers to research by Horst Brinkhaus.

22. Maurice Winternitz writes that the work "is not really a *Purāṇa*, but a *Māhātmya*." See Maurice Winternitz, *A History of Indian Literature* (Calcutta: University of Calcutta Press, 1933), II: 375f.

23. Vaidya, p. 265, ll. 1–6.

24. I am relying, here, on Burnouf's summary of the verse sūtra. See Burnouf, *L'Introduction*, p. 198.

25. Malla, *Classic Newari Literature: A Sketch* (India: Kathmandu Educational Enterprises, 1982), p. 4.

26. This supercedes Winternitz's judgment that the date of these sixteenth century manuscripts also represents the time of the work's original creation. See Winternitz, *A History of Indian Literature*, II: 376.

27. See Gellner, *Monk, Householder and Tantric Priest*, p. 21.

28. John K. Locke, *Karunamaya: The Cult of Avalokiteśvara-Matsendranath in the Valley of Nepal* (Kathmandu: Sahayogi Prakashan Research Centre, 1980), p. 281.

29. See Siegfried Lienhard, "Avalokiteśvara in the Wick of the Night-Lamp," *Indo-Iranian Journal* 36 (1993): 93. Lienhard gives no reason for this judgment in this article.

30. See F. Edgerton, *Buddhist Hybrid Sanskrit Grammar and Dictionary* (New Haven, CT: Yale University Press, 1953) I: xxv. The third class is one in which Middle-Indic or Prakritic forms have almost all been transposed into Sanskrit, leaving a residue of Prakritic grammatical peculiarities, as well as a distinctively Buddhist vocabulary. Other texts in this category include: *Mūlasarvāstivāda Vinaya, Divyāvadāna, Avadāna Śataka, Prātimokṣasūtra* of the Sarvastivādins, (*Ārya*) *Mañjuśrīmūlakalpa, Bodhisattvabhūmi, Aṣṭasāhasrikā Prajñāpāramitā Sūtra, Śatasāhasrikā Prajñāpāramitā Sūtra, Māhāmāyūrī, Bhikṣunīkarmavācanā, Laṅkāvatāra Sūtra, Vajracchedikā, Jātakamāla.*

31. Constantin Régamey, "Lexicological Gleanings from the Kāraṇḍavyūhasūtra," *Indian Linguistics* 16 (1965): 1.

32. The second of these two sets of fragments was identified by O. von Hinüber, in 1981, among the manuscripts from the Gilgit find labeled as belonging to the *Saṃghāṭasūtra*. See O. von Hinüber, *Die Erforschung der Gilgit-Handschriften—Neu Ergebnisse* (Wiesbaden: Zeitschrift der Deutschen Morgenlandischen Gesellschaft 131, 1981), p. 11.

33. See N. Dutt, *Gilgit Manuscripts* (Calcutta: Calcutta Oriental Press, 1939) I: 42. "The script used in the manuscripts is mostly Upright Gupta of a date little later than those used in the manuscript remains found in Eastern Turkestan and similar to the script found in the Bower manuscript. The script of the Bower manuscript is assigned to the sixth century A.C., and so the Gilgit manuscript may also be dated in the sixth or at the latest in the seventh century A.D."

See also O. von Hinüber, *Die Bedeutung des Handschriftes bei Gilgit*, Zeitschrift der Deutschen Morgenlandischen Gesellschaft Supplement V. 21 Deutsches Orientalistentag, Ausgew (Weisbaden: Vorträge, 1982), pp. 47–66, esp. pp. 52 and 61.

34. See N. Dutt, "Religion and Philosophy," in *The Age of Imperial Kanauj*, R. C. Majumdar, ed. (Bombay: Bharatiya Vidya Bhavan, 1955), p. 261.

35. Adelheid Mette, *Die Gilgitfragmente des Kāraṇḍavyūha* (Swisstal-Odendorf: Indica et Tibetaica Verlag, 1997).

36. Adelheid Mette, "Remarks on the Tradition of the Kāraṇḍavyūha," in *Aspects of Buddhist Sanskrit*, Proceedings of the International Symposium on the Language of Sanskrit Buddhist Texts, 1991 (Sarnath: Central Institute of Higher Tibetan Studies, 1993), p. 514 f.

37. David Snellgrove, *Indo-Tibetan Buddhism* (London: Serindia, 1987), p. 148f.

38. See Edward Conze, trans., *The Short Prajñāpāramitā Texts*, (London: Luzac 1973a), pp. 141 and 145.

39. He also writes that it seems reasonable that the *Suvarṇaprabhāsa* should belong to the tantras. He presents the *Mañjuśrīmūlatantra* as "the chief tantra of the Master of the Family," and the *Sarvatathāgatatattvasaṃgraha* as "the fundamental one of all the Yoga Tantras." See F. D. Lessing and A. Wayman, *mKhas-grub-rje's Fundamentals of the Buddhist Tantras* (The Hague/Paris: Mouton, 1978), pp. 107ff and p. 215.

40. David Snellgrove, *Buddhist Himālaya* (Oxford: Cassirer, 1957), p. 69.

41. N. Dutt, "Religion and Philosophy," p. 263.

42. Yukei Matsunaga, "On the Date of the *Mañjuśrīmūlakalpa*," in *Tantric and Taoist Studies in Honour of R. A. Stein*, Michel Strickman, ed. (Brussels: Institut Belge des Hautes Etudes Chinoises, 1985) 3: 887–894.

43. See Edward Conze, "The Development of Prajñāpāramitā Thought," in *Thirty Years of Buddhist Studies*, (1960; reprint, Oxford: Cassirer, 1967), p. 138.

44. See R. E. Emmerick, *The Sūtra of Golden Light* (Oxford: Pali Text Society, 1996), p. xii.

45. See, for instance, E. Obermiller, trans., *History of Buddhism, Being an English Translation of Bu ston's Chos 'Byung* (Delhi: Sri Satguru) II: 182ff; Tarthang Tulku, *Ancient Tibet* (CA: Dharma, 1986), p. 167f and p. 192; and George N. Roerich trans., *The Blue Annals* (1949; reprint, Delhi: Motilal Banarsidass, 1995), p. 38.

Mention of missionaries from Li, or Khotan, is found in *The Blue Annals* of Gos Lo tsa ba and the *Chos 'byung rin po che'i gter mdzod* of kLong chen rab 'byams.

46. Tarthang Tulku, for instance, argues that Lha tho tho ri is most likely to have been born in 374 C.E. See Tarthang Tulku, *Ancient Tibet*, p. 166f.

Hugh Richardson writes that the king "may be placed tentatively in the middle of the fifth century." See Hugh Richardson, "Some Monasteries, Temples and Fortresses in Tibet before 1950," in *High Peaks, Pure Earth*, by Hugh Richardson (London: Serindia, 1998), p. 319.

47. See Vaidya, p. 282, l. 8. This may, of course, refer to an actual historical event. I have, however, been unable to identify any such occurrence.

48. Vaidya, p. 281, ll. 23–32.

49. Vaidya, p. 298, ll. 2, 23, and 31.

50. Vaidya, p. 307, l. 23–25.

51. See, particularly, the "*samādhi*-contest" (*samādhivigrahaḥ*) between Avalokiteśvara and Samantabhadra (Vaidya, p. 306, ll. 1–18). The descriptions of Avalokiteśvara's body (Vaidya, pp. 288, l. 18–292, l. 8 and pp. 301, l. 15–303, l. 2), which contains worlds in its hair pores, is also clearly indebted to the conception of Samantabhadra's body found in the *Avataṃsaka Sūtra*. See Thomas Cleary, trans., *The Flower Ornament Scripture, A Translation of the Avataṃśaka Sūtra*, (Boston and London: Shambhala, 1993), p. 1510.

52. See Paul Williams, *Mahāyāna Buddhism*, (London: Routledge, 1989) p. 121: "The original texts translated as the *Avataṃsaka Sūtra* were brought to China from Khotan, in Central Asia. The texts refer to China and Kashgar, so it is likely that compilation and even authorship of at least some portions of the comprehensive work took place within the Indic cultural sphere of Central Asia."

53. The *Kāraṇḍavyūha Sūtra* does not, however, appear to be among those Mahāyāna works that have so far been found, mainly in fragmentary form, at Khotan. See R. E. Emmerick, *A Guide to the Literature of Khotan* (Tokyo: Studia Philologica

Buddhica, Occasional Paper Series III, 1979), pp. 15 ff. The text may, however, as we shall show in the course of this thesis, be linked to some of the works that seem to have been most widely represented at Khotan: for instance, the *Saddharmapuṇḍarīka Sūtra*, the *Sukhāvatīvyūha Sūtra* and the Prajñāpāramitā sūtras. Also, in the retelling of the *jātaka* story of Siṃhala and the man-eating *rākṣasīs*, the *Kāraṇḍavyūha* displays one of the characteristics of the Khotanese literature, "a continuing interest in the quasi-historical life of Śākyamuni Buddha and the stories of his previous rebirths." See Snellgrove, *Indo-Tibetan Buddhism*, p. 336 f.

54. See, for instance, Snellgrove, Ibid., p. 439f.

55. See Alexander Csoma de Kôrös, "Analysis of the Sher—'Phyin," in *Journal of the Asiatic Society of Bengal* 20, pt. 2 (1839): 440.

56. See D. L. Chattopadhyaya, ed., *Tāranātha's History of Buddhism in India* (1970; reprint, Delhi: Motilal Banarsidass, 1990), p. 259.

57. For the dating of this catalog, see Giuseppe Tucci, *Minor Buddhist Texts*, II (Rome: Istituto Italiano per il Medio ed Estremo Oriente, 1958), p. 48. For a full presentation of the contents of the catalogue, see Marcelle Lalou, "Les textes bouddhiques au temps du roi Khri Srong-lde-brtsan," in *Journal Asiatique* (1953): 313–353.

58. Thus, Régamey writes of an article written by Lalou in 1938: "A l'époque de la rédaction de cet article le *Kāraṇḍavyūha* était situé au IXe–Xe siècle parmi les textes du 'Mahāyāna décadent.' " See Régamey, "Motifs Vichnouites et Śīvaites dans le Kāraṇḍavyūha," in *Etudes Tibétaines Dediées à la Memoire de Marcelle Lalou* (Paris: Libraire d'Amérique et d'Orient, 1971), p. 420, n. 15. Régamey refers to Lalou, "A Tun-huang Prelude to the *Kāraṇḍavyūha*," *Indian Historical Quarterly* 14 (1938): 398–400.

See also Burnouf, 1844, p. 196: "Parmi les traites que je viens de désigner, il en est deux auxquels le titre de *sūtra* n'a vraisemblablement été appliqué qu'après coup, où, ce qui revient au même, qui, malgré leur titre de *Mahāyāna Sūtra*, ou sūtra servant de grand véhicule, ne peuvent prétendre à être classés au nombre des sūtras primitifs, ni même des sūtras developpés."

59. Régamey, "Motifs Vichnouites," p. 418f.: "Ces caractéristiques du contenu, de même que l'état corrompu de la langue dont certaines tournures syntaxiques font déjà penser aux structures néo-indiennes, étaient des raisons valables pour assigner à ce texte une date tardive, au moins celle du IXe siècle."

60. Taisho 1050 and Nanjio 782. T'ien Si Tsai was a Kashmiri who left the great Buddhist university of Nālandā for China in 980. The precise date of the translation of the sūtra is given in a catalogue of Buddhist texts translated into Chinese between 982 C.E. and 1011 C.E. See Y. Imaeda, "Note Préliminaire sur la Formule Oṃ Maṇi Padme Hūṃ dans les Manuscrits Tibétains de Touen-Houang," in *Contributions aux Études sur Touen-Houang* (Genève-Paris: Libraire Droz, 1979), p. 71.

61. See M. Lalou, "A Tun-huang Prelude," p. 400. Lalou refers to P. Pelliot, *T'oung Pao*, vol. 30, 1934, p. 174 and a reference in *Bibliographie Bouddhique*, 6, no. 273, whose judgment about the late date of the formula is probably based on the date of the Chinese translation of the *Kāraṇḍavyūha*. Lalou's article concerns a Tun Huang

text called the *"gShin lam bstan ba,"* or "Teaching on the Path of the Dead," which, like the text discussed by Imaeda, describes how a dead person may be prevented from taking an unfortunate rebirth. One of the striking features of this text is that Avalokiteśvara, who is said to be able to save the dead person from a great hell, is invoked not by the formula *Oṃ Maṇipadme Hūṃ*, but by *Oṃ hri hung pad ma pri ya sva hā*. The text also includes a shortened version of the *Bālāhajātaka*, a long version of which is also found in the *Kāraṇḍavyūha*, leading Lalou, on the basis of her belief in the late date of the sūtra, to dub the *gShin lam bstan ba*, "A Tun-huang Prelude to the *Kāraṇḍavyūha*."

62. See Imaeda, "Note Préliminaire sur la Formule."

63. See H. Karmay, *Early Sino-Tibetan Art* (Warminster: Aris and Phillips, 1975), p. 11.

64. I am grateful to Burkhard Quessel, Curator of the Tibetan Collections at the British Library, for drawing my attention to this article.

65. See bibliography for detailed references to these books and articles.

66. Guiseppe Tucci, "La Redazione," p. 605.

67. See Régamey, "Motifs Vichnouites," p. 418. "La composition du *Kāraṇḍavyūha* est très incohérente, même dans la rédaction des détails. La langue dans laquelle ce texte est rédigé, sans être ce qu'on appelle le 'sanskrit hybride,' est extrêmement incorrecte, dépassant par ses incongruités grammaticales et syntaxiques même la langue des Avadāna."

Also, Burnouf, *L'Introduction à l'Histoire*, p. 197: "D'ailleurs, le manuscrit du Karaṇḍa en prose est si incorrect, qu'il m'aurait été beaucoup plus difficile d'en donner un extrait parfaitement exact, qu'il ne me le serait de traduire intégralement le poème."

68. Adelheid Mette, "Remarks on the Tradition of the Kāraṇḍavyūha," p. 512.

69. Ibid., p. 511.

70. Ibid., p. 511.

71. Ibid., p. 511.

72. See, Ibid., p. 513, n. 1. According to p. 230 of Cecil Bendall's, *Catalogue of the Sanskrit Manuscripts in the British Museum* (London: Longmans, 1902), Sāmaśrami's edition is based on a palm leaf manuscript (No. 542 = Or. 3345) of the India Office Library, dated Newār 316 (1196 C.E.)

73. See Régamey, "Lexicological Gleanings," p. 1. Régamey was preparing a critical edition of the text based on Nepalese manuscripts dated from the fourteenth to the nineteenth centuries.

74. Mette, "Remarks on the Tradition of the Kāraṇḍavyūha," p. 513.

75. Régamey gave this translation high praise. See Régamey, "Le Pseudo-Hapax *ratikara* et la Lampe qui Rit dan le 'Sūtra des Ogresses' Bouddhique," *Études*

Asiatiques 18/19 (1965a): 176, n. 5. "C'est un document stupéfiant . . . se basant sur un seul manuscrit népalais (actuellement Bibl. Nat., Fonds Sanskrit No. 24) . . . fit en neuf jours . . . "

76. Mette, "Remarks on the Tradition of the Kāraṇḍavyūha," p. 514. Régamey remarks that the first Gilgit text is the most fantastical and incoherent of any manuscript known to him and that it is extremely carelessly edited with regard to grammar and spelling. See Régamey, "Motifs Vichnouites," p. 418 and Régamey, "Le Pseudo-Hapax," p. 183.

77. See Adelheid Mette, *Die Gilgitfragmente,* p. 87.

Chapter 2: Purāṇic Influence on the *Kāraṇḍavyūha*

1. A fuller discussion of the place of this couplet in the *Skanda Purāṇa* occurs later in this chapter.

2. Vaidya, p. 265, l. 6.

3. Vaidya, p. 265, l. 7f.

4. Régamey, "Motifs Vichnouites," p. 431, n. 49.

5. See Ibid., p. 432: "Il prouve que pour les textes dans le genre du *Kāraṇḍavyūha* ces sources sont à chercher avant tout dans la vaste littérature des Purāṇa."

6. Ludo Rocher, *The Purāṇas* (Wiesbaden: Otto Harrassowitz, 1986), p. 90.

7. Ibid., p. 90.

8. Ibid., p. 90.

9. Ibid., p. 90.

10. Ibid., p. 91.

11. Winternitz, *A History of Indian Literature,* I: 525.

12. Lienhard, "Avalokiteśvara in the Wick of the Night-Lamp," p. 93. He refers to the *Valāhassajātaka* in the Pali canon, the *Dharmalabdhajātaka* in the *Mahāvastu* and the *Siṃhalāvadāna* in the *Divyāvadāna*. The story appears, too, in various Nepalese, Tibetan, Chinese, Kotanese, and Japanese Buddhist works. It is also found in a Prakrit Jain text, the *Nāyādhammakahāo*. See Todd T. Lewis, *Popular Buddhist Texts from Nepal* (Albany: State University of New York Press, 2000), for a discussion of the use of the story of Siṃhala in contemporary Nepalese religion.

13. See the translation of the *"Saddharmapuṇḍarīka Sūtra"* by H. Kern, in *The Sacred Books of the East Series,* ed. Max Muller (Oxford: Oxford University Press, 1884), p. 406f.

14. Vaidya, p. 280, ll. 1–31.

15. The only Sukuṇḍala I am aware of is one of the one hundred sons of Dhṛtarāṣṭra listed in the Mahābhārata. See P. Lal, trans., *The Mahābhārata* (Calcutta: Writers Workshop, 1969), 12: 32.

16. Vaidya, p. 280, l. 29; Peking, p. 244b, l. 6. My rendering of the song of praise is quite free. The Sanskrit (Vaidya, p. 280, ll. 28 and 29) reads: *aho guṇamayaṃ kṣetraṃ sarvadoṣavivarjitam / adyaiva vāpitaṃ bījaṃ adyaiva phalasaṃpadam /*

17. Régamey, "Motifs Vichnouites," p. 402. "Les connaisseurs de cette littérature pourront-ils peut-être trouver également la source de la version du mythe de la 'Descent du Nain' raconté à sa manière par le *Kāraṇḍavyūha* . . . ?"

18. Deborah A. Soifer, *The Myths of Narasiṃha and Vāmana—Two Avatars in Cosmological Perspective* (Albany: State University of New York, 1991).

19. Ibid., p. 132

20. *Bhāgavata Purāṇa*, VIII. 19. 4. See the English translation, produced and edited by Ganesh Vasudeo Tagare (Delhi: Motilal Banarsidass, 1976).

21. *Bhāgavata Purāṇa*, VIII. 19. 21–25.

22. *Bhāgavata Purāṇa*, VIII. 19. 36–37.

23. *Bhāgavata Purāṇa*, VIII. 20. 2.

24. *Bhāgavata Purāṇa*, VIII. 20. 9–10.

25. *Bhāgavata Purāṇa*, VIII. 22. 9–11.

26. *Bhāgavata Purāṇa*, VIII. 22. 16–17.

27. *Skanda Purāṇa*, I. i. 18. 48–52. See the English translation, produced, and edited by Ganesh Vasudeo Tagare (Delhi: Motilal Banarsidass, 1994).

28. *Skanda Purāṇa*, I. i. 18. 59.

29. *Skanda Purāṇa*, I. i. 18. 69–73. One *ghaṭikā* is said to be equivalent in duration to twenty-four minutes.

30. *Skanda Purāṇa*, I. i. 18. 143.

31. *Skanda Purāṇa*, I. i. 18. 131–132.

32. *Skanda Purāṇa*, I. i. 19. 63.

33. *Skanda Purāṇa*, I. i. 19. 63–72.

34. Vaidya, p. 271, ll. 20–24.

35. Vaidya, p. 271, ll. 24–25.

36. Vaidya, p. 271, ll. 25–30.

37. Vaidya, p. 271, l. 31–p. 272, l. 23.

38. Vaidya, p. 275, l. 29–p. 276, l. 21.

39. Vaidya, p. 275, ll. 12–18.

40. Vaidya, p. 275, ll. 23–27.

41. Vaidya, p. 272, l. 28.

42. Vaidya, p. 272, l. 30.

43. Vaidya, p. 274, l. 31.

44. Vaidya, p. 274, l. 32.

45. Vaidya, p. 275, l. 1.

46. Vaidya, p. 275, l. 9f.

47. Rocher, *The Purāṇas,* p. 53.

48. Ibid., p. 237. Rocher refers to a manuscript, written in Gupta script, in the Durbar library in Kathmandu.

49. Alain Daniélou, *Polythéisme Hindou* (Paris: Buchet/Chastel, Corrêa, 1960), p. 452, n. 437.

50. *Skanda Purāṇa,* I. i. 8. 116.

51. *Skanda Purāṇa,* I. i. 32. 62f.

52. *Skanda Purāṇa,* I. i. 6. 34–35.

53. Vaidya, p. 273, l. 19–p. 274, l. 10.

54. Vaidya, p. 273, l. 28f.

55. Régamey, "Motifs Vichnouites," p. 425: "Les transformations de Nārāyaṇa en mouche, en abeille, en sanglier etc. proviennent de nouveau d'une autre légende."

56. Ibid., p. 425.

57. *Bhāgavata Purāṇa,* VIII. 19. 5–15.

58. *Bhāgavata Purāṇa,* VIII. 19. 14.

59. Vaidya, p. 265, l. 4ff.

60. See Snellgrove, *Indo-Tibetan Buddhism,* pp. 134–141.
For further discussion of this issue, see, for instance, Robert Mayer, *A Scripture of the Ancient Tantra Collection, The Phur-pa bcu-gnyis* (Oxford: Kiscadale, 1996), pp. 115–128.

61. Vaidya, p. 303, l. 32f.

62. See Snellgrove, *Indo-Tibetan Buddhism,* p. 140. To be absolutely precise, Śiva is called "Bhasmeśvaranirghoṣa," or "Soundless Lord of Ashes" in the *Sarvatathāgatatattvasaṃgraha.*
Vaidya, p. 304, l. 8 f.

63. Vaidya, p. 304, l. 16f.

64. Vaidya, p. 275, l. 23ff.

65. Vaidya, p. 281, ll. 24–32.

66. Vaidya, p. 281, l. 27f.

67. Vaidya, p. 281, ll. 28–31.

68. Vaidya, p. 281, l. 31f.

69. Vaidya, p. 273, l. 28.

70. *Śiva Purāṇa, Rudrasaṅhitā,* Section V, introduction to ch. 45.

71. Monier-Williams, *A Sanskrit-English Dictionary,* p. 881.

72. *Bhāgavata Purāṇa,* VIII. 18. 3.

73. Guy L. Beck, *Sonic Theology* (NC: University of South Carolina, 1993), p. 93. Beck quotes an English translation of the *Nādabindu Upaniṣad* (31–41).

74. *Śiva Purāṇa, Vidyeśvara Saṃhitā,* ch. 11, l. 20f. See the English translation, produced by a board of scholars and edited by Arnold Kunst and J. L. Shastri (Delhi: Motilal Banarsidass, 1970).

75. Vaidya, p. 258, l. 19.

76. Vaidya, p. 265, l. 1ff.

77. Vaidya, p. 268, l. 21f.

78. Vaidya, p. 299, l. 1f.

79. Vaidya, p. 262, l. 23f. See also Régamey, "Motifs Vichnouites," p. 426f.

80. *Skanda Purāṇa,* I. i. 18. 130.

81. *Skanda Purāṇa,* I. i. 19. 3ff.

82. See Jan Gonda, *Viṣṇuism and Śivaism, A Comparison* (London: Athlone Press, University of London, 1970), p. 103.

83. *Skanda Purāṇa,* vi, I, 26.

84. See Gonda, *Viṣṇuism and Śivaism,* p. 101f. He cites the *Rāmottaratāpanīya Upaniṣad,* I. 4.

85. *Kūrma Purāṇa,* I. 35. 9. See the English translation, translated, and edited by Ganesh Vadeo Tagare (Delhi: Motilal Banarsidass, 1981).

86. See Lokesh Chandra, *The Thousand-Armed Avalokiteśvara* (New Delhi: Indira Gandhi National Centre for the Arts, 1988), p. 279.

Chapter 3: Avalokiteśvara as the Buddhist *Īśvara*

1. As Gonda writes: "It was the term *īśvara* which was preferred when the concept of the personal God had arisen." See Gonda, "The Concept of a personal God in ancient Indian religious thought," *Selected Studies* (1968; reprint, Leiden: Brill, 1975), p. 7.

2. For discussion of the term *īśvara* see M. D. Shastri, "History of the word 'Īśvara' and its idea," in *Proceedings and Translations VIIth All-India Conference* (1933; reprint, Baroda: Oriental Institue, 1935), pp. 487–503; Gonda, *Selected Studies*, and "Concept of a personal God," Ibid.; and Gonda, "The Īśvara Idea," in *Change and Continuity in Indian Religion* (The Hague: Mouton & Co., 1965), pp. 131–163.

3. See p. vii of the introduction to the translation of the *Bhagavadgītā* by W. J. Johnson (Oxford: Oxford University Press, 1994).

4. *Bhagavadgītā*, iv, 6. All Sanskrit quotations from the *Bhagavadgītā* are taken from the edition edited by Christopher Chapple and translated by Winthrop Sargeant, published by the State University of New York, 1984. The English translation is that of W. J. Johnson, Ibid.

5. *Bhagavadgītā*, xv, 8.

6. *Śiva Purāṇa, Rudrasaṃhitā*, Section V, in the opening passage of ch. 49.

7. *Śiva Purāṇa, Rudrasaṃhitā*, Section I, ch. 4, l. 39f.

8. *Liṅga Purāṇa*, Part I, ch. 85, l. 13. See the English translation produced by a board of scholars and edited by Professor J. L. Shastri (Delhi: Motilal Banarsidas, 1973). The text has been dated to between the fifth and eleventh century C.E. See Rocher, *The Purāṇas*, p. 187f. It is worth recalling the observation, made in the last chapter, that the purāṇas are composite works and that individual sections of a text may be much earlier in origin than the date of the completed text.

9. Vaidya, p. 262, l. 29f.

10. Vaidya, p. 304, l. 2ff.

11. Vaidya, p. 304, l. 12.

12. Gonda, "The Īśvara Idea," p. 144.

13. Gonda, "The Concept of a personal God," p. 4.

14. See, for instance, *Śiva Purāṇa, Rudrasaṃhitā*, Section V, introduction to ch. 49.

15. *Siva Purāṇa, Rudrasaṃhitā*, ch. 23, 5.

16. See, for instance, *Bhagavadgītā*, x, 12, and 15; xi, 18, and 38.

17. *Bhagavadgītā*, xi, 3.

18. *Bhagavadgītā*, xv, 17.

19. *Ṛgveda*, x, 90, 12–14. Translated by R. C. Zaehner, *Hindu Scriptures* (1938; reprint, London: Dent, 1978), p. 10. The Sanskrit of the *puruṣasūkta* may be found in A. A. Macdonell, *A Vedic Reader for Students* (Oxford: Oxford University Press, 1917), pp. 195–203.

20. *Nārada Purāṇa*, I, 11, 33–35. Soifer's translation: see Deborah A. Soifer, *The Myths of Narasiṃha*, p. 136. The text has been dated to around the ninth century C.E. See Rocher, *The Purāṇas*, p. 203.

21. Vaidya, p. 274, l. 28.

22. Vaidya, p. 265, ll. 1–3.

23. *Ṛgveda*, x, 90, 1.

24. *Kūrma Purāṇa*, II. 5. 8. The text has been dated to around the eighth century C.E. See Rocher, *The Purāṇas*, p. 186.

25. See Zaehner, *Hindu Scriptures*, p. 209.

26. *Bhagavadgītā*, xi, 46.

27. Vaidya, p. 290, l. 14; Peking, 253a, l. 5f.: *lag pa brgya stong pa / mig bye ba brgya stong pa /* One *koṭi* is 10 million or, in Indian parlance, a *crore*.

28. Chandra, *The Thousand-Armed Avalokiteśvara*, p. 265. He refers to Taisho 1056, Nanjio 1383.

29. Vaidya, p. 290, l. 15.

30. In the *Viṣṇu Purāṇa*, for instance, Rudra (or Śiva) is said to have been born from the forehead of Brahmā, who was frowning at the indifference displayed towards his creation by his sons, Sanandana and others. Rudra is then said to have divided himself into a male and a female form, and the male form is, finally, said to have divided, once again, into eleven bodies.

31. Vaidya, p. 262, l. 17, and p. 300, l. 19.

32. For instance, Snellgrove, *Indo-Tibetan Buddhism*, p. 140, writes: ". . . Śiva, as lord of yogins, frequents cemeteries as a naked ascetic, covered in matted hair and besmeared with ashes."

33. Chandra, *The Thousand-Armed Avalokiteśvara*, p. 48.

34. Ibid., p. 50. See George Michell, *The Penguin Guide to the Monuments to India* (London: Penguin, 1989), I: 373.

35. Ibid., 1988, p. 48. He refers to Alice Matsunaga, *The Buddhist Philosophy of Assimilation* (Tokyo: Tuttle, 1969), p. 124.

36. Ibid., 1988, p. 50. He refers to Heather Karmay, *Early Sino-Tibetan Art* (Warminster: Aris and Phillips, 1975), p. 11, fig. 4; and Arthur Waley, *A Catalogue of Paintings Recovered from Tun-huang by Sir Aurel Stein* (London: British Museum, 1931), p. 53.

37. Taisho 1060; Nanjio 320; Korean Tripiṭika 294.

38. Taisho 1064 and 1113B. Neither version is cataloged in either the Nanjio or the Korean Tripiṭaka.

39. Taisho 1061; Korean Tripiṭaka 1270. It is not found in the Nanjio.

40. Narthang, folios 346a–400a.

41. Chandra, *The Thousand-Armed Avalokiteśvara*, p. 133. This version of the hymn is used, to this day, as one of the three basic texts for recitation in the Zen Buddhist monasteries of China, Korea and Japan. See Chandra, Ibid., p. 92.

42. Śiva is said to have deliberately swallowed some poison that appeared while the gods, in order to obtain ambrosia, were churning the ocean of milk. His throat turned blue when his consort Pārvatī put her hands around his neck in order to prevent the poison reaching his stomach. See T. A. G. Rao, *Elements of Hindu Iconography* (1914; reprint, Varanasi: Indological Book House, 1971) II: 48.

43. See Chandra, *The Thousand-Armed Avalokiteśvara*, p. 93.

44. Ibid., 1988, p. 274. He writes: "The attributes in the hymns make it clear that Hari-Hara is the subject of veneration."

45. Vaidya, p. 303, l. 4f.

46. Vaidya, p. 303, l. 5.

47. Vaidya, p. 303, l. 5f.

48. See Soifer, *Myths of Narasiṃha*, p. 297.

49. Monier-Williams, *A Sanskrit-English Dictionary*, p. 915. He, however, gives *vaḍava* as a corruption of *vaḍabā*, meaning "mare." He also writes that *vaḍabāmukha* is synonymous with *vaḍabāgni*, the fire of the mare, a compound which combines the sense of the opening of the mouth and the subterranean fire lying below.

50. See John Dowson, *A Classical Dictionary of Hindu Mythology and Religion, Geography, History and Literature* (London: Trubner, 1879), p. 330.

51. Vaidya, p. 262, ll. 5 and 7–9.

52. Régamey, 1971, p. 429.

53. Vaidya, p. 265, ll. 1–3.

54. Vaidya p. 265, l. 3f.

55. Vaidya, p. 268, ll. 18f. and 31f.

56. This figure is sometimes regarded as a *nāga* king and sometimes as a lord of the *yakṣas*, guardian of the north. He is also sometimes confused with Vaiśramaṇa [*sic*], the lord of wealth. See F. Edgerton, *Buddhist Hybrid Sanskrit*, II: 513.

57. Vaidya, p. 268, l. 15–p. 269, l. 3.

58. Vaidya, p. 265, ll. 3–5.

There is here, surely, an echo of the age-old Buddhist argument against the doctrine of the primordial creator god as found, for instance, in the *Brahmajāla Sutta*. See, for instance, *Dīgha Nikāya*, ed. T. W. Rhys Davids and J. Estlin Carpenter (London: Pali Text Society, 1890), I: 17f. I am grateful to Dr. Rupert Gethin for pointing this out to me.

Régamey provides an analysis of the peculiar grammar of the expression *ādideva ākhyāyase sraṣṭāraṃ kartāram* in Régamey, "Motifs Vichnouites," p. 428, n. 44.

59. Ibid., p. 430.

60. The doctrine of a kind of Buddhist creator is also evident, for instance, in a Tibetan work, the *Kun byed rgyal po'i mdo*, or "The Sūtra of the All-Creating Sovereign," the main scriptural source of the *sems sde*, or "mind class," teachings of the *rDzogs chen* system of Tibetan Buddhism. Here, the creator is the mind. According to Tibetan tradition the text was translated from Sanskrit into Tibetan in the eighth century, though no Sanskrit edition is extant. Like the *Kāraṇḍavyūha*, the *Kun byed rgyal po'i mdo* also straddles the divide between sūtra and tantra: though it declares itself to be a sūtra (*mdo*) in its title, it refers to its own sections as tantras and is usually referred to as a tantra by Tibetans. According to Eva K. Neumaier-Dargyay, the text was influenced by the doctrines of Kashmiri Śaivism. John Reynolds, however, while admitting that there is certain plausibility to this point of view, wants to resist it. He also argues against a theist understanding of the text.

See E. K. Neumaier-Dargyay, *The Sovereign All-Creating Mind* (Albany: State University of New York, 1992), pp. 2–14; and Reynolds, *The Golden Letters*, pp. 236–248.

61. *Śiva Purāṇa*, *Rudrasaṃhita*, i, 4, 33.

62. *Skanda Purāṇa*, III, iii, 1, 14, p. 244.

63. *Bhagavadgītā*, x, 20.

64. Vaidya, p. 290, ll. 15–17.

65. See Williams, *Mahāyāna Buddhism*, p. 98.

66. Vaidya, p. 264, l. 21f.

67. Vaidya, p. 267, l. 28f.

68. Vaidya, p. 269, l. 5–7 and p. 283, l. 17.

69. Vaidya, p. 292, l. 24f.

70. Vaidya, p. 292–297.

71. Vaidya, p. 293, l. 25.

72. See Williams, *Mahāyāna Buddhism*, pp. 238–241.

73. Vaidya, p. 292, l. 13.

74. See Williams, *Mahāyāna Buddhism*, p. 120.

75. Cleary, *The Flower Ornament Scripture,* p. 1510. See also P. L. Vaidya, ed., *Gaṇḍavyūha Sūtra* (Darbhanga: Mithila Institute, 1960), p. 427, ll. 18–22.

76. Cleary, *Flower Ornament Scripture,* p. 1510. Vaidya, 1960a, p. 427, l. 26ff.

77. Ibid., p. 1510. Vaidya, 1960a, p. 427, l. 22f.

78. Vaidya, p. 290, l. 17 f.

79. Vaidya, p. 306, l. 4f.

80. Vaidya, p. 305, l. 17f.

81. Cleary, *Flower Ornament Scripture,* p. 178, from the chapter called "The Meditation on the Enlightening Being Universally Good [Samantabhadra]."

82. Vaidya, p. 306, ll. 6–14.

83. Vaidya, p. 306, l. 14f.

84. Vaidya, p. 306, l. 15f.

85. See Williams, *Mahāyāna Buddhism,* p. 251.

86. See Gomez, *The Land of Bliss,* p. 97f., and 193.

87. The position of this sūtra in our argument is somewhat problematic, as though the work is said to have been translated into Chinese by Kālayaśas towards the beginning of the fifth century, no Sanskrit original survives, the reason being, it has been suggested, that no Sanskrit text ever existed, the sūtra being a Chinese composition originating in Central Asia or China itself. But, without wishing to enter into this particular argument, it is surely reasonable to suppose, even were the latter hypothesis to be true, that the doctrinal details of the text were, at the very least, influenced by the Indian Mahāyāna, there being a strong possibility that they may even be a faithful record of practices and beliefs that were common in India.

See J. F. Pas, "The Kuan-wu-liang-shou Fo-ching: its origins and literary criticism," in *Buddhist Thought and Asian Civilization,* L. S. Kawamura and K. Scott, eds. (CA: Emeryville, 1977).

I have used the English translation of the sūtra, entitled *The Sūtra of Contemplation on the Buddha of Immeasurable Life,* produced by the Ryukoku University Translation Centre, Kyoto, under the direction of Meiji Yamada, 1984.

88. Amitābha means "Endless Light," and Amitāyus "Endless Life." The two names of the Buddha are discussed in the longer *Sukhāvatīvyūha Sūtra*. See Gomez, *The Land*

of Bliss, p. 83. "And, Ānanda, the measure of the life span of the Blessed Amitābha the *Tathāgata* is immeasurable. . . . Therefore that *tathāgata* is called 'Amitāyus.' "

89. M. Yamada, *The Sūtra of Contemplation on the Buddha of Immeasurable Life* (Kyoto: Ryukoku University Translation Centre, 1984), p. 45.

90. "Amida" is a transcription of the Japanese rendering of "Amitābha" or perhaps even a simpler form such as "Amita."

91. Yamada, *Sūtra of Contemplation*, p. 77.

92. Vaidya, p. 295, ll. 19–22, and p. 295, ll. 30–p. 296, l. 2.

93. Vaidya, p. 297, ll. 7–9.

94. Vaidya, p. 266, l. 18f. and p. 303, ll. 24–29.

95. Cleary, *Flower Ornament Scripture*, p. 1275; Vaidya, 1960a, p. 159, l. 10f.:

. . . *sarvajagatsaṃgrahaviṣayaṃ mahāmaitrīmahākaruṇāmukhodyotaṃ nāma* . . . /

96. Cleary, *Flower Ornament Scripture*, p. 1276; Vaidya, 1960a, p. 160, l. 9:

. . . *mahākaruṇāmukhāvilambaṃ nāma* . . . /

97. Ibid., p. 1277; Vaidya, 1960a, p. 160, l. 32f.:

etamahaṃ kulaputra mahākaruṇāmukhāvilambasya
bodhisattvacaryāmukhasya lābhī /

98. Vaidya, p. 263, l. 23f. and p. 278, l. 2.

99. Vaidya, p. 270, l. 24.

100. Vaidya, p. 293, l. 7.

101. Vaidya, p. 300, l. 25f.

102. Vaidya, p. 268, l. 18–p. 269, l. 2.

103. Cleary, *Flower Ornament Scripture*, p. 1276.

104. I am following the scheme of chapters of the Sanskrit version of the sūtra reproduced by Kern, *Saddharmapuṇḍarīka Sūtra;* and P. L. Vaidya, ed., *Saddharmapuṇḍarīka Sūtra* (Darbhanga: Mithila Institute, 1960). The chapter on Devadatta was added, as a new twelfth chapter, to the Chinese translation of the sūtra made by Kumārajīva in 406 C.E., making the chapter on Avalokiteśvara the twenty-fifth in most editions of the Chinese version of the sūtra.

105. See Williams, *Mahāyāna Buddhism*, p. 142.

106. See Monier-Williams, *A Sanskrit-English Dictionary*, p. 1246.

107. Kern, *Saddharmapuṇḍarīka Sūtra*, p. 410f.

108. Vaidya, p. 268, l. 5f.

109. Vaidya, p. 268, ll. 6–9.

110. Kern, *Saddharmapuṇḍarīka Sūtra*, p. 407f.

111. Ibid., p. 410.

112. See Mayer, *A Scripture of the Ancient Tantra Collection*, p. 115. The Hindu deity Khaṇḍobā, he writes, takes on the accessories of Malla and Maṇi, and the Buddhist *herukas* take on the *kāpālika* apparatus of Rudra or Bhairava.

113. See Burnouf, *L'Introduction*, p. 201.

114. N. D. Mironov, for example, writes: "It cannot be doubted that Avalokitasvara was the original form, later supplanted by Avalokiteśvara." See N. D. Mironov, "Buddhist Miscellanea: Avalokiteśvara—Kuan-Yin," *Journal of the Royal Asiatic Society* (1927): 243.

115. Mironov, "Buddhist Miscellanea," p. 243.

116. The details of the above two paragraphs are taken from Chandra, *The Thousand-Armed Avalokiteśvara*, pp. 18–23.

117. See Ibid., p. 22f.

118. Samuel Beal, *Si-Yu-Ki, Buddhist Records of the Western World* (1884; reprint, Delhi: Motilal Banarsidass, 1981), part I, p. 128, n. 28.

119. Ibid., part I, p. 128, n. 28.

120. See James Legge, trans., *A Record of Buddhistic Kingdoms* (1886; reprint, New York: Dover, 1965), pp. 46 and 112. The bodhisattva's name appears as *Kwan-she-yin* in Legge's transliteration scheme.

121. See Baron A. von Staël-Holstein, "Avalokita and Apalokita," *Harvard Journal of Asiatic Studies* 3/4 (1936): 353f. He refers to the *Ta Fang Kuang Fo Hua-yen Ching Su*, Nanjio 1589.

122. von Staël-Holstein, "Avalokita and Apalokita," p. 353. He refers to the *Fan-i Ming-i Chi*.

123. Monier-Williams, *A Sanskrit-English Dictionary*, p. 1285.

124. Ibid., p. 103.

125. See Marie-Thérèse de Mallman, *Introduction à l'Étude d'Avalokiteśvara* (Paris: Annale du Musée Guimet, 1948), pp. 59f. and 68. She refers to Burnouf, *L'Introduction*, p. 226.

126. de Mallman, *Introduction à l'Étude*, p. 67. Renou's evidence took the form of a verbal communication to de Mallman.

127. Ibid., p. 68. She refers to L. de la Vallée Poussin in the *Encyclopaedia of Religion and Ethics* (Edinburgh—New York: 1909), p. 257, n. 4, where he writes: "*Parijita* (*Mahāvyutpatti*, 126, 63) seems quite clearly to mean *parijitavān*, and it is quite possible that there are other examples."

128. Samuel Beal, *A Catena of Buddhist Scriptures from the Chinese* (London: Trubner, 1871), pp. 389ff. Beal translates the Chinese version of the text made by Jñānagupta and Dharmagupta in 601 C.E.

129. See Giuseppe Tucci, "Buddhist Notes I: A Propos Avalokiteśvara," in *Mélanges Chinois et Bouddhique* 9 (1948): 174.

130. Vaidya, p. 303, ll. 24–29.

131. Vaidya, p. 307, l. 6f.

132. Vaidya, p. 303, ll. 26–28.
See also Vaidya, p. 266, ll. 21–27.

133. Tucci, "Buddhist Notes," p. 174.

134. Kern, *Saddharmapuṇḍarīka Sūtra,* p. 406.

135. Mironov, "Buddhist Miscellanea," p. 245.

136. Chandra, *The Thousand-Armed Avalokiteśvara,* p. 22. Many widely used folk etymologies of Sanskrit words are based on readings of the words that are, strictly speaking, grammatically incorrect, such as the understanding of the word *mantra* as something which "saves" (from *trā-*, to save, or rescue) whoever "meditates" on it (from *man-*, to think, or meditate). See Jan Gonda, *"The Indian Mantra,"* in *Selected Studies,* by Jan Gonda (1963; reprint, Leiden: Brill, 1975), p. 252.

137. Beal, *Si-Yu-Ki,* part I, p. 127, n. 26.

138. von Staël-Holstein, "Avalokita and Apalokita," p. 353, n. 6.

139. Chandra, *The Thousand-Armed Avalokiteśvara,* p. 18.
Bodhicaryāvatāra, ch. 2, v. 51: "Terrified I cried out in anguish to the Protector Avalokita whose conduct overflows with compassion. I have done evil. May he protect me." Translation by Kate Crosby and Andrew Skilton (Oxford: Oxford University Press, 1996).

140. Chandra, *The Thousand-Armed Avalokiteśvara,* p. 20.
The bodhisattva is often referred to in Tibetan texts as *sPyan ras gzigs dBang phyug*, the second part of the expression being a translation of *īśvara*.

141. See Yamada, *The Sūtra of Contemplation,* p. 132. This remark is based on the findings of an article by John Brough, "Comments on Third Century Shan-shan and the History of Buddhism," in *Bulletin of the School of Oriental and African Studies* 28, pt. 3 (1965): 607–611.

142. The bodhisattva is, it appears, specifically called a *lokeśvara* in the twenty-fourth chapter of the *Saddharmapuṇḍarīka Sūtra,* where he is referred to, at one point, as: *lokeśvara rāja nāyako*. See Vaidya, ed., *Saddharmapuṇḍarīka Sūtra,* p. 256; l. 17.

143. These painting are probably of eighteenth century origin. Bhattacharyya, for instance, writes: "The painting appears to be at least two hundred years old . . ." Texts describing an arrangement of one hundred and eight forms of Avalokiteśvara

(slightly different from the one depicted in the Macchandar Vahal temple) were, however, translated into Chinese in 985 C.E. and into Tibetan, anonymously, at an unknown date.

See Benoytosh Bhattacharyya, *The Indian Buddhist Iconography* (1924; reprint, Delhi: Cosmo, 1985), p. 33, and Lokesh Chandra, *The 108 Forms of Lokeśvara in Hymns and Sculptures* (New Delhi: International Academy of Indian Culture, 1981), p. 5.

144. Among the thirty-three forms of Kuan-yin, Nīlakaṇṭha Kuan-yin preserves the relationship between the bodhisattva and Śiva. See Chandra, *The Thousand-Armed Avalokiteśvara*, p. 45, and Piyasīlo, *Avalokiteśvara: Origin, Manifestations and Meanings* (Malaysia: Petaling Jaya, 1991), pp. 40ff.

Many of the forms of Kuan-yin are female, such as "White-robed Kuan-yin" related to Pāṇḍaravāsinī, "Leaf-robed Kuan-yin," related to Parṇaśavarī, and "Tārā Kuan-yin," related to Tārā. See Chandra, *The Thousand-Armed Avalokiteśvara*, pp. 44–47, and Piyasīlo, *Avalokiteśvara*, ch. 6. The absorption of such deities into the figure of Kuan-yin may account, at least in part, for the way in which the bodhisattva is often depicted, in the Far East, as a rather androgynous, asexual figure and is usually, in fact, conceived of as female.

145. See Chandra, *The Thousand-Armed Avalokiteśvara*, p. 43.

According to Piyasīlo, there are a number of accepted variations of her name: Cundi, Cundra, Candra, Canda, Cuṇḍāvajri. Lokesh Chandra refers to her as Cundī. Her popularity is attested to by the three separate Chinese translations of her extended *dhāraṇī* made at the end of the seventh and beginning of the eighth centuries. The extended *dhāraṇī* was translated by Divakara around 685 C.E. (Nanjio 344, Taisho 20, 185), by Vajrabodhi around 723 C.E. (Nanjio 345, Taisho 20, 173), and by Amoghavajra (Nanjio 346, Taisho, 20, 78). See Piyasīlo, *Avalokiteśvara*, p. 54.

146. See Vaidya, p. 301, ll. 12–14

Piyasīlo writes: "The first mention of Cuṇḍā Avalokiteśvara is in the Kāraṇḍavyūha, where we find her mantra: 'Oṃ cale cule cunde svāhā'." See *Avalokiteśvara*, Piyasīlo, p. 54.

Vaidya's Sanskrit edition seems to contain a misprint. There, the formula apears as: *Oṃ Cale Cule Cunye Svāhā*. The Peking edition of the Tibetan text, however, reads: *oṃ tsa le tsu le tsun de svāhā*. This corresponds to the version given by Piyasīlo: *Oṃ Cale Cule Cunde Svāhā*.

Chapter 4: *Oṃ Maṇipadme Hūṃ* and *Namaḥ Śivāya*

1. See Monier-Williams, *A Sanskrit-English Dictionary*, p. 963.

2. *Aṣṭasāhasrikā*, 335; Conze, *The Perfection of Wisdom*, p. 205.

3. See, for instance, Vaidya, p. 264, l. 24; p. 265, l. 11; p. 275, l. 24, and p. 304, l. 9 and 17, where the term *vidyācaraṇasaṃpanna* is applied, respectively, to the *tathāgatas* Vipaśyin, Śikhin, Śrī (Bali's future identify as a *tathāgata*), Bhasmeśvara (Maheśvara's future identify as a *tathāgata*) and Umeśvara (Umādevī's future identity as a *tathāgata*).

The epithet is also found throughout the Nikāyas. See, for instance, *Dīgha Nikāya*, vol. I, p. 49. I am grateful to Dr. Rupert Gethin for pointing this latter point out to me.

4. See, Vaidya, p. 263, l. 10, where Yama addresses Avalokiteśvara in this way.

5. *Aṣṭasāhasrikā*, 73; Conze, *The Perfection of Wisdom*, p. 108f.

6. Ibid., 75f.; Ibid. p. 109.

7. Ibid., 73; Ibid., p. 109.

8. See Conze, *The Short Prajñāpāramitā Texts*, p. 141. The *vidyā* is often prefixed by the additional syllable *Oṃ*.

9. See, for instance, the discussion of this issue by Alex Wayman in "The Significance of Mantras, from the Veda down to Buddhist tantric practice," in A. Wayman, *Buddhist Insight* (Delhi: Motilal Banarsidass, 1984).

10. Vaidya, p. 292, l. 11f.

11. Vaidya, p. 292, l. 16f.

12. Vaidya, part II, ch. 4.

13. Vaidya, p. 298, l. 3f.

14. Vaidya, part II, ch. 6.

15. Respectively, Vaidya, p. 297, l. 3 and p. 300, l. 23.

16. Vaidya, part II, ch. 3–6.

17. Vaidya, p. 260, l. 32.

18. Vaidya, p. 261, l. 24f.

19. Vaidya, part II, ch. 3–6.

20. Vaidya, p. 281, l. 1.

21. Vaidya, p. 285, l. 1f.

22. Vaidya, p. 268, ll. 5–14.

23. Vaidya, p. 275, l. 26f.

24. This is the first chapter of the third section, the *Brāhmottara Khaṇḍa*, of book three, the *Brāhma Khaṇḍa*.

25. Chapter 17 of the *Vidyeśvara Saṃhitā* near the beginning of the purāṇa.

26. Chapters 12–14 in the second section of the *Vāyavīyasaṃhitā*, near the end of the purāṇa.

27. Chapter 85 of the first part of the purāṇa.

28. *Skanda Purāṇa*, III, iii, 1, 1–4.

29. *Skanda Purāṇa*, III, iii, 1, 7.

30. *Skanda Purāṇa*, III, iii, 1, 8f.

31. *Skanda Purāṇa*, III, iii, 1, 10–15.

32. *Skanda Purāṇa*, III, iii, 1, 16–20.

33. *Skanda Purāṇa*, III, iii, 1, 20–27.

34. *Skanda Purāṇa*, III, iii, 1, 28–36.

35. *Skanda Purāṇa*, III, iii, 1, 37–40.

36. *Skanda Purāṇa*, III, iii, 1, 41–48.

37. *Skanda Purāṇa*, III, iii, 1, 49–59.

38. *Skanda Purāṇa*, III, iii, 1, 60–71.

39. See Ludo Rocher, "Mantras in the *Śivapurāṇa*," in *Understanding Mantras,* Harvey P. Alper, ed. (Albany: State University of New York, 1989), p. 180. "Occasionally, the *Śiva Purāṇa* speaks of *ṣaḍakṣaramantra* rather than *pañcākṣaramantra*. This is described as 'the *pañcākṣaravidyā* to which the *praṇava* is added' . . ." (*pañcākṣaramayīṃ vidyāṃ jajāpa praṇavānvitām*). *Śiva Purāṇa*, iv, 20, 45.

40. Vaidya, p. 292, ll. 19f and 25

41. *Liṅga Purāṇa*, I, 85, 39f.

42. *Śiva Purāṇa*, *Vāyavīyasaṃhitā*, 14, 51.

43. *Śiva Purāṇa*, *Vāyavīyasaṃhitā*, 13, 12.

44. *Liṅga Purāṇa*, I, 85, 39f.

It should be noted that the comparable Vaiṣṇavite formulae, the eight-syllable *Oṃ Namo Nārāyaṇāya* and the twelve-syllable *Oṃ Namo Bhagavate Vāsudevāya*, are described in the same all-encompassing terms. In the *Liṅga Purāṇa*, for instance, we read: "The mantra *Oṃ Namo Nārāyaṇāya* is the means for achieving all objects. Hence, one should repeat the mantra *Oṃ Namo Nārāyaṇāya* on all occasions." (*Liṅga Purāṇa*, ch. 7, ll. 9–14) The twelve-syllable formula, meanwhile, "destroys the great sins of those who read and listen to it. The man who repeats this unchanging twelve-syllabled mantra continuously attains the divine, incomparable great region of Viṣṇu even if he follows a sinful conduct." (*Liṅga Purāṇa*, ch. 7, ll. 28–33)

45. Vaidya, p. 292, l. 20.

46. Vaidya, p. 293, ll. 8–10.

47. Vaidya, p. 293, l. 16f.

48. Vaidya, p. 294, l. 4.

49. Vaidya, p. 300, l. 1.

50. Vaidya, p. 293, l. 18f.

51. *Śiva Purāṇa*, *Vāyavīyasaṃhitā*,12, 37.

52. *Śiva Purāṇa, Vāyavīyasaṃhitā,* 14, 74.

53. *Śiva Purāṇa, Vāyavīyasaṃhitā,* 14, 1–15.

54. Rocher, "Mantras," pp. 183 and 198.

55. *Śiva Purāṇa, Vidyeśvarasaṃhitā,* 18, 158.

56. *Śiva Purāṇa, Vidyeśvarasaṃhitā,* 10, 25f.

57. *Śiva Purāṇa, Vidyeśvarasaṃhitā,* 7, 2.
Rocher points out that the *sūta* explains to the sages that he knows the formula due to the mercy of Śiva (*śivasya kṛpayaiva*). See Rocher, "Mantras," p. 183.

58. Vaidya, p. 296, l. 16.

59. Vaidya, p. 293, l. 5f.

60. Vaidya, p. 298, ll. 12–14.

61. Vaidya, p. 296, l. 20f.

62. Vaidya, p. 292, l. 17f.

63. Vaidya, p. 292, l. 22f.

64. Vaidya, p. 292, ll. 23–25.

65. Vaidya, p. 297, l. 1f.

66. Vaidya, p. 300, l. 20f.

67. Vaidya, p. 296, l. 5.

68. Vaidya, p. 296, ll. 7–9.

69. Vaidya, p. 296, ll. 22–25.

70. Vaidya, p. 296, ll. 25f.

71. *Śiva Purāṇa, Vāyavīyasaṃhitā,* 14, 1.

72. *Śiva Purāṇa, Vidyeśvarasaṃhitā,* 17, 35.

73. Jan Gonda, "The Indian Mantra," *Oriens* 16 (1963): 278.

74. *Taittitīya Upaniṣas,* I, 8: *Oṃ iti brahma / Oṃ itīdaṃ sarvam /* See Zaehner, *Hindu Scriptures,* p. 135.

75. *Māṇḍūkya Upaniṣad,* 1. See Zaehner, *Hindu Scriptures,* p. 201.

76. *Śiva Purāṇa, Vidyeśvarasaṃhitā,* 17, 4–9. I have followed the discussion of this passage in Rocher, *The Purāṇas.* The subtle *praṇava* is itself subdivided into a long and a short form, the long one separating out the single sound of the short form into the components "A," "U," and "M."

77. *Kaṭha Upaniṣad,* II, 16. See Zaehner, *Hindu Scriptures,* p. 174.

78. *Śiva Purāṇa, Vidyeśvarasaṃhitā,* 17, 34.

79. *Śvetāśvatara Upaniṣad,* IV, 9. See Zaehner, *Hindu Scriptures,* p. 211.

80. So, too, was it said of the seventh-century South Indian Śaivite singer-saint Appar: "Just as the Vedas and their six branches were the precious jewel to the (ancient) Brāhmaṇas, so was *Namaḥ Śivāya* to himself (Appar) and his followers." See K. A. Nilakantha Sastri, "An historical sketch of Śaivism," in *The Cultural Heritage of India* (Calcutta: Ramakrishna Mission, 1956), IV: 70.

81. *Śiva Purāṇa, Vāyavīyasaṃhitā,*12, 23.

82. *Śiva Purāṇa, Vāyavīyasaṃhitā,*12, 39.

83. *Liṅga Purāṇa,* I, 85, 9.

84. Vaidya, p. 297, l. 17f.

85. Vaidya, p. 299, l. 13f.

86. Vaidya, p. 293, l. 19f.: . . . *sarvajñānasya akṣayaṃ nirdeśaṃ* . . . /

87. *Śiva Purāṇa, Vāyavīyasaṃhitā,* 12, 7.

88. *Liṅga Purāṇa,* I, 85, 32.

89. Strictly speaking, this work, also known as the *Talavakāra Upaniṣad Brāhmaṇa,* belongs to the *āraṇyaka,* or "forest treatise" literature that prefigures the more purely philosophical Upaniṣads. See Jan Gonda, *Vedic Literature* (Wiesbaden: Otto Harrassowitz, 1974), I: 319, and 431.

90. The text and its English translation are presented by Hanns Oertel, *Journal of the American Oriental Society* 16 (1896): 79–206.

See also a discussion of this passage in J. A. B. van Buitenen, "Akṣara," *Journal of the American Oriental Society* 79 (1959): 176–178.

91. Vaidya, p. 299, l. 31–300, l. 5.

92. See J. Takasaki, trans., *A Study of the Ratnagotravibhāga (Uttaratantra)* (Rome: Instituto Italiano per il Medio ed Estremo Oriente, 1966), p. 268f.

93. *Śiva Purāṇa, Vayavīyasaṃhitā,* 12, 40–43.

94. Vaidya, p. 296, l. 9f.

95. See Fredrick W. Bunce, *A Dictionary of Buddhist and Hindu Iconography* (New Delhi: Printworld, 1997) and Gosta Liebert, *Dictionary of the Indian Religions* (Leiden: Brill, 1976). The Tibetan translation is *rgyal po'i dbang po thams cad* (Peking, 260a, l. 3).

96. See for instance Sanjukta Gupta, "The Pāñcarātra Attitude to Mantra," in Alper, *Understanding Mantras,* p. 225f. "God's causal relation to the universe is regularly expressed in terms of his *śakti.* All creation is considered to be a special state of his being *(bhūti)* and a result of the action of his sovereign will, acting in the light of his omniscience. Thus, god's *śakti* is said to manifest herself in two aspects. Dynamically viewed, she is god's omnipotent creative activity, *kriyāśakti.* More statically viewed, she is god manifest as the creation, *bhūtiśakti.*"

97. *Śiva Purāṇa, Vāyavīyasaṃhitā,* 12, 24.

98. *Śiva Purāṇa, Vidyeśvarasaṃhitā,* 17, 132.

99. *Śiva Purāṇa, Vidyeśvarasaṃhitā,* 17, 135.

100. *Śiva Purāṇa, Vidyeśvarasaṃhitā,* 17, 43f.

101. *Śiva Purāṇa, Vidyeśvarasaṃhitā,* 17, 50. The term *śakti* is not actually used here, but the alternative *parā*. The essential point, I think, remains the same.

102. It seems likely that this was a well-known story: a footnote to the English translation of the *Skanda Purāṇa*, published by Motilal Banarsidass, states that it is also found in the *Pañcākṣara Māhātmaya* of the *Śiva Purāṇa,* although, perplexingly, it is, in fact, absent from the English translation of that purāṇa produced by the same publishers.

Chapter 5: *Oṃ Maṇipadme Hūṃ* and the Mahāyāna

1. Vaidya, p. 284, l. 1–p. 288, l. 11.

2. Vaidya, p. 283, ll. 1–30.

3. Vaidya, p. 307, l. 9f.

4. Vaidya, p. 307, l. 10–p. 308, l. 21.

5. Vaidya, p. 307, l. 10–13.

6. Lienhard, "Avalokiteśvara," p. 93.

7. Vaidya, p. 287, ll. 17–22.

8. Vaidya, p. 287, ll. 22f.

9. Vaidya, p. 287, l. 23f.

10. Vaidya, p. 287, ll. 24f.

11. Vaidya, p. 287, ll. 27–29.

12. Vaidya, p. 287, l. 29f.

13. Vaidya, p. 287, ll. 30–32.

14. Vaidya, p. 286, l. 32.

15. Vaidya, p. 288, l. 6f.

16. Vaidya, p. 288, l. 8f.

17. Vaidya, p. 288, ll. 9–11.

18. F. Edgerton, *Buddhist Hybrid Sanskrit,* II: 244 explains that *jñapti* refers to a "motion" or "proposal" put before the monastic assembly, usually in connection with

matters to do with initiation. The *jñaptimuktika*, or "isolated" *jñapti* refers to a proposal put forward without a separate question as to whether the monks approve and a *jñaptidvitīyam* to a proposal put forward with a single additional question. The *jñapticaturtham*, by extension, is a proposal put forward with three such questions.

19. Vaidya, p. 307, l. 14.

20. Vaidya, p. 307, l. 15; Peking, p. 273a, l. 4: *dge slong dag tshul khrims dang mi ldan pa'i dge slong gis ni sna tshogs kyi gnas su yang 'gro bar mi byin gsol ba dang / bzhi ba bya ba lta ci smos te /*

21. Vaidya, p. 307, l. 16. The Tibetan omits this sentence. Peking, p. 273a, l. 5: *de dag ni ston pa'i bstan pa 'jig par byed ba'o* / "They should not sit upon the teacher's seat."

22. Vaidya, p. 307, l. 17; Peking, p. 273a, l. 5. Monier-Williams, *A Sanskrit-English Dictionary*, p. 153, gives "conversation, communication" for *ālapa*, though the Tibetan translation indicates that it is the food of the *saṃgha* that is not to be given: *de dag la dge dun gyi zas kyang ni sbyin no* / H. A. Jäschke, *A Tibetan-English Dictionary* (London: Routledge and Kegan Paul, 1881), p. 487, gives "food, nourishment" for *zas*.

23. Vaidya, p. 307, l. 18; Peking, p. 273a, l. 6.

24. Vaidya, p. 307, l. 24f

25. Vaidya, p. 307, l. 25–28.

26. Vaidya, p. 307, l. 28–32.

27. Vaidya, p. 307, l. 32–p. 308, l. 10.

28. Vaidya, p. 307, ll. 21–24.

29. Vaidya, p. 298, ll. 10–12.

I am following Lalou's translation of the last of these epithets (*asaṃvṛtter-yāpathaḥ*). See Marcelle Lalou, *Les Religions du Tibet* (Paris: Presses Universitaires de France, 1957), p. 38: ". . . ce *dharmabhāṇaka* est né dans une mauvaise voie (*gati*); il a une conduite degradée; il est entouré d'épouses, de fils et de filles; son vêtement religieux est plein d'excréments et d'urine; il n'est pas un abstinent." The relevant Tibetan phrase (Peking p. 262a, l. 6) is: *spyod lam ma bsdams pa yin no.*

30. Vaidya, p. 298, ll. 6–9.

31. *Aṣṭasāhasrikā*, 483. See Conze, *The Perfection of Wisdom*, p. 278.

32. Kern, *Saddharmapuṇḍarīka Sūtra*, p. 216.

33. See Snellgrove, *Indo-Tibetan Buddhism*, p. 157

34. Vaidya, p. 299, l. 13.

35. Vaidya, p. 293, ll. 5–7.

36. Vaidya, p. 293, l. 8. The Tibetan (Peking, p. 256b, l. 4) reads: *de rigs 'dzin gyi 'khor los sgyur ba'i dbang thob par 'gyur ro /*

37. Vaidya, p. 296, ll. 7–9.

38. Vaiyda, p. 296, l. 9.

39. Vaidya, p. 296, ll. 10–12.

40. Vaidya, p. 296, ll. 12–14.
Monier-Williams translates *dhūpakaṭacchuka* as: "small spoon with frankincense." See Monier-Williams, *A Sanskrit-English Dictionary*, p. 517.

41. Vaidya, p. 296, ll. 14–16.
See the discussion of four "door guardians" in the *Vajradhātu* maṇḍala in the *Sarvatathāgatatattvasaṃgraha Tantra* in Snellgrove, *Indo-Tibetan Buddhism*, p. 222f.

42. See J. A. B. van Buitenen, "The Indian Hero as Vidyādhara," in *Studies in Indian Literature and Philosophy—Collected Articles of J. A. B. van Buitenen*, Ludo Rocher, ed. (1958; reprint, Delhi: Motilal Banarsidass, 1988), pp. 135–145.
On the *Bṛhatkathā*, see Felix Lacôte, *Essai sur Guṇāḍhya et la Bṛhatkathā* (Paris: Leroux, 1908). Lacôte (p. 276) writes that the conception of the *vidyādhara* is an amalgamation of the traits of the *gandharva*, the yogin and the *arhat*: ". . . création de l'imagination populaire où s'amalgament les traits de l'antique gandharva, du yogin at de l'arhat . . ."

43. *Ratnaguṇasaṃcayagāthā*, xxvii, 5. See Conze, *The Perfection of Wisdom*, p. 59.

44. See, for instance, Marcelle Lalou, "A La Recherche du Vidyādharapiṭaka: Le Cycle du Subāhuparipṛcchā-Tantra," in *Studies in Indology and Buddhology Presented in Honour of Professor Susumu Yamagachi* (Tokyo: Hozokan, 1955), pp. 68–72.

45. See Debiprasad Chattopadhyaya, ed., *Tāranātha's History of Buddhism in India* (1970; reprint, Delhi: Motilal Banarsidass, 1990), p. 151. "Their": Tāranātha is referring to important Buddhist philosophers of the fifth century C.E., such as Asaṅga and Vasubhandu.

46. See Ibid., p. 151.

47. See Jean Przyluski, "Les Vidyārāja, Contribution à l'Histoire de la Magie dans les Sectes Mahāyānistes," in *Bulletin de l'Ecole Francaise d'Extrème Orient* 23 (1923): 301–318.
See, also Snellgrove, *Indo-Tibetan Buddhism*, p. 135. He concludes: "These [the *vidyādharas*] can be human or supramundane beings, just as Bodhisattvas can be either. Thus, the term can be a synonym for *mahāsiddha*, 'great adept' in the sense of highly perfected yogin, or it can refer to powerful divinities of the kind that one might expect to find in Vajrapāṇi's following."

48. See Przyluski, "Les Vidyārāja," p. 306.

49. *Bhāgavata Purāṇa,* VIII, 18, 9f.

50. *Padma Purāṇa,* I, 30, 67f. See the English translation produced by N. A. Deshpande (Delhi: Motilal Banarsidass, 1988).

51. Vaidya, p. 299, ll. 21–23: *ye ca kulaputrā nānāsthāṇeṣu dīkṣante / mokṣārtheṣu nānāpaṭeṣu dīkṣante / tadyathā indrapaṭaṃ śvetapaṭaṃ dhyuṣitapaṭam / divasanirīkṣakā maheśvareṣu dīkṣante / bailmavegarudreṣu nagnaśramaṇeṣu ca / eṣu sthāneṣu dīkṣante / na teṣāṃ mokṣaṃ saṃvidyate / anādigatikānāmapi nāpi nāśo bhavat /*

The identity of the different sects listed here remains obscure, though the readings of Monier-Williams and Edgerton suggest they include both Śaivite and Jain groups.

52. Vaidya, p. 265, l. 5 f.

53. Vaidya, p. 303, l. 32–p. 304, l. 22.

54. Vaidya, p. 262, ll. 21–24.

55. Vaidya, p. 262, l. 24f.

56. Vaidya, p. 262, l. 25–27.

57. Vaidya, p. 280, l. 23f.

58. Vaidya, p. 280, l. 25f.

59. Vaidya, p. 282, l. 18f.

60. Vaidya, p. 282, l. 19–22.

61. Vaidya, p. 297, ll. 18–20.

62. *Aṣṭasāhasrikā,* 63–69; Conze, *The Perfection of Wisdom,* p. 107f.

63. Vaidya, p. 293, ll. 5–7.

64. Vaidya, p. 300, l. 8.

65. *Aṣṭasāhasrikā,* 81; Conze, *The Perfection of Wisdom,* p. 111 f.

66. *Aṣṭasāharikā,* 481–527; Conze, *The Perfection of Wisdom,* pp. 277–299.

67. Stephan Beyer, "Notes on the Vision Quest in Early Mahāyāna," in *Prajñāpāramitā and Related Systems,* Lewis Lancaster, ed. (CA: University of California, 1977), pp. 329–340.

68. Ibid., p. 332.

69. See Paul Harrison, trans., *The Samādhi of Direct Encounter with the Buddhas of the Present, An Annotated English Translation of the Tibetan Version of the Pratyutpannabuddha-saṃmukhāvasthitasamādhi Sūtra* (Tokyo: International Institute for Buddhist Studies, 1990), pp. 121–129.

70. I am using a reconstructed Sanskrit title for this Pure Land text, whose origins have been discussed briefly in chapter 3.

71. See Gomez, *The Land of Bliss*, pp. 66–80.

72. Beyer, "Notes on the Vision Quest," p. 331.

73. See Kern, *Saddharmapuṇḍarīka Sūtra*, pp. 354–363.

74. See Cleary, *The Flower Ornament*, p. 1174.

75. *Aṣṭasāhasrikā*, 481–492; Conze, *The Perfection of Wisdom*, pp. 277–283.

76. Vaidya, p. 294, ll. 3–30.

77. Vaidya, p. 284, ll. 27–29.

78. Vaidya, p. 292, l. 12f.

79. Vaidya, p. 292, l. 16f.

80. *Aṣṭasāhasrikā*, 526f.; Conze, *The Perfection of Wisdom*, p. 298f.

81. Vaidya, p. 300, ll. 22–25.

82. Vaidya, p. 301, l. 15.

83. *Aṣṭasāhasrikā*, 497f.; Conze, *The Perfection of Wisdom*, p. 285.

84. Ibid., p. 296.

85. Vaidya, p. 293, ll. 21–23.

86. See Kern, *Saddharmapuṇḍarīka Sūtra*, p. 379f.

87. See Cleary, *The Flower Ornament*, p. 1509.

88. Vaidya, p. 302, ll. 26–32.

89. Vaidya, p. 302, l. 9f.

90. Vaidya, p. 299, l. 29.

91. See, for instance, *Aṣṭasāhasrikā*, 254; Conze, *The Perfection of Wisdom*, p. 172.

92. Vaidya, p. 299, l. 30f.

93. Vaidya, p. 299, l. 31.

94. Vaidya, p. 296, l. 16–18.

95. See, for instance, Alexis Sanderson, "Vajrayānā: Origin and Function," from *Buddhism into the Year 2000: International Conference Proceedings* (Bangkok: Dhammakaya Foundation, 1994), pp. 87–102. Sanderson comments in detail on an initiation ceremony described in one of the Buddhist Yoginītantras, which involves throwing a flower into the center of a maṇḍala. He remarks (p. 92): "The present author's view is that almost everything concrete in the system is non-Buddhist in origin even though the whole is entirely Buddhist in its function."

96. See Snellgrove, *Indo-Tibetan Buddhism*, p. 110.

97. Ibid., pp. 192, and 240f.

98. Ibid., p. 192, n. 130.

99. See Gregory Schopen, "Sukhāvatī as a Generalised Religious Goal in Sanskrit Mahāyāna Sūtra Literature," in *Indo-Iranian Journal* 19 (1977): 177–210.

100. In the *Bhaiṣajyaguru Sūtra*, for instance, monks, nuns, laymen, and women who undertake a fast with the intention of being reborn in Sukhāvatī are said to achieve this end if, at the time of their death, they hear the name of the *tathāgata* Bhaiṣajyaguru-vaiḍūryaprabha, a buddha who has his own buddha field and who is not normally associated with Sukhāvatī. See Schopen, "Sukhāvatī," p. 177f.

101. See Schopen, "Sukhāvatī," pp. 201–204.

102. Vaidya, p. 269, ll. 15–22 and p. 306. l. 33–p. 307, l. 5.

103. Vaidya, p. 281, ll. 28–31.

104. Vaidya, p. 264, ll. 11–14.

105. Vaidya, p. 271, ll. 25–29. This passage appears neither in the Peking edition of the Tibetan translation, nor in Burnouf's French translation of the sūtra.

106. Vaidya, p. 276, l. 25f. Like the above, this passage appears neither in the Peking edition, nor in Burnouf's translation.

107. Vaidya, p. 266, ll. 1–3.

108. Vaidya, p. 266, l. 12f.

109. Vaidya, p. 303, ll. 14–17.

110. Vaidya, p. 303, l. 20–22.

111. Vaidya, p. 303, l. 23.

112. Vaidya, p. 297, l. 21f.: *yaḥ kulaputro vā kuladuhitā vā imāṃ ṣaḍakṣarīṃ mahāvidyāṃ japet, sa imān samādhīn pratilabhate / tadyathā—maṇidharo nāma samādhiḥ, . . .*

113. Peking, p. 260a, l. 1: *gyas phyogs su ni byang chub sems dpa' nor bu rin po che 'dzin par bgyi'o /*

Peking, p. 261b, l. 2: *nor bu rin po che 'dzin ces bya ba'i ting nge 'dzin dang /*

114. See Jäschke, *A Tibetan-English Dictionary,* p. 308.

115. See E. Conze, trans., *Abhisamayālaṅkāra* (Rome: Istituto Italiano per il Medio ed Estremo Oriente, 1954), i, 19. However, the Tibetan translation of *cintāmaṇi* here is not *nor bu rin po che*, but *yid bzhin nor bu*. See, Conze, *Materials for a Dictionary of the Prajñāpāramitā Literature*, p. 175.

116. Vaidya, p. 292, l. 26f.

117. Vaidya, p. 293, l. 5f.

118. Vaidya, p. 293, l. 14f.

119. Vaidya, p. 295, l. 12f.

120. Meritorious, also, are they who listen, meditate on, and mentally bear in mind the formula. Vaidya, p. 297, l. 15f.: *puṇyavastaste sattvā ya imaṃ ṣaḍakṣarīṃ mahāvidyāṃ japanti śṛṇvanti cintayanti adhyāśayena dhārayanti* /

121. Vaidya, p. 300, l.1.

122. Vaidya, p. 300, l. 8.

123. *Śiva Purāṇa, Vāyavīyasaṃhitā,* 14, 26–29. See also Rocher, *The Purāṇas*, p. 180, whose Sanskrit transliteration I have borrowed.

124. Schopen identifies one instance in which *japa*, as a surrogate practice to the offering of flowers to the *tathāgatas*, is linked to Sukhavatī. See Schopen, "Sukhāvatī," p. 188f.

125. See Gomez, *The Land of Bliss,* p. 19, and the Sanskrit in Vaidya's edition, 1961, p. 256, ll. 4–8

126. Vaidya, p. 276, l. 9–12.

127. Kern, *Saddharmapuṇḍarīka Sūtra*, p. 406. Vaidya, 1960, p. 250, l. 8.

128. Ibid., p. 406. Ibid., p. 250, l. 8.

129. Ibid., p. 406. Ibid., p. 250, l. 11.

130. Ibid., p. 407. Ibid., p. 250, l. 21.

131. Ibid., p. 408. Ibid., p. 250, l. 31.

132. Ibid., p. 408. Ibid., p. 251, l. 4.

133. Ibid., pp. 413–418. Ibid., p. 252–257.

134. Ibid., p. 409. Ibid., p. 251, l. 16.

135. Vaidya, p. 289, l. 32–p. 290, l. 2.

136. Vaidya, p. 292, ll. 6–8.

137. Vaidya, p. 268, ll. 5–9.

138. Vaidya, p. 275, ll. 19–22.

139. Vaidya, p. 278, l. 30–p. 279, l. 6 and p. 289, ll. 8–11.

140. Vaidya, p. 279, l. 6–13.

141. Vaidya, p. 291, l. 16 f.

142. Schopen, "Sukhāvatī," p. 184. Schopen points out that such ambiguity is common in the Prajñāpāramitā literature and may also be observed in passages from the *Samādhirāja Sūtra* and the *Gaṇḍavyūha Sūtra*.

143. Vaidya, p. 292, ll. 11–13.

144. Vaidya, p. 294, l.3f.

145. Vaidya, p. 300, ll. 9–11.

146. Vaidya, p. 292, ll. 6–8.

147. Vaidya, p. 292, l. 10f.

148. Vaidya, p. 292, l. 11f.

149. Vaidya, p. 292, l. 11f.: *ye ca tasya ṣaḍakṣarīmahāvidyānāmānusmaranti, tadā teṣu romavivareṣu jāyante /*

150. Vaidya, p. 290, ll. 14–21.

151. Beyer, "Notes on the Vision Quest," p. 337: ". . . a wave of visionary theism sweeping over the whole of northern India, influencing Hindu contemplatives as well as the [Buddhist] *yoga* masters of Kashmir."

152. Ibid., p. 338.

153. *Bhagavadgītā*, ix, 17 and xi, 43.
Saddharmapuṇḍarīka Sūtra, xv, 21 (Kern, 1884, p. 309, and Vaidya, 1960, p. 195, l. 13).

154. *Bhagavadgītā*, xi, 30.
Saddharmapuṇḍarīka Sūtra, ch. 20—beginning of prose section (Kern, 1884, p. 364)

155. *Bhagavadgītā*, ix, 26–28.
Saddharmapuṇḍarīka Sūtra, ii, 93 (Kern, 1884, p. 51f. and Vaidya, 1960, p. 36, l. 23ff.)

156. *Bhagavadgītā*, ix, 29.
Saddharmapuṇḍarīka Sūtra, ch. 5—the parable of the rain (Kern, 1884, p. 119).

157. Beyer, "Notes on the Vision Quest," p. 333f.

158. *Bhagavadgītā,* vii, 23.

159. *Bhagavadgītā*, viii, 5.

160. *Bhagavadgītā*, viii, 6.
Bhagavadgītā, viii, 7.
Bhagavadgītā, viii, 9 and 10.

161. *Bhagavadgītā*, viii, 13.

162. Beyer, "Notes on the Vision Quest," p. 334. Once again, we are arguing that even if this Pure Land text was composed outside India, it is not unlikely that its contents reflect practices that did originate in India.
See Yamada, *The Sūtra of Contemplation*, p. 101.

163. *Bhagavadgītā*, xi, 47.

164. *Bhagavadgītā*, xi, 54.

165. Beyer, "Notes on the Vistion Quest," p. 334f.

166. Ibid., p. 334.

167. *Bhagavadgītā*, xi, 7.

168. *Bhagavadgītā*, xi, 15.

169. *Bhagavadgītā*, xi, 46.

170. *Bhagavadgītā*, xi, 54.

171. *Bhagavadgītā*, xi, 45.

172. *Bhagavadgītā*, xi, 52.

173. *Bhagavadgītā*, xi, 52.

174. *Bhagavadgītā*, xi, 8.

175. *Bhagavadgītā*, xi, 54.

176. *Bhagavadgītā*, xi, 30.

177. *Bhagavadgītā*, xi, 27.

178. *Bhagavadgītā*, xi, 21.

179. *Bhagavadgītā*, xi, 23.

180. *Bhagavadgītā*, xi, 24.

181. *Bhagavadgītā*, xi, 36.

182. *Bhagavadgītā*, xi, 49.

183. *Bhagavadgītā*, xi, 32.

184. Vaidya, p. 290, ll. 22–24.

185. Vaidya, p. 290, ll. 23–25.

186. Vaidya, p. 290, ll. 29–31.

187. Vaidya, p. 290, l. 14.

188. Vaidya, p. 288, l. 19f.

189. Vaidya, p. 291, l. 19f.

190. Vaidya, p. 301, l. 27f.

191. Vaidya, p. 302, l. 21ff.

192. Kṛṣṇa is twice identified as the *puruṣa* in the chapter: *Bhagavadgītā*, xi, 18, and 38.

193. Vaidya, p. 290, l. 3f.

194. Vaidya, p. 290, l. 4f.

195. Vaidya, p. 290, ll. 6–8.

196. Vaidya, p. 290, l. 12f.

197. Vaidya, p. 290, l. 14.

198. Vaidya, p. 292, l. 11f.

199. Vaidya, p. 302, l. 30–32.

200. Vaidya, p. 290, l. 16f.

201. Vaidya, p. 292, l. 11f.

202. Rocher, *The Purāṇas,* p. 83.

203. Ibid., pp. 184–186.

204. *Kūrma Purāṇa*, II, iii, 7.

205. *Kūrma Purāṇa*, II, v, 11.

206. *Kūrma Purāṇa*, II, v, 8.

207. *Kūrma Purāṇa*, II, iv, 5.

208. *Kūrma Purāṇa*, II, iv, 7.

209. *Kūrma Purāṇa*, II, iv, 2.

210. *Kūrma Purāṇa*, II, v, 28.

211. *Kūrma Purāṇa*, II, vi, 50

212. Vaidya, p. 290, ll. 18–22.

Chapter 6: The Meaning of *Oṃ Maṇipadme Hūṃ*

1. See Alper, "The Cosmos as Śiva's Language Game," *passim*.

2. Gonda, "The Indian Mantra," p. 253f.
Gonda also comments on the folk etymology of *mantra* as that which "saves" (from *trā-*, "to save," or "rescue") whoever "meditates" on it (from *man-*, "to think," or "meditate").

3. Ibid., p. 253.

4. Namkhai Norbu, *Dzogchen,The Self-Perfected State* (London: Arkana, 1989), p. 9.

5. Gonda, "The Indian Mantra," p. 252f.

6. Vaidya, p. 292, l. 11f.

7. Vaidya, p. 304, l. 2f.

8. Vaidya, p. 284, l. 28.

9. Vaidya, p. 297, ll. 21–29.

10. Vaidya, p. 300, l. 22.

11. Vaidya, p. 300, ll. 24–28.

12. Vaidya, p. 300, l. 25f.

13. Vaidya, p. 293, l. 5–7.

14. Vaidya, p. 267, ll. 1–27

15. Vaidya, p. 304, l. 29 - p. 305, l. 17.

16. Vaidya, p. 304, l. 28f.

17. Vaidya, p. 294, l. 6 - p. 295, l. 16.

18. Vaidya, p. 267, ll. 11–14.

19. Vaidya, p. 294, ll. 6–8.

20. In his esssay on the Indian mantra, Gonda reminds us that the use of the name of Jesus in the Christian tradition (Mark, xvi, 17) is believed to be a means of exorcising demons. See Gonda, "The Indian Mantra," p. 256.

21. See Kern, *Saddharmapuṇḍarīka Sūtra*, pp. 405–407.

22. *Śiva Purāṇa, Vāyavīyasaṃhitā,* 12, 62.

23. Vaidya, p. 293, l. 3f.

24. Vaidya, p. 293, l. 5f.

25. Vaidya, p. 282, l. 4 - p. 283, l. 28.

26. Vaidya, p. 292, l. 20.

27. Vaidya, p. 293, l. 3–5.

28. Vaidya, p. 294, l. 4.

29. Vaidya, p. 299, l. 31.

30. Vaidya, p. 300, l. 1.

31. Vaidya, p. 293, l. 19f.

32. Vaidya, p. 297, l. 16f.

33. Vaidya, p. 299, l. 14.

34. Vaidya, p. 299, l. 32.

35. See, for instance, Bokar Rinpoche, *Chenrezig, Lord of Love* (San Francisco: Clearpoint Press, 1991), pp. 39–41, where the six syllables are also related to six impure "veils," to six wisdoms, to six buddhas and, lastly, to five aspects of buddhahood, the final syllable *hūṃ* being used, in this instance, to "gather the grace" of those different aspects.

36. *Śiva Purāṇa, Vidyeśvarasaṃhitā*, 17, 16ff.

37. Liṅga Purāṇa, I, 85, 47ff.

38. Vaidya, p. 293, l. 7.

39. See Vaidya, p. 297, l. 26.

40. Vaidya, p. 300, l. 8.

41. Vaidya, p. 293, l. 18.

42. See Gonda, "The Indian Mantra," p. 256. He refers to *ṚgVeda*, i, 67, 4; vii, 7, 6, and vii, 32, 13.

43. See, for instance, Marylin Rhie and Robert Thurman, *Wisdom and Compassion, The Sacred Art of Tibet* (New York: Abrams, 1991), p. 34: "OM! the jewel in the lotus (itself a symbol of the union of compassion and wisdom, male and female, and so on) HUM."

44. See, for instance, Daniel Cozort, *Highest Yoga Tantra* (New York: Snow Lion, 1986), p. 177: "For instance, in the mantra of Avalokiteśvara, OṂ MAṆI PADME HŪṂ, Avalokiteśvara is the jewel (MAṆI) that arises in the lotus (PADME), that is, the deity that appears at the heart."

45. See R. S. Bucknell and Martin Stuart-Fox, *The Twilight Language* (London: Curzon, 1986), pp. 132–134: ". . . we have here a *dvandva* or "co-ordinative," compound, *maṇi-padme*, meaning 'jewel and lotus.' On this interpretation, the mantra is simply a list of five items: *Oṃ*, jewel, lotus, *Hūṃ*, *Hrīḥ*. This list contains two of the the five *dhyāni* Buddha emblems (jewel and lotus) and three of the five *bījas* (*Oṃ*, *Hūṃ*, *Hrīḥ*)."

46. See, for instance, Bokar Rinpoche, *Chenrezig*, p. 38: "Saying MANI PADME names Chenrezig through his attributes: 'the one who hold the jewel and the lotus'."

47. Edgerton notes the occasional use of nominative singular endings (*-o*, *-u*, and perhaps *-e*) for vocative of stems in *-a*. See Edgerton, *Buddhist Hybrid Sanskrit*, I: 8, 28.

48. Vaidya, p. 296, l. 11.

49. See Snellgrove, *Indo-Tibetan Buddhism*, p. 193.

50. See, for instance, F. W. Thomas, "Oṃ Maṇi Padme Hūṃ," *Journal of the Royal Asiatic Society* (1906): 464: "On the analogy of other *dhāraṇīs* such as *Oṃ Vajragandhe hūṃ*, *Oṃ Vajraloke Hūṃ*, *Oṃ Vajrapuṣpe hūṃ*, would it not be more probable that *maṇipadme* is a vocative referring to a feminine counterpart of that Bodhisattva, that is, Tārā?"

51. See Benoytosh Bhattacharya, ed., *The Indian Buddhist Iconography*, p. 180.

52. See, for instance, Agehananda Bharati, *The Tantric Tradition* (London: Rider, 1965), 133f.

53. See Bhattacharya, *The Indian Buddhist Iconography*, p. 178.

54. See Benoytosh Bhattacharya, ed., *Sādhanamāla* (Baroda: Oriental Institute, 1968) I: 30, and B. Bhattacharya, *The Indian Buddhist Iconography*, (1924), p. 33f. As we would expect, Ṣaḍakṣarī Lokeśvara holds a lotus in the left hand, a rosary in the right, with the other two hands held together against the breast (*vāmataḥ padmadharaṃ dakṣiṇato 'kṣaṣūtradharaṃ aparābhyām hastābhyāṃ hṛdi sampuṭāñjalisthitaṃ dhyāyāt*).

55. See Peking *bsTan 'gyur, rgyud 'gre Du*, p. 90b, l. 4–92a, l. 4.

56. The four-armed Avalokiteśvara that has become popular in the Tibetan tradition involves another slight modification of this form. While the bodhisattva continues to hold a string of prayer beads in right hand and lotus flower in left, the jewel is held between the two central hands. Amitābha is also often seated in miniature in the headdress of the bodhisattva. See, for instance, the statue described on p. 145 of Rhie and Thurman, *Wisdom and Compassion,* and the *'gro don mkha' ma*, "For All Beings Throughout Space," the famous *sādhana* composed by the fourteenth- and fifteenth-century Tibetan yogin Thang stong rgyal po. See Janet Gyatso, "An Avalokiteśvara Sādhana," in *Religions of Tibet in Practice,* Donald S. Lopez, ed. (NJ: Princeton University Press, 1997), pp. 266–270.

Avalokiteśvara also appears with Amitābha in his headdress in the *Kāraṇḍavyūha Sūtra*. Bali addresses the bodhisattva as "you who have the form of Amitābha on your head" (*amitābhamūrte śirasā*). See Vaidya, p. 275, l. 13f. The *dharmabhāṇaka* also sees him as "the one with the omniscient one on his head" (*sarvajñaśirasikṛtaṃ*), which is, I think, another reference to the same detail. See Vaidya, p. 300, l. 19.

57. Gomez, *The Land of Bliss*, p. 100; Vaidya, 1961, p. 247, l. 1.

58. Kern, *Saddharmapuṇḍarīka Sūtra*, p. 296; Vaidya, 1960, p. 20. The form *paduma* is a common middle Indic form *padma*. See Edgerton, *Buddhist Hybrid Sanskrit*, II, p. 317.

59. Kern, *Saddharmapuṇḍarīka Sūtra*, p. 239; Vaidya, 1960, p. 154, l. 23f.

60. Cleary, *The Flower Ornament*, p. 1281; Vaidya, 1960a, p. 167, l. 17.

61. Ibid., p. 1184; Ibid., p. 52, l. 4.

62. Ibid., p. 1184; Ibid., p. 52, l. 19ff.

63. Ibid., p. 1231; Ibid., p. 105, l. 5f.

64. Kern, *Saddharmapuṇḍarīka Sūtra*, p. 395f; Vaidya, 1960, p. 245, l. 14.

65. Gomez, *The Land of Bliss*, p. 85; Vaidya, 1961, p. 236, l. 26.

66. Ibid., p. 103; Ibid., p. 248, l. 21.

67. Ibid., p. 85; Ibid., p. 236, l. 26.

68. Ibid., p. 103; Ibid., p. 248, l. 21.

69. Cleary, *The Flower Ornament*, p. 1184; Vaidya, 1960a, p. 52, ll. 14–19.

70. Ibid., p. 1184; Ibid., p. 52, l. 23f.

71. Ibid., p. 1243; Ibid., p. 120, l. 19f.

72. Ibid., p. 1247; Ibid., p. 126, l. 3f.

73. Ibid., p. 1503; Ibid., p. 420, l. 21.

74. Cleary, The Flower Ornament, p. 1505; Ibid., p. 422, l. 10.

75. Ibid., p. 1507; Ibid., p. 424, l. 18.

76. Kern, *Saddharmapuṇḍarīka Sūtra*, p. 248; Vaidya, 1960, p. 159, l. 25.

77. Ibid., p. 249; Ibid., p. 160, l. 2.

78. Cleary, *The Flower Ornament,* p. 1418; Vaidya, 1960a, p. 325, ll. 14 and 27.

79. Ibid., p. 1317; Ibid., p. 207, l. 27f.

80. Ibid., p. 1493; Ibid., p. 410, l. 20.

81. Gomez, *The Land of Bliss,* p. 85; Vaidya, 1961, p. 236, l. 28.

82. See Robert A. F. Thurman, trans., *The Holy Teaching of Vimalakīrti* (PA: Pennsylvania State University, 1976), p. 19; Étienne Lamotte, *The Teaching of Vimalakīrti* (Oxford: Pali Text Society, 1976), p. 24.

83. Kern, *Saddharmapuṇḍarīka Sūtra*, p. 248; Vaidya, 1960, p. 159, l. 18f.

84 Ibid., p. 389; Ibid., p. 242, l. 12.

85. Cleary, *The Flower Ornament*, p. 1518; Vaidya, 1960a, p. 436, l. 5f.

86. Gomez, *The Land of Bliss*, p. 104; Vaidya, 1961, p. 248, l. 31f, and p. 249, l. 4.

87. Vaidya, p. 262, l. 30.

88. Vaidya, p. 275, l. 13f.

89. Vaidya, p. 300, l. 19.

90. Vaidya, p. 304, l. 3.

91. Vaidya, p. 304, l. 12.

92. Vaidya, p. 289, l. 1, and p. 291, ll. 12 and 26.

93. Vaidya, p. 261, l. 12.

94. Vaidya, p. 262, l. 8f.

95. Vaidya, p. 266, l. 16.

96. Vaidya, p. 266, l. 18, and p. 303, l. 29. In the first instance, the lotuses are "brilliant and shining, with golden stems and a thousand petals" (*sahasrapatrāṇi padmāni suvarṇadaṇḍāni vaidūryanirbhāsāni gṛhītvā*).

97. Vaidya, p. 268, l. 4ff.

98. Vaidya, p. 268, l. 11.

99. Vaidya, p. 270, l. 27

100. Cleary, *The Flower Ornament*, p. 1373; Vaidya, p. 273, l. 3f.

101. Dalai Lama, "Oṃ Maṇi Padme Hūṃ," in *Kindness, Clarity and Insight* (New York: Snow Lion, 1984), p. 117.

102. Quoted in Mark S. G. Dyczkowski, *The Doctrine of Vibration: An Analysis of the Doctrines and Practices of Kashmir Shaivism* (Albany: State University of New York, 1987), p. 202. See also pp. 185–188 for a further discussion of the significance of *Ahaṃ* as a mantra.

103. Quoted in Harvey P. Alper, "The Cosmos as Śiva's Language Game: 'Mantra' According to Kṣemarāja's *Śivasūtravimarśinī*," in Alper, *Understanding Mantras*, p. 280.

104. See P. C. Verhagen, "The *Mantra 'Oṃ maṇi-padme hūṃ'* in an Early Tibetan Grammatical Treatise," *Journal of the International Association of Buddhist Studies* 13 no. 2 (1990): 133–138.

105. This is the translation of *padme* in the *Kāraṇḍavyūha Sūtra*. See Vaidya, p. 268, l. 11, and Peking, p. 243b, l. 4.

106. Alexandra David-Neel, *Initiations and Initiates in Tibet* (London: Rider, 1931), p. 77. *bde ba can* is the Tibetan for Sukhāvatī, which is believed to be located in the west (*nub*).

Conclusion

1. Beatrice Lane Suzuki, "The School of Shingon Buddhism, Part II," *The Eastern Buddhist* (May 1936): 1–38 and Beatrice Lane Suzuki, "The School of Shingon Buddhism, Part III," *The Eastern Buddhist* (June 1937): 177–213.

2. Suzuki, "School of Shingon Buddhism," p. 198.

Appendix: Annotated Précis of the *Kāraṇḍavyūha*

1. Vaidya, p. 258, l. 4; Peking, p. 222a, l. 8. The Tibetan omits the preliminary praises and merely transliterates the simple title *Ārya Kāraṇḍavyūha Nāma Mahāyāna Sūtra*, in Tibetan, *'phags pa za ma tog bkod pa zhes bya ba theg pa chen po'i mdo /*

2. Vaidya, p. 258, l. 8; Peking, p. 224b, l. 2.

3. Vaidya, p. 258, l. 18; Peking, p. 224b, l. 8.

4. Vaidya, p. 260, l. 31; Peking, p. 227b, l. 4.

5. Vaidya, p. 261, l. 13; Peking, p. 228a, l. 2.

6. Vaidya, p. 261, l. 17; Peking, p. 228a, l. 5.

7. Vaidya, p. 261, l. 25; Peking, p. 228b, l. 1.

8. Vaidya, p. 262, l. 2; Peking, p. 228b, l. 5.

9. Vaidya, p. 262, l. 9; Peking, p. 229a, l. 2.

10. Monier-Williams, *A Sanskrit-English Dictionary*, p. 272, gives "assuming any shape at will" for *kāmarupin*.

11. Vaidya, p. 262, l. 20; Peking, p. 229a, l. 6. The Tibetan omits the last two epithets.

12. Vaidya, p. 262, l. 22. Nārayaṇa is referred to by the title *pañcamahāsamudra-namaskṛtasya*, or "he who is paid homage to by the five great oceans." The Tibetan omits this title.

13. Vaidya, p. 262, l. 24. Rāvaṇa is described as *pratidvandvī*, whilst Régamey's edition describes him as *nārāyaṇapratispardhin*. See Régamey, "Motifs Vichnouites," p. 426, n. 38.

14. Vaidya, p. 262, l. 27; Peking, p. 229b, l. 1.

15. Vaidya, p. 262, l. 30; Peking, p. 229b, l. 2.

16. Vaidya, p. 263, l. 13; Peking, p. 230a, l. 5.

17. Vaidya, p. 263, l. 22; Peking, p. 230b, l. 2.

18. Vaidya, p. 264, l. 11; Peking, p. 231a, l. 1.

19. Vaidya, p. 264, l. 16: Peking, p. 231a, l. 3.

20. Vaidya, p. 264, l. 22; Peking, p. 231a, l. 5.

21. Vaidya, p. 264, l. 27. Peking, p. 231a, l. 8. Both the Vaidya and Peking editions omit a passage in the text used by Burnouf, in which the "eyes" of Avalokiteśvara are said to be the same as those of all the *tathāgatas* (*sarvatathāgatasya eva mahāvalokiteśvarasya cakṣuṣo*).

22. Vaidya, p. 265, l. 8; Peking, p. 231b, l. 5.

23. Vaidya, p. 265, l. 15; Peking, p. 231b, l. 8.

24. Vaidya, p. 265, l. 25; Peking, p. 232a, l. 4.

25. Vaidya, p. 265, l. 27. This paragraph is not in the Peking edition.

26. Vaidya, p. 266, l. 3; Peking, p. 232a, l. 7.

27. Vaidya, p. 266, l. 13; Peking, p. 232b, l. 4.

28. Vaidya, p. 266, l. 27; Peking, p. 233a, l. 4.

29. Vaidya, p. 266, l. 29; Peking, p. 233a, l. 5.

30. Vaidya, p. 267, l. 9; Peking, p. 233a, l. 8.

31. Vaidya, p. 267, l. 17; Peking, p. 233b, l. 5.

32. Vaidya, p. 267, l. 25; Peking, p. 234a, l. 3.

33. Vaidya, p. 268, l. 5; Peking, p. 234a, l. 8.

34. Vaidya, p. 268, l. 11; Peking, p. 234b, l. 4: *chos kyi ros bskyod nas de nyid du pad ma'i nang du skye bar 'gyur te /*

35. Vaidya, p. 268, l. 14; Peking, p. 234b, l. 5.

36. Monier-Williams, *A Sanskrit-English Dictionary*, p. 1026: "a patriarch (esp. of Kubera and Rāvaṇa)."

37. Vaidya, p. 269, l. 2; Peking, p. 235b, l. 1.

38. Vaidya, p. 269, l. 7; Peking, p. 235b, l. 3.

39. Vaidya, p. 269, l. 13; Peking, p. 235b, l. 5.

40. Vaidya, p. 269, l. 18f.; Peking, p. 235b, l. 6f. The five acts of immediate retribution are: the killing of mother, father, or an *arhat*, causing dissension in the order of monks or deliberately causing the blood of a *tathāgata* to flow.

41. Vaidya, p. 269, l. 22; Peking, p. 235b, l. 8. However, the Tibetan refers only to an elaborate canopy and makes no mention of a *siṃhāsanaṃ*, or "lion throne."

42. Vaidya, p. 269, l. 27; Peking, p. 236a, l. 2.

43. Vaidya, p. 270, l. 13; Peking, p. 236a, l. 8. The men, presumably, have been reborn as animals.

44. Vaidya, p. 270, l. 19; Peking, p. 236b, l. 2.

45. Vaidya, p. 270, l. 22; Peking, p. 236b, l. 3.

46. Vaidya, p. 270, l. 26. This epithet is not found in the Peking edition.

47. Vaidya, p. 270, l. 26; Peking, p. 236b, l. 5.

48. Vaidya, p. 271, l. 9; Peking, p. 236b, l. 7.

49. Vaidya, p. 271, l. 10; Peking, p. 236b, l. 8: *. . . rin po che'i khri . . . /*

50. Vaidya, p. 271, l. 19; Peking, p. 237a, l. 2.

51. Vaidya, p. 271, l. 30. This paragraph is found neither in the Peking edition nor in Burnouf's translation.

52. Vaidya, p. 272, l. 23; Peking, p. 237b, l. 6.

53. Vaidya, p. 272, l. 29; Peking, p. 238a, l. 1.

54. Vaidya, p. 272, l. 30. These instrumental compounds are omitted in the Peking edition.

55. Vaidya, p. 273, l. 18; Peking, p. 238b, l. 2.

56. Vaidya, p. 273, l. 30; Peking, p. 238b, l. 8.

57. Vaidya, p. 274, l. 10; Peking, p. 239a, l. 6.

58. Vaidya, p. 274, l. 21; Peking, p. 239b, l. 3: *de nas mthu bo ches des par sbyin pa la 'gyod par 'gyur ro /*

59. Vaidya, p. 274, l. 23; Peking, p. 239b, l. 4.

60. Vaidya, p. 274, l. 28; Peking, p. 239b, l. 7. Régamey has "terre" instead of the sun and adds "flèches" to the list of weapons. Vaidya's edition, however, corresponds to the Peking edition at this point.

61. Vaidya, p. 274, l. 32; Peking, p. 240a, l. 1.

62. Vaidya, p. 275, l. 2; Peking, p. 240a, l. 2.

63. Vaidya, p. 275, l. 11; Paking, p. 240a, l. 6.

64. Vaidya, p. 275, l. 13. I take this epithet (not found here in the Peking edition) to be a reference to the common iconographical feature of Avalokiteśvara, in which the bodhisattva is depicted as carrying a small image of Amitābha in his head-dress. See, for instance, Rhie and Thurman, *Wisdom and Compassion*, p. 136.

65. Vaidya, p. 275, l. 18; Peking, p. 240b, l. 1.

66. Vaidya, p. 275, l. 22; Peking, p. 240b, l. 4.

67. Vaidya, p. 275, l. 28; Peking, p. 240b, l. 8.

68. Vaidya, p. 276, l. 8; Peking, p. 241a, l. 7.

69. Vaidya, p. 276, l. 12: Peking, p. 241a, l. 8. The third and fourth of these sins of omission are not found in the Peking edition.

70. Vaidya, p. 276, l. 21; Peking, p. 241b, l. 6.

71. Vaidya, p. 276, l. 32. This paragraph is found neither in the Peking edition nor in Burnouf's translation.

72. Vaidya, p. 277, l. 4; Peking, p. 241b, l. 7.

73. Vaidya, p. 277, l. 22; Peking, p. 242a, l. 8.

74. Vaidya, p. 278, l. 2; Peking, p. 242b, l. 4.

75. Vaidya, p. 278, l. 24; Peking, p. 243a, l. 6.

76. Vaidya, p. 279, l. 13; Peking, p. 243b, l. 6.

77. Vaidya, p. 279, l. 17; Peking, p. 243b, l. 7.

78. Vaidya, p. 279, l. 31; Peking, p. 244a, l. 2.

79. Vaidya, p. 280, l. 4; Peking, p. 244a, l. 3.

80. Vaidya, p. 280, l. 11; Peking, p. 244a, l. 6.

81. Vaidya, p. 280, l. 22; Peking, p. 244b, l. 3.

82. Vaidya, p. 280, l. 29; Peking, p. 244b, l. 6. My rendering of the song of praise is quite free. The Sanskrit (Vaidya, p. 280, ll. 28 and 29) reads: *aho guṇamayaṃ kṣetraṃ sarvadoṣavivarjitam / adyaiva vāpitaṃ bījaṃ adyaiva phalasaṃpadam /*

83. Vaidya, p. 281, l. 12; Peking, p. 245a, l. 2.

84. Vaidya, p. 281, l. 21; Peking, p. 245a, l. 5.

85. Vaidya, p. 281, l. 24; Peking, p. 245a, l. 5. The Tibetan phrase used in the place of Vārāṇasī is: *'jig gi grong khyer chen po*. The same comparison may be made elsewhere, for instance between: Vaidya, p. 298, l. 2, and Peking, p. 261b, l. 8; Vaidya, p. 298, l. 23, and Peking, p. 262b, l. 4.

86. Vaidya, p. 281, l. 32; Peking, p. 245a, l. 8. The Tibetan merely states that they are reborn as bodhisattvas called Sugandhamukha: . . . *kha na spos kyi dri* . . . /

87. Vaidya, p. 282, l. 23; Peking, p. 245b, l. 7.

88. Vaidya, p. 283, l. 4; Peking, p. 246a, l. 7.

89. Vaidya, p. 283, l. 11; Peking, p. 246b, l. 4.

90. Vaidya, p. 283, l. 21; Peking, p. 246b, l. 8.

91. Vaidya, p. 283, l. 28; Peking, p. 247a, l. 3.

92. Vaidya, p. 284, l. 30; Peking, p. 248a, l. 5.

93. Vaidya, p. 285, l. 22; Peking, p. 248b, l. 7.

94. Vaidya, p. 285, l. 24; Peking, p. 248b, l. 8. See Régamey, "Le Pseudo-Hapax," and Lienhard, "Avalokiteśvara," for a detailed discussion of the etymology and meaning of this word.

95. Vaidya, p. 286, l. 7; Peking, p. 249a, l. 6.

96. Vaidya, p. 286, l. 16; Peking, p. 249b, l. 3.

97. Vaidya, p. 286, l. 20; Peking, p. 249b, 5.

98. Vaidya, p. 287, l. 6; Peking, p. 250a, l. 5.

99. Vaidya, p. 287, l. 14; Peking, p. 250a, l. 8.

100. Vaidya, p. 287, l. 22; Peking, p. 250b, l. 4.

101. Vaidya, p. 287, l. 23; Peking, p. 250b, l. 5.

102. Vaidya, p. 288, l. 4; Peking, p. 251a, l. 2.

103. Vaidya, p. 288, l. 11; Peking, p. 251a, l. 5.

104. Vaidya, p. 288, l. 16; Peking, p. 251a, l. 8.

105. Vaidya, p. 288, l. 20; Peking, p. 251b, l. 1: *de dag 'khor ba'i sdug bsngal bar mi 'gyur zhing . . .* / This does not mean that these *gandharvas* are fully enlightened buddhas. Rather, it shows that they have reached the first of the ten stages of the bodhisattva path outlined by the *Daśabhūmika Sūtra*, the so-called stage of joy, upon which the bodhisattva is said to be "cut off from all evil and states of misery." See Cleary, *The Flower Ornament*, p. 703.

106. Vaidya, p. 288, l. 26; Peking, p. 251b, l. 2.

107. Vaidya, p. 289, l. 1; Peking, p. 251b, l. 7.

108. Vaidya, p. 289, l. 11; Peking, p. 252a, l. 6.

109. Vaidya, p. 289, l. 24; Peking, p. 252b, l. 4.

110. Vaidya, p. 289, l. 27; Peking, p. 252b, l. 5.

111. Vaidya, p. 290, l. 2; Peking, p. 253a, l. 1.

112. Vaidya, p. 290, l. 8; Peking, p. 253a, l. 4.

113. Vaidya, p. 290, l. 21; Peking, p. 253b, l. 2.

114. Vaidya, p. 290, l. 31; Peking, p. 253b, l. 8.

115. Vaidya, p. 291, l. 18; Peking, p. 254a, l. 6.

116. Vaidya, p. 292, l. 8; Peking, p. 255b, l. 1.

117. Vaidya, p. 292, l. 13; Peking, p. 255b, l. 5.

118. Vaidya, p. 292, l. 25; Peking, p. 256a, l. 3.

119. Vaidya's Sanskrit actually reads that those who wander in this world do know the formula. However, this makes little sense, in view of the preceding passage in which even *tathāgatas* are said not to know it, and is surely a mistake. The Peking edition of the Tibetan translation says that those who wander in this world do not know the formula. Vaidya, p. 292, l. 25f.: *yo 'apyayaṃ paribhramati jaganmandale kaścijjānīte ṣaḍakṣarī mahāvidyām* / Peking, p. 256a, l. 4: *'gro ba'i dkyil 'khor na yongs su 'khyam yang / sus kyang yi ge drug pa'i rig sngags chen mo sus kyang mi shes so* /

120. Vaidya, p. 293, l. 1; Peking, p. 256a, l. 8.

121. Vaidya, p. 293, l. 10 and 11. Neither *vastrasparśanena* nor *darśanamātreṇa* have an object, but I have assumed that they refer to the *dharmabhāṇaka* or guru who has the authority to bestow the formula.

122. Vaidya, p. 293, l. 14: Peking, p. 256b, l. 8.

123. Vaidya, p. 293, l. 24; Peking, p. 257a, l. 5. Once again, the text does not specify the identity of the subject of the sentence. In this instance, it is indisputably the guru or *dharmabhāṇaka* who bestows the formula.

124. Vaidya, p. 294, l. 5; Peking, p. 257b, l. 5.

125. I have used hours, minutes, and seconds instead of the Indian units of time specified in the text. Vaidya, p. 295, l. 2:... *muhūrta-* (48 minutes) *nāḍī-* (24 minutes) *kalāḥ* (1.6 minutes).

126. Vaidya, p. 295, l. 6; Peking, p. 258b, l. 6. Although Vaidya's edition omits the term "*ekajāpasya*," meaning "of (or in) one recitation," I have kept this phrase in my précis because it does appear both in Burnouf's translation and in the Peking edition:... *lan cig bzlas pa*... /

127. Vaidya, p. 295, l. 16; Peking, p. 259a, l. 3. Once again Vaidya's edition omits the term "*ekajāpasya*." This time, I have remained faithful to his version, because although Burnouf's translation does include the phrase ("... ne fut ce même qu'une seule fois..."), the Peking version also omits the term.

128. Vaidya, p. 295, l. 22; Peking, p. 259a, l. 7.

129. Vaidya, p. 295, l. 29; Peking, p. 259b, l. 3.

130. Vaidya, p. 296, l. 2; Peking, p. 259b, l. 6.

131. Vaidya, p. 296, l. 7; Peking, p. 259b, l. 8.

132. Vaidya, p. 296. l. 16; Peking, p. 260a, l. 5.

133. Vaidya, p. 296, l. 21; Peking, p. 260a, l. 8.

134. Vaidya, p. 296, l. 26; Peking, p. 260b, l. 3.

135. Vaidya, p. 297, l. 12; Peking, p. 261a, l. 4.

136. Vaidya, p. 297, l. 19; Peking, p. 261a, l. 8:... *nyin cig tu ring srel 'jug pa*... /

137. Vaidya, p. 297, l. 24. According to Monier-Williams, *A Sanskrit-English Dictionary*, p. 954, the Sanskrit verb *vikṛ* can also mean "to destroy, annihilate." The Tibetan, Peking, p. 261b, l. 3, reads: *'thor ba zhes bya ba'i ting nge 'dzin dang* / Jäschke, *A Tibetan-English Dictionary*, p. 246, translates *'thor ba* as "to be scattered, to fly asunder, to be dispersed, to fall to pieces, to decay, to burst..."

138. Vaidya, p. 297, l. 25; Peking, p. 261b, l. 4: *bsam gtan gyi rgyan ces bya ba'i ting nge 'dzin dang* /

139. Vaidya, p. 297, l. 25; Peking, p. 261b, l. 4: *chos kyi shing rta la 'jug pa zhes bya ba'i ting nge 'dzin dang* /

140. Vaidya, p. 297, l. 26. The Sanskrit word *vatsa* as well as "year," can also be translated as "calf," a meaning which seems to have been reproduced by the Tibetan (Peking, p. 261b, l. 7): *mtha' yas be'u zhes bya ba'i ting nge 'dzin*. "Endless calf"? See Monier-Williams, *A Sanskrit-English Dictionary*, p. 915.

141. Vaidya, p. 297, l. 29; Peking, 261b, l. 7.

142. Vaidya, p. 298, l. 4; Peking, p. 262a, l. 1:... *tshul bzhin yid la byed pa* ... /

143. Vaidya, p. 298, l. 7. This phrase is omitted in the Peking version.

144. Vaidya, p. 298, l. 11; Peking, p. 262a, l. 5: *tshul khrims nyams pa / spyod pa nyams pa* / In translating these two phrases, I have tried to convey the fact that the *dharmabhāṇaka*'s mode of behavior may break certain taboos, but is not wicked.

145. Vaidya, p. 298, l. 12; Peking, p. 262a, l. 6. I am following Lalou's translation of the last of these epithets (*asaṃvṛtteryāpathaḥ*). See Lalou, *Les Religions du Tibet,* p. 38, quoted above in note 29 of chapter five. The relevant Tibetan phrase is: *spyod lam ma bsdams pa yin no* /

146. Vaidya, p. 299, l. 3; Peking, p. 263a, l. 4.

147. Vaidya, p. 299, l. 4; Peking, p. 263, l. 5: *rigs kyi bu khyod 'gyod pa ma sked cig*. Monier-Williams, *A Sanskrit-English Dictionary*, p. 315, gives "evil doing, wickedness," and "repentance" for *kaukṛtya*. The former meaning seems more fitting in this context, even though Jäschke, *A Tibetan-English Dictionary*, p. 98, gives "to repent, to grieve for, repentance" for *'gyod pa*, which is the Tibetan equivalent.

148. Vaidya, p. 299, l. 5; Peking, p. 263a, l. 5.

149. Vaidya, p. 299, l. 8; Peking, p. 263a, l. 7.

150. Vaidya, p. 299, l. 16; Peking, p. 263b, l. 4.

151. Vaidya, p. 299, l. 21; Peking, p. 263b, l. 7. The Tibetan for the last of these is: *rtag tu lha rnams 'dod par byed pa'i tshig go* /

152. Vaidya, p. 299, l. 26; Peking, p. 264a, l. 2.

153. Vaidya, p. 299, l. 26f. The Sanskrit mistakenly uses a masculine relative pronoun here. The Tibetan differs at this point too, stating that the motive for gaining the formula is in order to apply oneself diligently towards liberation. Peking, p. 264a, l. 2f:... *thob par 'gyur thar pa la gzhol bar 'gyur* /

154. Vaidya, p. 299, l. 31; Peking, p. 264a, l. 4.

155. Vaidya, p. 300, l. 6; Peking, p. 264a, l. 8.

156. Vaidya, p. 300, l. 11; Peking, p. 264b, l. 4.

157. Vaidya, p. 300, l. 15; Peking, p. 264b, l. 6: *de nas chos smra pa de sgra ga las byung zhes bsams pa dang* /

158. Vaidya, p. 300, l. 17; Peking, p. 264b, l. 7.

159. Vaidya, p. 300, l. 23; Peking, p. 265a, l. 1.

160. Vaidya, p. 300, l. 28; Peking, p. 265a, l. 4. In the Tibetan, these *samādhis* are:... *mi zad ba'i chos nyid* ... *byams pa dang nying rje dang dga' ba* ... *rnal 'byor*

spyod . . . thar pa la 'jug par 'jog . . . thams cad snang par byed . . . bkod pa'i rgyal po . . . chos 'dzin pa . . . /

161. Vaidya, p. 301, l. 6; Peking, p. 265b, l. 1.

162. Vaidya, p. 301, l. 8. No title is given to this chapter in Vaidya's edition.

163. Vaidya, p. 301, l. 14; Peking, p. 265b, l. 3. The Tibetan transliteration of the *dhāraṇī* is slightly different, reading: *oṃ tsa le tsu le tsun de svāhā* (= . . . *cunde svāhā* in Sanskrit).

164. Vaidya, p. 301, l. 23. The Peking edition diverges quite significantly at this point, omitting any reference to *cittaprasādaṃ* and describing a slightly different sequence of events, in which, having brought to mind the formula, the bodhisattvas reach *nirvāṇa*, where they perceive seven *tathāgatas*. They then see Avalokiteśvara, thereby generating faith. Peking, p. 265b, l. 7ff.

165. Vaidya, p. 301, l. 26; Peking, p. 266a, l. 2.

166. Vaidya, p. 302, l. 2; Peking, p. 266a, l. 6.

167. Vaidya, p. 302, l. 10; Peking, p. 266b, l. 2: . . . *stong pa nyid dang mtshan ma med pa la sems te /*

168. Vaidya, p. 302, l. 13; Peking, p. 266b, l. 4.

169. Vaidya, p. 302, l. 20; Peking, p. 267a, l. 2.

170. Vaidya, p. 303, l. 2; Peking, p. 267b, l. 3.

171. See also Vaidya, p. 295, l. 5.

172. Vaidya, p. 303, l. 9; Peking, p. 267b, l. 7.

173. Vaidya, p. 303, l. 13; Peking, p. 268a, l. 1.

174. Vaidya, p. 303, l. 22; Peking, p. 268a, l. 4.

175. Vaidya, p. 303, l. 31; Peking, p. 268b, l. 2.

176. Vaidya, p. 304, l. 4; Peking, 268b, l. 6. The others are: . . . *parivṛtāya . . . jagadāsvādanakarāya . . . pṛthivīvaralocanakarāya . . . prahlādanakarāya . . . /*

177. Vaiyda, p. 304, l. 10; Peking, p. 269a, l. 2. Bhasmeśvara, it is said, will appear in a particular realm, called *vivṛtāyāṃ lokadhātau*, "the realm of the opened ones" (?). The Tibetan, Peking, p. 269a, l. 1, reads: *'jig rten gyi khams phye pa zhes bya bar. . . .* According to Jäschke, *A Tibetan-English Dictionary*, p. 398, *kha phye ba* can mean "to open, to begin to bloom."

178. Vaidya, p. 304, l. 19; Peking, p. 269b, l. 1.

179. Vaidya, p. 304, l. 22; Peking, p. 269b, l. 2.

180. Vaidya, p. 305, l. 17; Peking, p. 270b, l. 1.

181. Vaidya, p. 305, l. 32; Peking, p. 271a, l. 2.

182. Vaidya, p. 306, l. 18; Peking, p. 272a, l. 1.

183. Vaidya, p. 306, l. 24; Peking, p. 272a, l. 5.

184. Vaidya, p. 307, l. 8; Peking, p. 272b, l. 8.

185. Vaidya, p. 307, l. 13; Peking, p. 273a, l. 3.

186. Vaidya, p. 307, l. 14. Edgerton, *Buddhist Hybrid Sanskrit,* II, p. 244 explains that *jñapti* refers to a "motion," or "proposal" put before the monastic assembly, usually in connection with matters to do with initiation. The *jñaptimuktika,* or "isolated" *jñapti* refers to a proposal put forward without a separate question as to whether the monks approve and a *jñaptidvitīyam* to a proposal put forward with a single additional question. The *jñapticaturtham* mentioned here is, by extension, a proposal put forward with three such questions.

187. Vaidya, p. 307, l. 15; Peking, p. 273a, l. 4: *dge slong dag tshul khrims dang mi ldan pa'i dge slong gis ni sna tshogs kyi gnas su yang 'gro bar mi byin gsol ba dang / bzhi ba bya ba lta ci smos te /*

188. Vaidya, p. 307, l. 16. The Tibetan omits this sentence. Peking, p. 273a, l. 5: *de dag ni ston pa'i bstan pa 'jig par byed ba'o* / "They should not sit upon the teacher's seat."

189. Vaidya, p. 307, l. 17; Peking, p. 273a, l. 5. Monier-Williams, *A Sanskrit-English Dictionary,* p. 153, gives "conversation, communication" for *ālapa,* though the Tibetan translation indicates that it is the food of the *saṃgha* that is not to be given: *de dag la dge dun gyi zas kyang ni sbyin no* / Jäschke, *A Tibetan-English Dictionary,* p. 487, gives "food, nourishment" for *zas.*

190. Vaidya, p. 307, l. 18; Peking, p. 273a, l. 6.

191. Vaidya, p. 307, l. 21; Peking, p. 273a, l. 7: *nga mya ngan las 'das nas lo sum brgya na de 'dra ba'i sbyin gnas dag 'byung ste /*

192. Vaidya, p. 307, l. 23; Peking, p. 273b, l. 1: *dge 'dun dag gi nye bar sbyod pa la gshad pa dang / bci bar byed do /*

193. Vaidya, p. 307, l. 24. The Tibetan is quite different here. Peking, p. 273b, l. 1: *mchil ma dag kyang 'dor zhing las kyi rnam par smin pa mi zhes so / gang dge 'dun kyi nye bar spyod ba la mchil ma 'dor ba de dag ni le bcu gnyis su shid sa la'i 'tshal du kha khab kyi mig tsam gyi srog chags su skye'o /*

194. Vaidya, p. 307, l. 25. The Tibetan is also slightly different here. Peking, p. 273b, l. 2: *gang dge' dun na gyi so shing la spyod du ma 'os pa la spyod ba de dag ni ru sba (?) la dang /*

195. Vaidya, p. 308, l. 11; Peking, p. 274a, l. 6.

196. Vaidya, p. 308, l. 18; Peking, p. 274a, l. 8.

197. Vaidya, p. 308, l. 29; Peking, p. 274b, l. 4. The Tibetan ending is shorter and reads simply: *'phags pa za ma tog bkod pa zhes bya ba theg pa chen po'i mdo rdzogs so /*

BIBLIOGRAPHY

The Main Text and Translation

Kāraṇḍavyūha Sūtra. In *Mahāyāna-Sūtra-Saṃgraha*. Edited by P. L. Vaidya, 258–308. Darbhanga: Mathila Institute, 1961.

Za Ma Tog bKod Pa. In *bKa' 'Gyur*. Peking ed., *Mdo Chu*, 224a, 7–274b, 4. In the *Tibetan Tripiṭaka*, 91–112. Tokyo: Suzuki Research Foundation, 1964.

Burnouf, E., trans. 1837. *Kāraṇḍavyūha Sūtra*. Paris: Fonds Sanskrit No. 24, Bibliothèque Nationale.

Mahāyāna Sūtras and Translations

Cleary, T., trans. 1993. *The Flower Ornament Scripture, A Translation of the Avataṃsaka Sūtra*. Boston and London: Shambhala.

Conze, Edward, trans. 1973. *The Perfection of Wisdom in Eight Thousand Lines & its Verse Summary*. San Francisco: Four Seasons Foundation.

———. trans. 1973a. *The Short Prajñāpāramitā Texts*. London: Luzac.

———. 1954. *Abhisamayālaṅkāra*. Rome: Istituto Italiano per il Medio ed Estremo Oriente.

Emmerick, R. E., trans. 1996. *The Sūtra of Golden Light*. Oxford: Pali Text Society.

Gomez, Luis, trans. 1996. *The Land of Bliss, The Paradise of the Buddha of Measureless Light*. Honolulu: University of Hawaii Press.

Harrison, P., trans. 1990. *The Samādhi of Direct Encounter with the Buddhas of the Present, An Annotated English Translation of the Tibetan Version of the Pratyutpannabuddhasaṃmukhāvasthitasamādhi Sūtra*. Tokyo: International Institute for Buddhist Studies.

Kern, H., trans. 1884. "*Saddharmapuṇḍarīka Sūtra*." In The Sacred Books of the East Series. Edited by M. Muller. Oxford: Oxford University Press.

Lamotte, Étienne, trans. 1976. *The Teaching of Vimalakīrti*. Oxford: Pali Text Society.

Takasaki, J., trans. 1966. *A Study of the Ratnagotravibhāga (Uttaratantra)*. Rome: Instituto Italiano per il Medio ed Estremo Oriente.

Thurman, Robert A. F., trans. 1976. *The Holy Teaching of Vimalakīrti*. PA: Pennsylvania State University.

Vaidya, P. L., ed. 1961. *Sukhāvatīvyūha Sūtra*. In *Mahāyānasūtrasaṃgraha*. Vol. I: 221–253. Darbhanga: Mithila Institute.

———. 1960. *Saddharmapuṇḍarīka Sūtra*. Darbhanga: Mithila Institute.

———. 1960a. *Gaṇḍavyūha Sūtra*. Darbhanga: Mithila Institute.

Yamada, M., trans. 1984. *The Sutra of Contemplation on the Buddha of Immeasurable Life*. Kyoto: Ryukoku University Translation Centre.

Purāṇas and Translations

Kūrma Purāṇa. 1981. Translated and edited by Ganesh Vadeo Tagare. Delhi: Motilal Banarsidass.

Padma Purāṇa. 1988. Translated by N. A. Deshpande. Delhi: Motilal Banarsidass.

Bhāgavata Purāṇa. 1976. Translated and edited by Ganesh Vasudeo Tagare. Delhi: Motilal Banarsidass.

Liṅga Purāṇa. 1973. Translated by a board of scholars and edited by Professor J. L. Shastri. Delhi: Motilal Banarsidass.

Śiva Purāṇa. 1970. Translated by a board of scholars and edited by Arnold Kunst and J. L. Shastri. Delhi: Motilal Banarsidass, 1970.

Skanda Purāṇa. 1994. Translated and edited by Ganesh Vasudeo Tagare. Delhi: Motilal Banarsidass.

Other

Alper, H. P. 1989. "The Cosmos as Śiva's Language Game: 'Mantra' According to Kṣemarāja's Śivasūtravimarśinī." In *Understanding Mantras*. Edited by H. P. Alper, 249–294. Albany: State University of New York.

Beal, Samuel, 1981. *Si-Yu-Ki, Buddhist Records of the Western World*. 1884. Reprint, Delhi: Motilal Banarsidass.

———. 1871. *A Catena of Buddhist Scriptures from the Chinese*. London: Trubner.

Beck, Guy L., 1993. *Sonic Theology, Hinduism and Sacred Sound*. NC: University of South Carolina.

Bendall, C. 1902. *Catalogue of the Sanskrit Manuscripts in the British Museum*. London: Longmans.

Beyer, Stephan. 1977. "Notes on the Vision Quest in Early Mahāyāna," in *Prajñāpāramitā and Related Systems*. Edited by Lewis Lancaster, 329–340. CA: University of California.

Bharati, Agehananda. 1965. *The Tantric Tradition*. London: Rider.

Bhattacharya, Benoytosh. 1985. *The Indian Buddhist Iconography*. 1924. Reprint, Delhi: Cosmo Publications.

———. Ed. 1968. *Sādhanamāla*. Baroda: Oriental Institute.

Bokar Rinpoche. 1991. *Chenrezig, Lord of Love*. San Francisco: Clearpoint Press.

Brough, J. 1965. "Comments on Third Century Shan-shan and the History of Buddhism." *Bulletin of the School of Oriental and African Studies* 28, pt. 3: 607–611.

Bucknell, R. S., and Martin Stuart-Fox. 1993. *The Twilight Language*. 1986. Reprint, London: Curzon Press.

van Buitenen, J. A. B. 1959. "Akṣara," *Journal of the American Oriental Society* 79: 176–187.

———. 1958. "The Indian Hero as Vidyādhara," *Journal of American Folklore* 71: 305–311; also in Rocher, Ludo, ed. 1988. *Studies in Indian Literature and Philosophy. Collected Articles of J. A. B. van Buitenen,* 135–145. Delhi: Motilal Banarsidass.

Bunce, F. W. 1997. *A Dictionary of Buddhist and Hindu Iconography*. New Delhi: Printworld.

Burnouf, Eugène. 1844. *L'Introduction à l'Histoire du Bouddhisme Indien*. Paris: Imprimerie Royale.

Chandra, Lokesh. 1988. *The Thousand-Armed Avalokiteśvara*. New Delhi: Indira Gandhi National Centre for the Arts.

———. 1981. *The 108 Forms of Lokeśvara in Hymns and Sculptures*. New Delhi: International Academy of Indian Culture.

Chapple, C., ed. and W. Sargeant, trans. 1984. *Bhagavadgītā*. Albany: State University of New York.

Chattopadhyaya, A. 1967. *Atiśa and Tibet*. Delhi: Motilal Banarsidass.

Chattopadhyaya, D., ed. 1990. *Tāranātha's History of Buddhism in India*. 1970. Reprint, Delhi: Motilal Banarsidass.

Conze, Edward. 1967. *Materials for a Dictionary of the Prajñāpāramitā Literature*. Tokyo: Suzuki Research Foundation.

———. 1960. "The Development of Prajñāpāramitā Thought." In *Buddhism and Culture dedicated to Dr. Daisetz Teitaro Suzuki in Commemoration of his Ninetieth Birthday*. Edited by S. Yamaguchi, 24–45. Tokyo: Suzuki Research Foundation; also in Conze, E. 1967. *Thirty Years of Buddhist Studies*. 123–147. Oxford: Cassirer.

Cozort, Daniel. 1986. *Highest Yoga Tantra*. New York: Snow Lion.

Crosby, K., and A. Skilton, trans. 1996. *The Bodhicaryāvatāra*. Oxford: Oxford University Press.

Csoma de Kôrös, Alexander. 1839. "Analysis of the Sher-'Phyin," *Journal of the Asiatic Society of Bengal* 20, pt. 2: 393–552.

Dalai Lama. 1984. "Oṃ Maṇi Padme Hūṃ." In *Kindness, Clarity and Insight*. 116–117. New York: Snow Lion.

Daniélou, A. 1960. *Polythéisme Hindou*. Corrêa, Paris: Buchet/Chastel.

David-Neel, A. 1931. *Initiations and Initiates in Tibet*. London: Rider.

Douglas, Nick, and Meryl White. 1976. *Karmapa: The Black Hat Lama of Tibet*. London: Luzac.

Dowson, J. 1879. *A Classical Dictionary of Hindu Mythology and Religion, Geography, History and Literature*. London: Trubner.

Dudjom (bDud 'joms) Rinpoche. 1991. *The Nyingma School of Tibetan Buddhism*. Boston: Wisdom.

Dutt, N. 1955. "Religion and Philosophy." In *The Age of Imperial Kanauj*. Edited by R. C. Majumdar, 257–287. Bombay: Bharatiya Vidya Bhavan.

———. 1939. *Gilgit Manuscripts*. Vol. I. Calcutta: Calcutta Oriental Press.

Dyczkowski, Mark S. G. 1987. *The Doctrine of Vibration: An Analysis of the Doctrines of Kashmir Shaivism*. Albany: State University of New York.

Edgerton, F. 1953. *Buddhist Hybrid Sanskrit Grammar and Dictionary*. New Haven, CT: Yale University Press.

Ekvall, Robert. 1964. *Religious Observances in Tibet: Pattern and Function,*. Chicago: University of Chicago Press.

Emmerick, R. E. 1979. *A Guide to the Literature of Khotan*. Tokyo: Studia Philologica Buddhica, Occasional Paper Series III.

Gellner, David. 1992. *Monk, Householder and Tantric Priest*. Cambridge: Cambridge University Press.

Gonda, Jan. 1975. *Selected Studies*. 1–26; 248–301. Leiden: Brill.

———. 1974. *Vedic Literature*. Wiesbaden: Otto Harrassowitz.

———. 1970. *Viśṇuism and Śivaism, A Comparison*. London: Athlone Press, University of London.

———. 1968. "The Concept of a personal God in ancient Indian religious thought." *Studia Missionalia* 17 (Rome, 1968): 111–136.

———. 1965. "The Īśvara Idea." In *Change and Continuity in Indian Religion*. 131–163. The Hague: Mouton.

———. 1963. "The Indian Mantra." *Oriens* 16: 244–295.

Govinda, Anagarika Lama. 1969. *Foundations of Tibetan Mysticism*. London: Rider.

Gupta, S. 1989. "The Pāñcarātra Attitude to Mantra." In *Understanding Mantras*. Edited by H. P. Alper, 224–248. Albany: State University of New York.

Gyatso, Janet. 1997. "An Avalokiteśvara Sādhana." In *Religions of Tibet in Practice*. Edited by Donald S. Lopez, 266–270. NJ: Princeton University Press.

———. 1981. *The Literary Transmission of the Traditions of Thang stong rgyal po: A Study of Visionary Buddhism in Tibet*. Ph. D. diss, University of California.

von Hinüber, O. 1982. *Die Bedeutung des Handschriftes bei Gilgit*. 47–66. Wiesbaden: Zeitschrift der Deutschen Morgenlandischen Gesellschaft Supplement V. 21 Deutsches Orientalistentag, Ausgew. 47–66. Wiesbaden: Vorträge.

———. 1981. *Die Erforschung der Gilgit-Handschriften—Neu Ergebnisse*. 9–11. Zeitschrift der Deutschen Morgenlandischen Gesellschaft 131.

Holt, J. C. 1991. *Buddha in the Crown, Avalokiteśvara in the Buddhist Traditions of Sri Lanka*. Oxford: Oxford University Press.

Imaeda, Y. 1979. "Note Préliminaire sur la Formule Oṃ Maṇi Padme Hūṃ dans les Manuscrits Tibétains de Touen-Houang." In *Contributions aux Études sur Touen-Houang*. Edited by M. Soymie, 71–76. Genève-Paris: Libraire Droz.

Jäschke, H. A. 1881. *A Tibetan-English Dictionary*. London: Routledge and Kegan Paul.

Jerstad, Luther G. 1969. *Maṇi Rimdu: Sherpa Dance Drama*. Washington: University of Washington Press.

Johnson, W. J., trans. 1994. *Bhagavadgītā*. Oxford: Oxford University Press.

Kapstein, M. 1992. "Remarks on the Maṇi bKa' 'bum and the Cult of Avalokiteśvara in Tibet." In *Tibetan Buddhism, Reason and Revelation*. Edited by Steven D. Goodman and Ronald M. Davidson, 79–94. Albany: State University of New York.

Karmay, H. 1975. *Early Sino-Tibetan Art*. Warminster: Aris and Phillips.

Khyentse, Dilgo. 1992. *The Heart Treasure of the Enlightened Ones*. Boston: Shambhala.

Lacôte, F. 1908. *Essai sur Guṇāḍhya et la Bṛhatkathā*. Paris: Leroux.

Ladner, Lorne. 2000. *Wheel of Great Compassion: The Practice of the Prayer Wheel in Tibetan Buddhism*. Somerville: Wisdom.

Lal, P., trans. 1969. *The Mahābhārata*. Calcutta: Writers Workshop.

Lalou, Marcelle. 1957. *Les Religions du Tibet*. Paris: Presses Universitaires de France.

———. 1955. "A la Recherche du Vidyādharapiṭaka: le Cycle du Subāhuparipṛcchā-Tantra." In *Studies in Indology and Buddhology Presented in Honour of Professor Susumu Yamaguchi*. 68–72. Tokyo: Hozokan.

———. 1953. "Les textes bouddhiques au temps du roi Khri Srong-lde-brtsan." *Journal Asiatique*: 313–353.

———. 1938. "A Tun-huang Prelude to the Kāraṇḍavyūha," *Indian Historical Quarterly* 14: 398–400.

Legge, James, trans. 1965. *A Record of Buddhistic Kingdoms*. 1886. Reprint, New York: Dover.

Lessing, F. D., and A. Wayman. 1978. *mKhas-grub-rje's Fundamentals of the Buddhist Tantras*. The Hague/Paris: Mouton.

Lewis, T. T. 2000. *Popular Buddhist Texts from Nepal: Narratives and Rituals of Newar Buddhism*. Albany: State University of New York Press.

Liebert, G. 1976. *Dictionary of the Indian Religions*. Leiden: Brill.

Lienhard, Siegfried. 1993. "Avalokiteśvara in the Wick of the Night-Lamp." *Indo-Iranian Journal* 36: 93–104.

Locke, John. K. 1980. *Karunamaya: The Cult of Avalokiteśvara-Matsendranath in the Valley of Nepal*. Kathmandu: Sahayogi Prakashan Research Centre.

Lopez, D. S. 1998. *Prisoners of Shangri La, Tibetan Buddhism and the West*. Chicago: University of Chicago Press.

Losty, Jeremiah P. 1988. *An Early Indian Manuscript of the Kāraṇḍavyūhasūtra, Studies in Art and Archaeology of Bihar and Bengal*. Delhi: Sri Satguru Publications.

Macdonell, A. A. 1917. *A Vedic Reader for Students*. Oxford: Oxfozrd University Press.

Majumder, P. C. 1948. "The Kāraṇḍavyūha: Its Metrical Version." *Indian Historical Quarterly* 24: 293–299.

Malla, 1982. *Classic Newari Literature: A Sketch*. Kathmandu: Kathmandu Educational Enterprises.

de Mallman, Marie–Thérèse. 1948. *Introduction à l'Étude d'Avalokiteśvara*. Paris: Annale du Musée Guimet.

Matsunaga, A. 1969. *The Buddhist Philosophy of Assimilation*. Tokyo: Tuttle.

Matsunaga, Yukei. 1985. "On the Date of the Mañjuśrīmūlakalpa." In *Tantric and Taoist Studies in Honour of R. A. Stein*. Edited by Michel Strickman, 3: 882–894. Brussels: Institut Belge des Hautes Etudes Chinoises.

Mayer, Robert. 1996. *A Scripture of the Ancient Tantra Collection, The Phur-pa bcu-gnyis*. Oxford: Kiscadale.

Mette, Adelheid. 1997. *Die Gilgitfragmente des Kāraṇḍavyūha*. Swisttal-Odendorf: Indica et Tibetica Verlag.

———. 1993. "Remarks on the Tradition of the Kāraṇḍavyūha." In *Aspects of Buddhist Sanskrit, Proceedings of the International Symposium on the Language of Sanskrit Buddhist Texts*. 510–519. 1991. Sarnath: Central Institute of Higher Tibetan Studies.

Michell, G. 1989. *The Penguin Guide to the Monuments to India*. London: Penguin.

Mironov, N. D. 1927. "Buddhist Miscellanea: Avalokiteśvara—Kuan-Yin." *Journal of the Royal Asiatic Society*: 241–252.

Monier-Williams, Monier. 1899. *A Sanskrit-English Dictionary*. Oxford: Oxford University Press.

Neumaier-Dargyay, E. K. 1992. *The Sovereign All-Creating Mind*. Albany: State University of New York.

Norbu, Namkhai. 1997. *Journey Among the Tibetan Nomads*. Dharamsala: Library of Tibetan Works and Archives.

———. 1991. *The Dzogchen Ritual Practices*. London: Kailash Editions.

———. 1989. *Dzogchen, The Self-Perfected State*. London: Arkana.

Obermiller, E., trans. 1986. *History of Buddhism, Being an English Translation of Bu ston's Chos 'Byung*. 1932. Reprint, Delhi: Sri Satguru.

Oertel, H., trans. 1896. *Jaiminīya Upaniṣad Brāhmaṇa, Journal of the American Oriental Society* 16: 79–260.

Pas, J. F. 1977. "The Kuan-wu-liang-shou Fo-ching: its origins and literary criticism." In *Buddhist Thought and Asian Civilization*. Edited by L. S. Kawamure and K. Scott, 144–218. CA: Emeryville.

Pelliot, P. 1934. "Note on Oṃ Maṇipadme Hūṃ." *T'oung Pao* 30: 174.

Piyasīlo. 1991, *Avalokiteśvara: Origin, Manifestations and Meanings*. Malaysia: Petaling Jaya.

Przyluski, Jean. 1923. "Les Vidyārāja, Contribution à l'Histoire de la Magie dans les Sectes Mahāyānistes." *Bulletin de l'Ecole Francaise d'Extrème Orient* 23: 301–368.

Rao, T. A. G. 1971. *Elements of Hindu Iconography*. 1914. Reprint, Varanasi: Indological Book House.

Régamey, Constantin. 1971. "Motifs Vichnouites et Sīvaites dans le Kāraṇḍavyūha." In *Études Tibétaines Dediées à la Memoire de Marcelle Lalou*. 411–432. Paris: Libraire d'Amérique et d'Orient.

———. 1965. "Lexicological Gleanings from the Kāraṇḍavyūhasūtra." *Indian Linguistics* 16: 1–10.

———. 1965a. "Le Pseudo-Hapax ratikara et la Lampe qui Rit dan le 'Sūtra des Ogresses' Bouddhique." *Études Asiatiques* 18, No. 19: 175–206.

———. 1954. "Randbemerkungen zur Sprache und Textuberlieferung des Kāraṇḍavyūha." In *Asiatica, Festschrift Friedrich Weller*. 514–527. Leipzig: Otto Harrassowitz.

Reynolds, John. 1996. *The Golden Letters*. New York: Snow Lion.

Rhie, Marylin and Robert Thurman. 1991. *Wisdom and Compassion, The Sacred Art of Tibet*. New York: Abrams.

Rhys Davids, T. W., and J. Estlin Carpenter, ed. 1890. *Dīgha Nikāya*. London: Pali Text Society.

Richardson, Hugh. 1998. "Some Monasteries, Temples and Fortresses in Tibet before 1950." In *High Peaks, Pure Earth*. Edited by H. Richardson. London: Serindia.

Rocher, Ludo 1989. "Mantras in the Śivapurāṇa." In *Understanding Mantras*. Edited by H. P. Alper, 177–203. Albany: State University of New York.

———. 1986. *The Purāṇas*. Wiesbaden: Otto Harrassowitz.

Rockhill, W. W. 1900, *The Journey of Friar William of Rubruck to the Eastern Parts of the World, 1253–55, as Narrated by Himself*. London: Hakluyt Society.

Roerich, G., trans. 1995. *The Blue Annals*. 1949. Reprint, Delhi: Motilal Banarsidass.

Sanderson, A. 1994. "Vajrayānā: Origin and Function." In *Buddhism into the Year 2000: International Conference Proceedings*. 87–102. Bangkok: Dhammakaya Foundation.

Sastri, K. A. N. 1956. "An Historical Sketch of Śaivism." In *The Cultural Heritage of India*. Edited by H. Bhattacharya. Vol. 4: 63–78. Calcutta: Ramakrishna Mission.

Schopen, Gregory. 1977. "Sukhāvatī as a Generalised Religious Goal in Sanskrit Mahāyāna Sūtra Literature." *Indo-Iranian Journal* 19: 177–210.

———. 1975. "The phrase '*sa pṛthivīpradeśaś caiityabhūto bhavet*' in the Vajracchedikā: notes on the cult of the book in the Mahāyāna." *Indo-Iranian Journal* 17: 147–181.

Shastri, M. D. 1935. "History of the word 'Īśvara' and its idea." in *Proc. and Trans. VIIth All-India Conference*. 487–503. 1933. Reprint, Baroda: Oriental Institute, Oriental Institute.

Snellgrove, David. 1987. *Indo-Tibetan Buddhism: Indian Buddhists and their Tibetan Successors*. London: Serindia.

———. 1957. *Buddhist Himālaya*. Oxford: Cassirer.

Soifer, Deborah A. 1991. *The Myths of Narasiṃha and Vāmana—Two Avatars in Cosmological Perspective*. Albany: State University of New York.

von Staël-Holstein, A. 1936. "Avalokita and Apalokita." *Harvard Journal of Asiatic Studies* 3, No. 4 (1936): 350–362.

Suzuki, Beatrice Lane. 1936. "The School of Shingon Buddhism, Part II." *The Eastern Buddhist* (May 1936): 1–38.

———. 1936. "The School of Shingon Buddhism, Part III." *The Eastern Buddhist*. (June 1937): 177–213.

Tarthang Tulku, ed. 1986. *Ancient Tibet*. CA: Dharma.

Thomas, F. W. 1906. "Oṃ Maṇi Padme Hūṃ." *Journal of the Royal Asiatic Society*: 464.

Tucci, Giuseppe. 1958. Minor Buddhist Texts, II. Rome: *Istituto Italiano per il Medio ed Estremo Oriente*.

———. 1948. "Buddhist Notes I: A Propos Avalokiteśvara." *Mélanges Chinois et Bouddhique* 9: 173–219.

———. 1922–23. "La Redazione Poetica del Kāraṇḍavyūha." *Atti della Reale Accademia delle Scienze di Torino, Classe di Scienza di Morali, Storiche e Filologique* 58: 605–630.

Verhagen, P. C. 1990. "The Mantra 'Oṃ maṇi-padme hūṃ' in an Early Tibetan Grammatical Treatise." *Journal of the International Association of Buddhist Studies* 13, No. 2: 133–138.

Waley, Alex 1931. *A Catalogue of Paintings Recovered from Tun-huang by Sir Aurel Stein*. London: British Museum.

Wayman, A. 1984. "The Significance of Mantras, from the Veda down to Buddhist Tantric Practice." In *Buddhist Insight*. By A. Wayman, 413–430. Delhi: Motilal Banarsidass.

Williams, Paul. 1989. *Mahāyāna Buddhism*. London: Routledge.

Winternitz, M. 1933. *A History of Indian Literature*. Calcutta: University of Calcutta Press.

Zaehner, R. C. 1978. *Hindu Scriptures*. 1938. Reprint, London: Dent.

Zopa, Thubten. 2001. *Teachings from the Mani Retreat*. Boston: Lama Yeshe Wisdom Archive.

INDEX

INDEX TO APPENDIX

Précis of *Kāraṇḍavyūha Sūtra*